POSSESSED LANDSCAPES

CULTURE, PLACE, AND NATURE
Studies in Anthropology and Environment
K. Sivaramakrishnan, Series Editor

Centered in anthropology, the Culture, Place, and Nature series encompasses new interdisciplinary social science research on environmental issues, focusing on the intersection of culture, ecology, and politics in global, national, and local contexts. Contributors to the series view environmental knowledge and issues from the multiple and often conflicting perspectives of various cultural systems.

Possessed Landscapes

EXPERIMENTS IN CONSERVATION AND
SOVEREIGNTY IN SOUTHEAST MYANMAR

Tomas Cole

UNIVERSITY OF WASHINGTON PRESS

Seattle

This book is freely available in an open access edition with funds received from the 2025 Arcadia Open Access Publishing Award, granted to the University of Washington Press by the American Council of Learned Societies with generous support from Arcadia.

Additional support for this publication was provided by the Samuel and Althea Stroum Endowed Book Fund.

Copyright © 2026 by Tomas Cole

Composed in Warnock Pro, typeface designed by Robert Slimbach

The digital edition of this book may be downloaded and shared under a Creative Commons Attribution Non-Commercial No Derivatives 4.0 international license (CC-BY-NC-ND 4.0). For information about this license, see https://creativecommons.org/licenses/by-nc-nd/4.0. This license applies only to content created by the author, not to separately copyrighted material. To use this book, or parts of this book, in any way not covered by the license, please contact the University of Washington Press.

Photographs by the author.

UNIVERSITY OF WASHINGTON PRESS | uwapress.uw.edu

LIBRARY OF CONGRESS CATALOGING-IN-PUBLICATION DATA

Names: Cole, Tomas author

Title: Possessed landscapes : experiments in conservation and sovereignty in Southeast Myanmar / Tomas Cole.

Description: Seattle : University of Washington Press, [2025] | Series: Culture, place, and nature | Includes bibliographical references and index

Identifiers: LCCN 2025022975 | ISBN 9780295754192 hardcover | ISBN 9780295754208 paperback | ISBN 9780295754215 ebook

Subjects: LCSH: Indigenous peoples—Land tenure—Burma | Protected areas—Social aspects—Burma | Protected areas—Political aspects—Burma | Land use—Social aspects—Burma | Land use—Political aspects—Burma | Ethnoscience—Social aspects—Burma | Ethnoscience—Political aspects—Burma | Conservation of natural resources—Social aspects—Burma | Conservation of natural resources—Political aspects—Burma

Classification: LCC GN449.3 .C65 2025 | DDC 959.1—dc23/eng/20250615

LC record available at https://lccn.loc.gov/2025022975

For EU product safety concerns please contact Easy Access System Europe Oü 16879218, Mustamäe tee 50, 10621, Tallinn, Estonia, gpsr.requests@easproject.com, +372 56 98939.

∞ This paper meets the requirements of ANSI/NISO Z39.48-1992 (Permanence of Paper).

For my parents and all the elders who went before me

CONTENTS

Foreword by K. Sivaramakrishnan ix

Acknowledgments xiii

Introduction: Radical Experiments in Conservation and Sovereignty 1

PART I
POSSESSION

ONE
Possessed Landscapes
Negotiating Histories and Specters 29

TWO
Alternating Ownership
Ephemeral, Nesting, and Patchwork Lands 52

THREE
Spectral Sovereignty
Negotiations of State, Power, and Politics 69

PART II
DISPOSSESSION/REPOSSESSION

FOUR
Countermovements
Dispossession, Repossession, and Translation 93

FIVE
Alter-Politics
Revolution, Conservation, and Conviviality   118

SIX
Liberation Conservation
Messing with the Scales of Conservation and Revolution   142

EPILOGUE
Pugmarks in the Sand   171

Notes   183

References   189

Index   211

FOREWORD

K. SIVARAMAKRISHNAN

In this study, so relevant to the times, Tomas Cole offers an examination of how Indigenous people participate in building peace and sovereignty amid political violence, forest conservation initiatives, and the relentless intrusion of the forces of capitalism in contested landscapes. He does this work in the highlands of southeast Myanmar, an area rich in forests and their lore. This is a region known by long-term residents as an embattled home where strife is seared into their memory. Repossessing the land is, Cole shows, about making peace with ancestors and spirits. It also requires the Indigenous residents, working with Karen activists, to find ways to refashion and create programs of nature conservation, all while negotiating national integration and maintaining a measure of political autonomy in Myanmar.

This is research that is particularly resonant with other work in many parts of the world where Indigenous people struggle to secure lands rights and recognition of their homelands. There is now a considerable literature on this topic in the Americas, Canada, Australia, and, to some extent, Africa. Such inquiries in Asia are fast emerging as a key topic for political and environmental anthropology. Cole takes an approach that is both well suited to the history of such movements and struggles in Myanmar (and more generally for highlands of mainland Southeast Asia) and can offer some new directions to scholars interested in these questions elsewhere. He does so by examining the multiple valences of possession in and of the land where human corporeal rights and more-than-human spiritual or spectral dwelling meet in the forests.

Forests have long been considered places of wonder and dread, holding treasures and threats, across cultures. In the history of Western civilization, this has been well discussed in the writings of Robert Harrison.[1]

Much of the mystery, generating both attraction and trepidation, of forests extended to forest people. Across Asia the conquest of forest peoples and the control of forests often became part of a civilizing process undertaken by regional agrarian polities and, later, colonial empires. Studies of colonial efforts to command and exploit forests in Asia detail some of these developments.[2] But this large-scale history often conceals the continuing inhabitation of forests by people, spirits, and powers that locally remain salient to the reproduction of social relations, patterns of forest use, and conflicts over forest management.

Through skillful and patient ethnography, Cole turns to these obscured histories and cultural politics. As in the case of research that is questioning the erasure of Native American ideas and values, as well as rights and claims, in the development of protected areas in North America, Cole wishes to uncover how externally initiated conservation might meet and even be modified by Indigenous ideas, political assertion, and conservation projects.[3] He carries out this work by considering local Indigenous ideas of forest inhabitation by the spirits of ancestors and how they come to inform forest conservation initiatives in the Salween Peace Park. In this way, Cole offers a whole new perspective on what has been discussed as community-based conservation. He does so by focusing on the meanings and practices emergent from within the community rather than the efforts to decentralize or delegate externally designed conservation projects to local entities either organic (village authority) or synthetic (forest committees and self-help groups).

Cole is also offering a novel history of peace parks. In the past, critical studies of peace parks and advocacy for them as desirable conservation initiatives have often emphasized their crucial role in promoting both environmental values and peacebuilding in conflict-ravaged areas. These have often been contentious international border zones.[4] For some scholars, peace parks are a borderland manifestation of placing conservation at the service of promoting the political hegemony of regional states. Across Asia researchers have drawn attention to such processes in China, Korea, Thailand, Vietnam, India, Indonesia, the Philippines, and Pakistan. But for others, especially conservation scientists, peace parks hold a unique possibility that can promote peacebuilding in borderlands, which are often rife with conflict. To such idealistic visions peace parks might be the way to mitigate and even avert the deadly conflicts that may become more severe in times of climate change.[5]

The Salween Peace Park is formed in a borderland in Myanmar but in the context of the animosities and warfare between the Myanmar state and ethnic minorities. A region redolent with the history of colonial forestry (mostly for teak) is now contested terrain where conservation is a vehicle for state intrusion and the assertion of local claims on the forest and enactment of self-government. As Cole notes, the sharply undulating terrain of the highlands in southeast Myanmar is fragmented by many ridges and valleys. Each fold in this wrinkled topography becomes an ecologically and socially distinct site for the larger peace and conservation initiatives to play out in terms of specific local mobilizations.

What Cole does well here is to build a careful examination of the different ways in which forests are inhabited and possessed by Indigenous people and their ancestors while recounting the ways in which these forms of dwelling were altered and reasserted in response to forces of dispossession driven by government consolidation and international resource mining efforts. Throughout the book, Cole dwells in the struggles for sovereignty that implicate people and the spirits of their ancestral dead, as well as the way the pragmatic approaches to forest management embedded in and emergent from these struggles are elevated from local immediacy to more durable regional outcomes in the Salween Peace Park.

This project was born concurrently with the hopeful democratization that began in Myanmar fifteen years ago. In the last few years Myanmar has fallen into more difficult times. However, the politics of sovereignty and Indigenous efforts to shape conservation in keeping with their beliefs will remain vital to the future of Myanmar and the prospects for various Indigenous people in the region. In a time when Indigenous efforts to reimagine how humans might live in the world are gaining attention across continents, this study offered by Tomas Cole is a timely contribution to the wider conversation.

NOTES

1. Robert Pogue Harrison, *Forests: The Shadow of Civilization* (University of Chicago Press, 1992).
2. The work of Raymond Bryant is particularly relevant here. See, for instance, Raymond L. Bryant, "Romancing Colonial Forestry: The Discourse of 'Forestry as Progress' in British Burma," *Geographical Journal* 162, no. 2 (1996): 169–78, https://doi.org/10.2307/3059874.
3. Examples of recent efforts to recognize Native heritage in protected areas in North America, for instance, may be found in Rochelle Bloom and Douglas Deur, "Through a Forest Wilderness: Native American Environmental Management at Yosemite and Contested Conservation Values in

America's National Parks," and Paul Berne Burow, "Nature's Belonging: Landscape, Conservation, and the Cultural Politics of Place in the Great Basin," both in *Public Lands in the Western US: Place and Politics in the Clash Between Public and Private*, ed. Kathleen M. Sullivan and James H. McDonald (Lexington Press, 2021).

4. See, for instance, Bram Büscher, *Transforming the Frontier: Peace Parks and the Politics of Neoliberal Conservation in Southern Africa* (Duke University Press, 2013).

5. One such view can be found in Aishwarya Maheshwari, "Ease Conflict in Asia with Snow Leopard Peace Parks," *Science* 367, no. 6483 (2020): 1203, https://doi.org/10.1126/science.aba9882.

ACKNOWLEDGMENTS

This book has been percolating for well over a decade, since I first stepped out into the Thai-Myanmar borderlands in 2010 and experienced Pwakanyaw hospitality. The following list of thanks is therefore far from comprehensive. My deepest apologies to anyone I have missed.

First and foremost, I would like to extend my most heartfelt thanks to all the people of the Myanmar-Thai borderlands who helped me along the way over the years and who made this book possible. I owe my greatest debt of gratitude to the residents of the village I call Ta K'Thwee Duh ("Misty Village") and the surrounding Mutraw highlands. Thank you, from the very bottom of my heart, for your countless acts of generosity: constantly bringing me fruit, vegetables, and lashings of rice alcohol; caring for me when I was sick; telling me stories that made me laugh until my sides hurt; sharing your hearths, histories, and lives with me, all while dealing with my endless stream of questions with such grace and good humor. During my time in the United States, I am also eternally grateful to the generosity of spirit and dazzling wit of the Pwakanyaw living in upstate New York and to Katheryn Stam and Chris Sunderlin who took me in, found me a home, and filled my days with joy. In Chiang Mai I was continually bowled over by the kindness, brilliance, and resilience of the activists from the Karen Environmental and Social Action Network (KESAN) and Tenasserim River and Indigenous Peoples' Network (TRIP NET), who also facilitated my access and travel to the Mutraw hills. While none of your real names feature in this book, your passion, verve, and intelligence have seeped into every page. The same goes for my field assistant, whom I call here Naw Paw. Your boundless humor, keen intellect, and warmth of heart shine throughout this book. The way the residents of these borderlands continue to face down apocalypse after apocalypse, without losing their warmth and good humor, is a perpetual source of inspiration to me. Ta plu doh ma!

Several brilliant scholars were instrumental in making this book happen. Paramount among them are Beppe Karlsson and Johan Lindquist, who have acted as advisers and later colleagues of the highest caliber, supporting me at each stage of the process. This work would have never come to fruition without their searing intellect and warm encouragement throughout. At the Department of Social Anthropology, Stockholm University, I have been blessed with the best colleagues imaginable. Ivana Maček, Shahram Khosravi, Hege Leivestad, Anna Gustafsson, Karin Ahlberg, Annika Rabo, Alireza Behtoui, Johan Nilsson, Andrew Alan Johnson, and my fellow PhD cohort of Isabella Strömberg, Victor Nygren, Simon Johansson, Igor Petričević, Siri Schwabe, Tekalign Ayalew, Rasmus Rodineliussen, and Jonathan Krämer have all, in ways both great and small, made this text infinitely more readable and my life more livable.

In Ithaca, I am immensely grateful to Thamora Fishel at the Southeast Asian Program (SEAP) and Magnus Fiskesjö at Cornell University who both helped me find my feet practically, intellectually, and morally. My stay in Chiang Mai was made possible thanks in no small measure to the good graces of Chayan Vaddhanaphuti, who facilitated my time at the Regional Center for Social Science and Sustainable Development (RSDC) and constantly provoked me to rethink my ideas. At Chiang Mai University, I also had the good fortune of meeting and learning from Kwanchewan Buadaeng, Bobby Farnan, Ekraj Sabur, and Emily Teera-Hong and received unfailing administrative help from Chanida Puranapun. My stay was also greatly enriched by the company of Ashley South, who so generously offered his time, a friendly ear, and a critical eye throughout. I would also like to thank Tine Gammeltoft and Alexander Horstmann from my time at the University of Copenhagen.

Parts of chapters 2 and 3 were presented at a workshop at the Danish Institute for International Studies (DIIS) in Copenhagen and the SOAS-Oxford Graduate Workshop in Oxford, both in 2018. The scholarly generosity and engagement of Matthew Walton, Mandy Sadan, Izzy Rhoads, Courtney Wittekind, Ardeth Thawnghmung, Shona Loong, Elisabeth Olivius, and Helene Kyed all left a deep impression on these chapters. Parts of chapters 4 and 6 also greatly benefited from feedback provided at the Land, Law, and Nationalism Workshop in Stockholm and the Varieties of Peace Asia Conference in Jakarta, both in 2019. A special thanks to Kevin Woods, Geoff Aung, Nick Cheesman, Andrew Ong, Michelle Miller, and Jenny Hedström. Jenny in particular has been an outstanding friend, neighbor, and inspiration throughout the years for what an academic/activist should look like. The same can be said of Camelia Dewan.

Magnus Fiskesjö, Mark Graham, Martin Saxer, Mikael Gravers, Claudia Merli, and Danielle Drozdzewski have all read and commented on early versions of this book and helped vastly improve it. I reserve special thanks to the two anonymous reviewers for their careful, insightful, and inspired comments and suggestions that greatly assisted me in turning this text into the best version of itself. I am also deeply indebted to the keen editorial eye and steady hand of Amy Bonnaffons, without whom this book may have never seen the light of day. I am also exceedingly grateful to the editorial team at the University of Washington Press, K. Sivaramakrishnan, Caitlin Tyler-Richards, and Dandi Meng for their careful readings, constructive suggestions, and warm encouragement throughout the publishing process. It is possible to trace the deep imprints of all these intellectual contributions throughout this book. That said, any mistakes herein are wholly of my own making.

The fieldwork this book is based on was made possible by generous grants from the Swedish Society for Anthropology and Geography (SSAG), the Axel and Margaret Helge Ax:son Johnson Foundation for Public Benefit, and the Stockholm Center for Global Asia. I am especially thankful to the latter, and to Eva Hansson in particular, for a grant allowing me to dedicate several months to preparing my manuscript. I would surely have perished long ago without this steady help.

Finally, I would like to thank my family and friends, near and far, for sticking with me and supporting me through thick and thin. None of this would have been possible without my elders who went before me, especially my parents who mean the world to me. Last, but far from least, thank you to my beloved Aga, for everything.

POSSESSED LANDSCAPES

INTRODUCTION

Radical Experiments in Conservation and Sovereignty

CLANK. Clank. Clank. In lieu of a hammer, Hpa Kha Pa used a machete to nail a sign onto the side of a tree. The sign, once part of a biscuit tin, read, "Protected Forest: It is prohibited to eat or kill any living creature."

It was the middle of the monsoon season up in the mountainous Mutraw District of southeast Myanmar, toward the end of my fieldwork there, in August 2017. I was invited to accompany Hpa Kha Pa and two other men from a small nearby village as they went about conserving a patch of deep forest. All the men were wearing traditional striped tunics, out of respect to the ancestors who resided there, they told me. Yet Wee Daw, a slightly built fellow who never appeared entirely comfortable in his own skin, had paired his tunic with a baseball cap inexplicably bearing the word *Fuck*. Giant trees towered over us, and we had to talk loudly to be heard over the din of a thousand trilling insects.

This patch of forest was known as the *loh* or *ta lay* (the dwelling place of the dead; see figure 1). The men explained to me how when a person dies, their shade (*k'la*) travels to this area and takes up residence. Traipsing through the thick undergrowth, we stumbled over broken objects, left in neat piles here and there: a ripped umbrella sheltering a knife without a handle and several smashed alcohol jugs as well as three sticks driven into the earth, with a filthy piece of striped fabric draped over them, tarpaulin-like. Hpa Kha Pa, who was filming everything on his mobile phone, told me that these objects belonged to local residents who had passed away. They were conveyed here and purposefully destroyed because, in the dwelling place of the dead, everything is *koh kee* (backward, inverted), so what is broken is whole and the dead are still living. In their realm, the structure of cloth-draped sticks was someone's home, and this whole stretch of forest,

FIGURE 1. The *loh*, the dwelling place of the dead.

including the small stream that runs through it, was "their place." They possessed this forest both in the sense that they haunted it and in the sense that it belonged to them.

We were gathered here on this particular dark and rainy August afternoon to attempt to protect the forest once and for all. For many years, local people feared that outsiders might not realize the objects left here belong to the dead and take them home. Such acts risked provoking the ire of these dearly departed. People also worried that the plethora of species that called this patch of thick forest home were being over-fished and over-hunted. Following several failed experiments in conservation—attempting to get local authorities to recognize this area as a community forest, even calling in Buddhist monks from Thailand to ordain the trees there in order to protect them—they decided to take matters into their own hands. In addition to hanging signs, they also prayed and made libations to the spectral owners of this area, entreating them to protect the animals, plants, and items that belonged to the dead. Following this intervention, all the villagers I spoke to agreed that this patch of forest was safe from harm—at least for the time being.

I first met these three men nine months earlier, at a so-called consultation meeting in Mutraw's administrative center Deh Bu Noh. During this meeting we learned that a wide-ranging Indigenous-led conservation project was afoot. This project, called the Salween Peace Park, aimed to support and build on Indigenous efforts to protect patches of forest, like those carried out in the *loh*, to create a sprawling protected area. Projects such as the Salween Peace Park that experimented with different modes and scales of conservation across Myanmar's southeasterly highlands were increasingly becoming intertwined with long-standing struggles for autonomy and peacebuilding efforts. While the men in the forest that day did not see this particular effort to protect the *loh* as explicitly tied to the peace park—and, in fact, sometimes voiced reservations about the project—their actions, and the intricately layered understanding of landscapes and specters that animated them, were emblematic of the spirit behind the Salween Peace Park and other similar experiments.

These divergent efforts to protect the environment in southeast Myanmar occurred during a period of unprecedented hope in a nation long wracked by civil war. Between 2011 and 2021, Myanmar entered a faltering process of transition to democracy. Rolling ceasefires were signed between armed groups across the country, and in 2015, free elections were held for the first time in decades. Notwithstanding an overwhelming and pervasive skepticism as to the real intentions of these shifts—especially among Indigenous communities—this moment of transition elicited a flurry of radical experiments in alternative modes of conservation, governance, and sovereignty. Many of these endeavors worked to repossess highly contested landscapes upended by conflict.[1] This flurry of activity is significant not only for understanding the region more deeply but also for contemplating novel methods of peacebuilding and Indigenous sovereignty in war zones.

In this book I explore how, on multiple scales—from highly localized ad hoc solutions to transnational struggles—Indigenous people have drawn on understandings of possessing landscapes as a negotiation with spectral owners in order to not only conserve ecologies but also strive for greater autonomy, pushing back against state encroachment and capitalist predation. I begin exploring these radical experiments in conservation and autonomy in southeast Myanmar by delving into Indigenous practices and cosmologies of possessing landscapes, arguing that they be approached as alternative modes of both ownership and sovereignty. I then trace how these practices and cosmologies of possession were negotiated, translated, and rescaled to transform contested and conflictual landscapes into large-scale Indigenous-run protected areas. I examine how the playful and improvisational spirit of local experiments in environmental protection and self-determination were rescaled into conservation projects envisioning federal futures of transnational significance. In this manner, Indigenous-run protected areas became gardens for growing and prefiguring radical alternatives to armed conflict and top-down conservation. In the process, I posit that the playful experimentation with Indigenous sovereignty underpinning them has the potential to unsettle not only established notions of conservation but also self-determination and peacebuilding in southeast Myanmar and beyond.

The path to these findings was far from unerring—littered with detours and dead ends along the way. My attention was first drawn to the highlands of southeast Myanmar, and the radical experiments with conservation and sovereignty that were taking place there, as I was about to embark on an initial phase of multi-sited fieldwork, starting off in upstate New York in 2016, where I was to spend three months among former refugees who had been resettled by the United Nations High Commissioner for Refugees (UNHCR) from the sprawling refugee camps along the Thailand-Myanmar border. This fieldwork would build on previous research I had conducted in and around one of these camps in 2013. I was interested in how translocal entanglements and remittances played into ecological and political landscapes in the war zones of southeast Myanmar.

Around this time, I first became aware of these experiments in conservation and sovereignty through a press release announcing the Salween Peace Park's arrival onto the world stage. The press release opens by asking the reader rhetorically, "Can a battlefield be turned into an indigenous-run protected area for scores of endangered species like tiger, gibbons and wild cattle?" and immediately answers emphatically, "Yes it can."[2] It proceeds to state the key aspirations of the peace park: "to end and avoid violent conflict; to protect the environment; to ensure the preservation of ethnic cultural resources; and to help post-conflict communities recover and rebuild." It then quotes a local military leader from the revolutionary movement the Karen National Union (KNU), poignantly concluding that "with the Salween Peace Park, we can survive as a nation." This press release captivated my interest, refusing to let it go. When I stepped out into the field, its promises of radically different approaches to both revolutionary politics and conservation continued to haunt me. I was not sure whether or how it related to my current work but felt compelled to learn more.

After returning from upstate New York, I set out on the second phase of fieldwork to trace flows of cash, knowledge, and affect back to remittance-receiving communities in the Myanmar-Thai borderlands. Here I swiftly learned that people were far less preoccupied with their translocal entanglements with kin and kith abroad than they were with the ever more pressing threats of dispossession by transnational organizations and the Tatmadaw (the Myanmar state military-cum-military state). At the very heart of the protracted cycles of armed conflict in southeast Myanmar lay differing, overlapping, and often conflicting perspectives on and claims over how land was and could be owned and controlled.

The most pertinent questions on people's lips pertained to how they might resolve growing conflicts over the landscapes they lived in and sustained themselves with. These questions brought my mind back to the description I had read of the Salween Peace Park's assertion that conservation and preservation could help communities "survive and rebuild" after conflict. Gradually, I began contemplating taking my research in a new direction. I contacted and struck up a conversation with the Indigenous and ecological activists behind the Salween Peace Park to learn more about how they approached issues of conflicting claims on and rights to land in southeast Myanmar. From our ongoing conversations, I started to grasp how the activists, in partnership with both local communities and the KNU, intended to demonstrate one way in which both self-determination and peacebuilding might be achieved in practice. At this point it is important to note that in day-to-day life, understandings of who was considered an "activist" were highly fluid and situational. While the majority of people developing the peace park were professionals, working full-time for the activist organization Karen Environmental and Social Action Network, many had their roots in Indigenous subsistence farming communities (something I explore in more detail in chapter 6). Likewise, as I dwell on a little longer in chapters 4 and 5, upland rotational cultivators were on occasion drawn into activism.

These KESAN activists were, and still are, in the process of transforming 6,747 km2 (slightly larger than Brunei and a little under half the size of East Timor) of highly contested terrain in southeast Myanmar into an Indigenous-run conservation zone (see map 1).[3] As the first flyer of the Salween Peace Park proclaims, they were carving out a place for "all living things sharing peace." To achieve these goals, Indigenous practices and modes of dwelling, as well as small-scale efforts to protect ecologies, were translated and rescaled into both government and conservation policy. My curiosity piqued, I decided to move away from a focus on diasporic entanglements to concentrate on struggles over land, conservation, and sovereignty, focusing on the mountainous Mutraw District where the Salween Peace Park was being enacted.

Together with the activists, we settled on one village to act as a base for my fieldwork—"where many of Indigenous practices are still strong," as

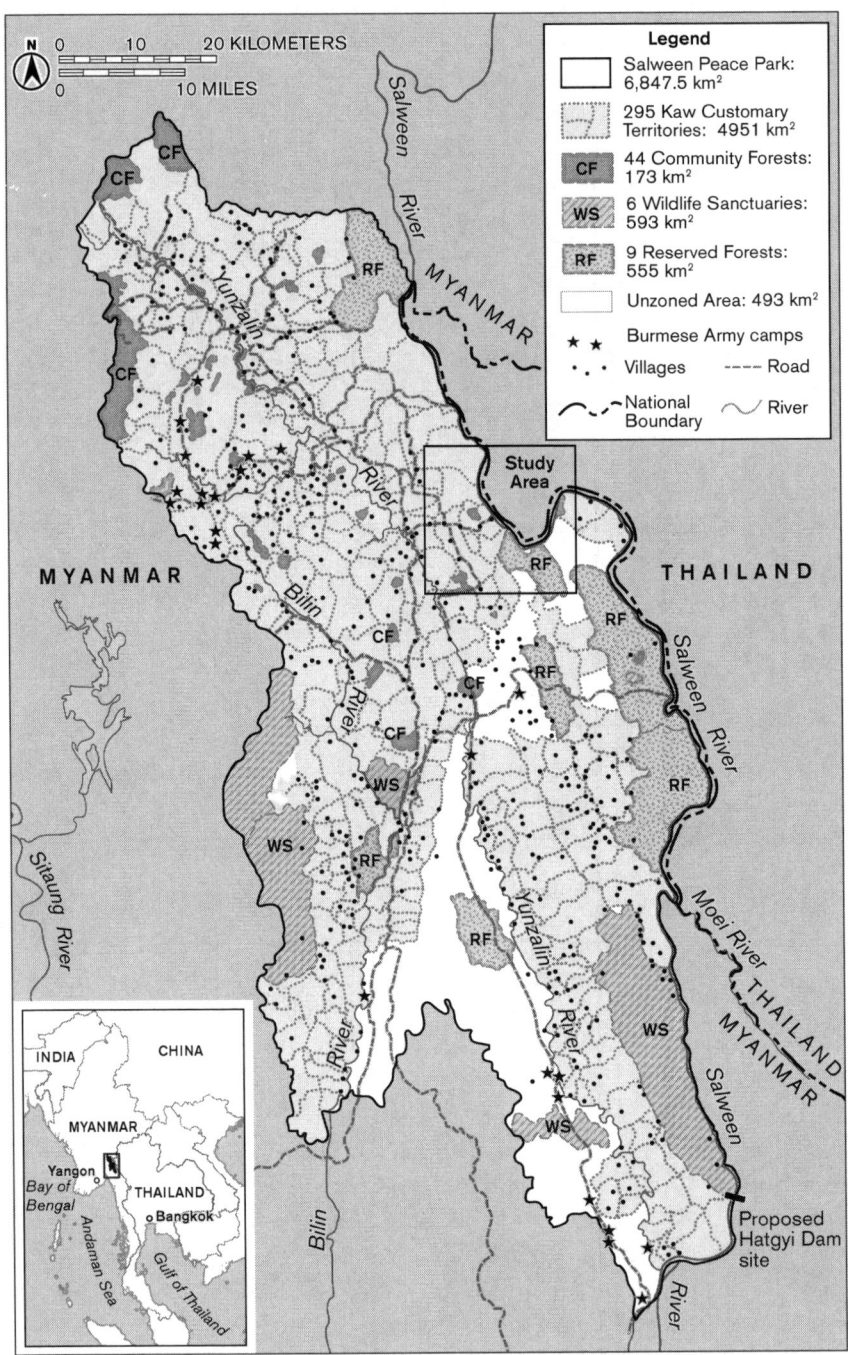

MAP 1. The Salween Peace Park. Map by Ben Pease (based on a map by the Karen Environmental and Social Action Network).

Doh K'Oh, one of the activists, put it. Given my initial frustrated attempts at multi-sited fieldwork, the physical restraints imposed on my movement by the monsoon season, and continued threats of warfare, I decided to stick to one particular area in the Mutraw highlands along the Salween River. As such, I spent nearly eight months (from January to September 2017) in and around the village I call Ta K'Thwee Duh, or Misty Village. The village sits high atop the Bu Thoe ridge that, at 1,200 meters above sea level, towers over the Salween River in the east (200 meters above sea level) while lying close to a KNU-built road (which I discuss in more detail in chapters 2 and 3).

While the village is nestled in an area ridden with armed conflict, which the Tatmadaw referred to as an insurgent "black zone" and "free fire zone" until the ceasefire of 2012 (KHRG 2009; Smith 1999), much of the heavy fighting passed around the village. The residents of Ta K'Thwee Duh and the other villages across this ridgetop were overwhelmingly subsistence farmers, sustaining themselves and their families primarily though swidden/shifting cultivation. The highlands along the Salween River are, however, far from uniformly of high altitude and instead divided into valleys and hills. As I shall demonstrate, topographic differences had significant effects on the political landscape of the Mutraw District. Capital from development and infrastructure projects, be they of KNU or non-governmental organizations (NGOs), tended to "jump over" the Bu Thoe ridge and remain in the regional centers that were often found at lower elevations.

From the vantage point of this one village, I could begin exploring vexed, overlapping, and highly indeterminate perspectives on how landscapes were and could be possessed, and highly localized ad hoc attempts to protect ecologies, in a region that was slowly becoming incorporated into the Salween Peace Park. Woven into this more classic anthropological fieldwork are my ongoing conversations with central figures from within Indigenous ecological activist groups, mostly based in Chiang Mai in Thailand, along with conversations with other activists, military figures, and local academics—periodically shifting back and forth between the highlands of southeast Myanmar and Chiang Mai. This work was supplemented with desk research on archival sources and analysis of policy documents such as land laws and charters and, to a lesser degree, my initial fieldwork in upstate New York.

LANDSCAPES OF POSSESSION AND REPOSSESSION

Spending time in Ta K'Thwee Duh, I learned how the Indigenous people regularly treated landscapes as *possessed* in the double and entangled senses of the word: as occupied or haunted by unseen more-than-human presences and as owned by these presences. Not only the *loh*, but all lands and waters were understood as, ultimately, borrowed by humans from their spectral owners, to be returned at a later date. Here I use the term *spectral* to denote something whose presence, while sensed, was never quite seen, understood to be just off the visual spectrum, yet felt in the effects they have on people's lives.[4] By *spectral* I allude not simply to "ghosts" that go bump in the night, but rather to all unseen yet powerful presences that can hold dominion over a certain area.

Part 1 of this book, "Possession," focuses on the area around Ta K'Thwee Duh and on Indigenous practices and cosmologies of possession and power. Chapter 1 delves deeper into the notion of "possessed landscapes," while chapters 2 and 3 explore the implications of this notion on regimes of ownership and sovereignty, respectively. Part 2, "Dispossession/Repossession," tacks back and forth across the border, delving deeper into growing threats of dispossession and the way various activists/Indigenous people experimented with these alternative modes of ownership and sovereignty to repossess their landscapes. Chapter 4 traces processes of dispossession in southeast Myanmar and the ways Indigenous practices were being pragmatically translated into burgeoning countermovements, while chapter 5 analyzes in situ struggles to reterritorialize the Mutraw hills as a mode of alter-politics. The sixth and final chapter then focuses on the Salween Peace Park itself, exploring how by rescaling these struggles into a large-scale protected area, the activists behind it were prefiguring alternative, more peaceful, futures.

Throughout, I take Indigenous practices, cosmologies, and concepts of possession seriously. I treat notions and practices of living together with humans and more-than-humans alike—what I describe as *conviviality*—as situated and radically alternative regimes of ownership and sovereignty: radically alternative in the sense that they present another way forward, beyond hegemonic regimes of individual ownership, state sovereignty, and extractivism that had left Myanmar bogged down in intractable conflict for decades. To paraphrase Saidiya Hartman (2019, xvii), the wild idea that animates this book is that these activists/Indigenous people are radical thinkers who tirelessly imagined other ways to live and tirelessly never failed to consider that the world might be otherwise.

Much like the Indigenous people and activists themselves, I attempt to hold in focus the two meanings of *possession*: the cosmological sense of the landscapes as occupied or haunted by more-than-human beings and the political-ecological sense of control and ownership of contested landscapes.

The title of this book plays on these entwined and contested connotations of *possessed*. In combining these different senses of possession, the Indigenous experiments with conservation and sovereignty I describe emerge as highly sophisticated ways of looking anew at the protracted political impasse in southeast Myanmar. They gesture toward and prefigure radically new approaches to securing peace and protecting biodiversity. At the same time, as the quote from the KNU general suggests, these experiments also continue seven decades of struggle for Indigenous autonomy. Furthermore, in speaking of possessed landscapes, I take landscapes as "a starting point" in order to study the "structural synchronicities between ecology, capital, and the human and more-than-human-histories" (Tsing, Mathews, and Bubandt 2019, 186). And following Munira Khayyat, I find that thinking through landscapes helps to "ethnographically grasp war's continuing presence in the warp and weft of living" (2022, 27). As I show, in southeast Myanmar everyday life, conflict, conservation, and revolution have become increasingly interwoven.

PERSPECTIVES AND POSITIONS

Three overarching and overlapping themes emerge out of my understanding of possession and run throughout this book: violent contact zones; spectral subjects and sovereignties; and experiments in translation, scale, and autonomy. While, for the sake of clarity, I divide these into three separate streams, they are intricately entwined.

Violent Contact Zones

Over the years pathbreaking work has been carried out in highland areas of Southeast Asia such as those in southeast Myanmar. In this body of scholarship, upland spaces are understood in relation to galactic polities and the geo-bodies of nation-states (Tambiah 1976; Winichakul 1994) and grasped in terms such as *borderworlds, non-state spaces,* or (capitalist) *frontiers* (Li 2014a; Sadan 2013; Scott 2009; Tsing 2005). This book brings such work into dialogue with the notion of contact zones. It ethnographically examines both historical and day-to-day encounters along the Salween and how such encounters have shaped and continue to shape landscapes. In drawing on the work of Mary Louise Pratt (1991, 2008) and James Clifford (1997), this book explores how these highlands are not only sites of domination but also of continuing relations, shot through with experimentation, improvisation, negotiation, and co-option. These are ongoing "contact histories" and "stories of struggle" that are disruptive, where power imbalances are not resolved but endure into the future (Clifford 1997, 193). Furthermore, contact zones are not only sites of violence and struggle but also of intimacy, desire, and dependency (Faier 2009; Yeoh and Willis 2005; Wilson 2019), where negotiation takes place between humans and more-than-humans alike (Haraway 2007; see also Govindrajan 2018).

Beginning in chapter 1, I show how practices and cosmologies along the Salween River were always interwoven with histories of violence, leaving them constantly unsettled and unsettling. Armed conflict undoes and refigures people's relations with one another, with their landscapes, and with the more-than-human world, remaking not only societies and ecologies but also the cosmos itself (cf. Ruiz-Serna 2023). Practices and cosmologies were constantly coming unstuck and open to renegotiation—in the grips of "continuous birth" (Ingold 2011, 68). Contact zones are "relational ensembles sustained through processes of cultural borrowing, appropriation and translation—multidirectional processes" (Clifford 2003, 34). Yet, in the midst of these processes of renegotiation, I found that many histories and practices endured, passed down through the generations. I attempt to grasp them less as hybrid (Latour 1993) or plural (McConnachie 2014)—which would suggest the finished products of these processes—but more as ongoing, unsettled, and highly flexible.

Spectral Subjects and Sovereignties

As I have already hinted, people in the highlands of Mutraw regularly treated their landscapes as teeming with more-than-human life, both biotic—from microbes to elephants—and spectral. In deploying the term *spectral*, I lean on its other ramifying connotations, to attempt to draw out a sense of these unseen more-than-humans as perpetually ineffable and indeterminate, almost impossible to pin down (cf. Bubandt 2017, 125). I explore how people could never be certain of their identity. People could only intuit these beings by sensing their presence on their own bodies, in dreams, and in their effects on everyday life by way of active experimentation.

In taking this perspective, in chapter 1, I bring it into conversation with scholarship on the ways in which, in many places around the world, both animals and specters are regularly treated as fellow persons, with whom humans were continually engaged in social relations (Chao 2022; Descola 2013; Kimmerer [2013] 2020). Much akin to other groups of Indigenous peoples across the globe, the residents of the Mutraw highlands constantly strove to *ray daw* (make friends)—that is to say, make and maintain good relations with one another and their environments (cf. Govindrajan 2018; TallBear 2019; Wildcat 2013). I gloss these processes, as mentioned above, as conviviality, or living with and living well with others (Büscher and Fletcher 2020; Illich [1973] 1975).

One corollary of landscapes busy with spectral persons, which I explore in depth in chapter 2, was that the human residents regularly spoke of the land they lived and farmed on as *hee loh* (borrowed) from its "real" spectral owners, intimating a logic of custodianship. This became particularly evident in the case of specters referred to as *k'sah*, or "owners," said to own certain trees, lakes, the lands around a village, or even all land and waterways.

I conceptualize the continual striving for conviviality between humans, animals, plants, and specters by describing these highlands as possessed landscapes, in the dual and entangled sense mentioned previously: of unseen persons both occupying and haunting landscapes as well as controlling and owning them. Returning to the notion of contact zones, in this book I understand possessed landscapes as naturalcultural or "more-than-human contact zones" (Haraway 2007; Isaacs and Otruba 2019) between the human and the spectral realms, where people are perpetually negotiating with specters: avoiding certain areas where they are said to reside; strictly observing *ta du ta htu*, or "taboos," so as not to vex them; and conducting *lu ta* that, while literally meaning "to feed," entails making offerings, propitiating, and entreating them.

To this end, in chapter 2, I argue that practices and cosmologies of possessed landscapes delineate alternative modes of both ownership and sovereignty. Chapter 3 explores how along the lower reaches of the Salween River, the Myanmar government remained distant, such that the KNU acted as a de facto state, with its own state departments and laws. However, at higher elevations, such as along the Bu Thoe ridge, its sovereignty also grew threadbare. Nevertheless, I found it difficult to square the ethnography I had collected with common portrayals of such highland areas as pockets of "anarchy" (Gibson and Sillander 2011; Scott 2009). Insofar as the term *anarchy* comes from the Greek for "no ruler" (Morris 2014, 62) or "without government" (Barclay 1998, 8–10), it was not so much the case that sovereignty was lacking but rather that sovereignty was held in spectral hands. I describe this mode of politics as "spectral sovereignty."

Experiments in Translation, Scale, and Autonomy

Riffing off Kevin Woods's (2011) notion of "ceasefire capitalism," I describe the startling uptick in violence and dispossession that shadowed the 2012 ceasefire agreements (see also Aung 2018; Barbesgaard 2019; Woods 2019) as a form of ceasefire territorialization. As I show, the Tatmadaw continued its counterinsurgency against villagers in these highlands—only now visited upon them by other means, through expanding economic and religious spheres. In response, growing ensembles of Indigenous people, activists, and armed revolutionary groups began pushing back against these new threats of dispossession by experimenting with Indigenous modes of conservation and autonomy.

In chapter 4, I delve into how these ensembles of villagers-cum-activists were enacting this pushback through pragmatic translations of Indigenous politics of possession. They were experimenting with translating local practices and cosmologies into "customary territories" and conservation zones and creating "counter-maps" (Peluso 1995; see also Chao 2022, 51–73). In this manner, they were able to begin repelling encroachments onto their lands from both the Myanmar state and actors from within the KNU state. Chapter 5 goes on to explore how Indigenous people in the Mutraw hills were increasingly experimenting with spectral sovereignty as a way to protect their landscapes from dispossession, creating ad hoc conservation areas and pockets of autonomy. I follow Ghassan Hage (2015) in describing these actions as alter-politics that gesture toward radically different ways of being enmeshed in the world. Furthermore, I draw on the notion of "symbiotic events" (Stengers 2011, 60) to show how these experiments with Indigenous conservation, in creating tiny pockets of autonomy, were not only clashing with but also intermittently becoming aligned with the KNU's long struggle for greater self-determination. I end this book by showing how KESAN was building on these fleeting moments of alignment to compose the Salween Peace Park.

In the final chapter, I show how the activists from KESAN experimented with rescaling Indigenous practices of possessed landscapes, tirelessly laboring to adapt small-scale in situ practices in the Mutraw hills so as to make them legible (Scott 1998) on the scale of national and transnational politics. They also worked top-down, lobbying to create laws and policies, clearing a space within the KNU's legal landscape where such alternative modes of ownership and sovereignty could take root (Hong 2017). By working across scales, they were playfully "messing" with scale to suit the situation at hand, unsettling and subverting both geographical and political levels of action in the process. In this manner, they prefigured alternative futures that upended established notions of conservation and revolution (cf. Krøijer 2010; Maeckelbergh 2009).

The Salween Peace Park, I argue, is thus a form of "liberation conservation," in which the demand to create an Indigenous-run protected area is deeply wedded to the demand for self-determination. Before getting into the nitty-gritty of how I approached these themes in my fieldwork, let me first contextualize this book with an abridged history of chronic conflict in highland southeast Myanmar, which I braid together with Indigenous histories.

HISTORIES OF CONTACT, WAR, AND REVOLUTION

The borderlands along the lower Salween River are steeped in deep histories of contact and violent conflict. Upland areas oscillated between sites of violent territorial tussles and largely autonomous buffer zones between successive city-states and empires for hundreds, if not thousands, of years (Gravers 1999; Scott 2009; South 2008). Located at the interstices of nation-states and of human and more-than-human realms, I follow Pratt (2008, 7–8) in describing this area as a contact zone where "cultures meet, clash and grapple with each other, often in contexts of highly asymmetrical relations of power." The "contact history" perhaps most pertinent to the current political predicaments along the Salween River, which I focus on here, followed the colonization of this area by the British Empire. As I show in chapter 1, people still live in and with the ruins of this particular historical conjuncture.

In the mid-nineteenth century, following the Second Anglo-Burmese War, the lower Salween highlands were forcibly annexed to British India and officially designated as a "frontier area." Following this designation, the newly minted Salween District was placed under indirect rule, with day-to-day governance left to "tribal chieftains" (Furnivall 1960, 12). Described in British colonial records as a "wilderness of mountains" (Burma Gazetteer 1910, 1), the Salween District covered most of modern-day Northern Karen State, bordered by the Thaton (Doo Tha Htoo) District to the south, the Toungoo (Ta-Oo) Division and the Karenni State to the north, and Thailand to the east. By some accounts, this area, particularly the area now known as the Mutraw District, has never been brought fully under centralized state rule and continues to be largely autonomous from the Myanmar state to this day (Jolliffe 2016, 9). The creation of these frontier zones and the resulting "indirect" governance were, however, part of what Mikael Gravers describes as a colonial "political and economic policy of divide and rule" to segregate certain groups and make them more governable (1999, 30–31).[5] This "indirect" rule was by no means tantamount to people being left to their own devices, isolated from the rest of Burma (proper). On the contrary, the classification of these highlands as a frontier initiated a massive intensification of (violent) contact—first with missionaries and venture capitalists and steadily with the colonial state in the guise of the forestry department.

The majority of the people living in the Mutraw highlands refer to themselves and their language as Pwakanyaw, literally meaning "human" or "humankind." As Violet Cho suggests, this term denotes "human becoming" (2023, 17n1) as a process rather than a fixed identity. Consequently, throughout this book, I refer to my interlocutors as Pwakanyaw in accord with the practices of the people themselves and the scholars who write about them (Cho 2014, 2023; Trakansuphakon 2006). Following the intensification of contact between Pwakanyaw (and other Karenic-language speakers across Burma) with colonial and missionary practices and discourses under British rule, this identification began to shift. Increasingly, these dispersed and heterogeneous peoples began to speak of themselves as belonging to a wider group, denoted by the exonym "Karen."

This notion of shared "Karen-ness" was initially articulated as *daw k'lu*, or "all the tribes" (Fujimura 2020, 321–22; Christie 2000), by missionaries and missionary-educated Pwakanyaw intellectuals such as Dr. T. Thanbyah, who studied theology in upstate New York. Consequently, missionaries and churches were, and continue to be, pivotal in the Karen movement (Christie 2000; Gravers 2007; Horstmann 2011a). Yet cases of missionary appropriation and co-option are rarely so simple, nor are those being preached to so passive: Proselytizing is a multidirectional process (cf. Clifford 2003, 34). As the notion of a separate "Karen People" began to take root across colonial Burma, reinforced by the growing power of Karen church groups, it was accompanied by a crescendo of calls for a corresponding homeland in which these people could reside. This new homeland, a "Karen Country" originally located in what is now known as the Tanintharyi Region of southern Myanmar (San C. Po 1928, 79), was later christened Kawthoolei. This name may be translated as either "the land of the *thoo lei* flower," a kind of crêpe ginger that my interlocutors explained indicates soil fertility, or "the earth burned black," intimating that the land is well suited for swidden cultivation—which involves clearing areas of forest for farming with the help of controlled burning (Gravers 2007, 245).

By 1881, the Karen National Association (KNA) was established. The KNA then began to flesh out and amplify calls for Karen nationhood, a place for "all the tribes" to live together. While vague assurances of Karen nationhood were made by colonial authorities throughout their reign, no provisions were made for an autonomous Karen homeland when Burma gained its independence in 1948, following several years under Japanese occupation during World War II (Walton 2008, 896–97). During the occupation, communities along the Salween River overwhelmingly sided with the British colonists, becoming embroiled in a bloody guerrilla war against both the Japanese Empire and their allies, the Burma Independence Army (BIA). This guerrilla war and the resulting violent reprisals visited on the civilian population cost countless lives and displaced whole villages (South 2008, 22–23).

When many of the central figures (the "thirty comrades") behind the BIA such as Aung San (Aung San Suu Kyi's father) and Ne Win (who later became the country's dictator) quickly took leadership positions (as prime minister and chief of staff of the armed forces, respectively) in the newly independent Union of Burma, many Karen were understandably wary. The KNA and three other Karen organizations joined forces in 1947 to form the KNU, and following a series of reprisal attacks that turned into intercommunal violence between Karen and Burman villages in 1948, the KNU went underground. An armed wing of the KNU, the Karen National Liberation Army (KNLA), was formed, and revolution was officially declared on January 31, 1949.

This revolutionary war was, however, slow to reach up into the Mutraw highlands. As many of the villagers who were alive at this time attested to me, the 1950s were a period of relative calm, punctuated by sporadic armed clashes between the KNU and the Tatmadaw. After the original heart of the revolution, the Irrawaddy Delta in southwestern Burma, fell to the resurgent Tatmadaw, by the mid-1950s these still largely autonomous "frontier areas" in Mutraw became the new "nucleus" of the Karen struggle (Furnivall 1960, 105–6; Lintner 2015). The situation changed dramatically in the mid-1960s when the county's ascendant dictator General Ne Win (who, as noted, was one of the "thirty comrades") began to enact a counterinsurgency program to "liquidate the insurgents" (Smith 1999, 258), known as *pya ley pya*, or the "four cuts."

The aim of this counterinsurgency program was to "cut" the four main links between the revolution and their civilian bases: food, funds, intelligence, and recruits (Smith 1999, 258). This was to be carried out by dispossessing villages and resettling them out of reach of the revolutionary movements. In one fell swoop, upland communities in much of southeast Myanmar became "black zones" of "hard-core" insurgency. The Tatmadaw were then given carte blanche to use any means necessary to remove the civilian population and transform an area into a "white zone" or "peace area." While sustained fighting never quite reached the top of the Bu Thoe ridge (where I conducted the lion's share of my research), many of the villagers' kin and kith living closer to the Salween River witnessed this counterinsurgency firsthand. One specific example, which I detail in chapter 4, occurred in the area of Thee Mu Hta, a short distance from Ta K'Thwee Duh and where many of the villagers' kin resided.

After a drawn-out battle, the Tatmadaw wrested control of Thee Mu Hta, and this hamlet and former KNLA base was declared a white zone.⁶ The Tatmadaw then began making regular visits to the nearest village of Dweh Kee Duh, demanding taxes and insisting that the residents relocate to the newly established so-called peace area. My neighbor's oldest brother, Hpu Htoo, who still lived in Dweh Kee Duh, explained that when the villagers refused, the Tatmadaw burned their rice fields and their granaries to the ground to intimidate them into moving. Martin Smith has shown that this was the case throughout Burma; in the "four cuts" campaign, "there [was] no such thing as an innocent or neutral villager. Every community must fight, flee or join the Tatmadaw" (1999, 260). All villagers living in "black zones" were classified as potential KNLA combatants or collaborators and thus legitimate targets. In the wake of this strategy, villagers all along the Salween faced shoot-on-sight orders, and their homes and fields were regularly plundered and razed to the ground, with the remains littered with landmines in scorched earth tactics (KHRG 2009, 2012)—giving new meaning to the translation of the shared Karen homeland of Kawthoolei as "earth burned black." These tactics were intended to force civilians to flee from such black zones where the KNU/KNLA were most active, either across the border or to newly established white zones/peace areas that acted much like the "strategic hamlets" the United States employed in Laos and Vietnam, insulated from the revolution (Smith 1999). I learned that, while many of the original residents of the area around Dweh Kee Duh had fled to the refugee camps across the river in Thailand, the KNLA, who retained a strong presence in this area, were able to eventually push the Tatmadaw back to their barracks and surround them with landmines hemming them in.

In the wake of these brutal counterinsurgency tactics, hundreds of thousands of civilians, much like the residents of Dweh Kee Duh, were forced to flee to the refugee camps in Thailand from the 1980s onward. Unable to return home, a whole new generation came into contact not only with more missionaries but also with a wide array of international non-governmental organizations (INGOs) that provided education and training steeped in notions of human and Indigenous rights and ecological sustainability. While a ceasefire was brokered between the KNU and the Tatmadaw in 2012, armed conflict and dispossession did not abate; as outlined in chapter 4, the fighting simply became more insidious. Increasingly, under the pretext of so-called development and conservation, the Tatmadaw were remobilizing in ceasefire areas to "secure" such projects, effectively dispossessing civilians and establishing control over earlier KNU territories (Woods 2011, 2019).

In the wake of this wave of mass dispossession, a new generation of revolutionaries was emerging. This new generation carried on their forebears' struggle for self-determination but by other means—moving away from armed insurgency to edge ever closer to Indigenous and ecological activism, as evidenced by the Salween Peace Park (I explore this project in detail in chapter 6). This, however, is but one way of narrating this history. The Indigenous people of these highlands had their own particular manner of telling this story, which is often left out of "official" accounts.

Indigenous Histories

Along the Salween River, people often spoke of themselves and their practices as Moh La Pa Lah, "people who feed and follow the practices of their ancestors" (cf. Buadaeng 2003), or Thoo Hkoh. While the literal translation of *Thoo Hkoh* is "black heads," American missionary Jonathan Wade defines this term aptly as "worldly people, unbelievers" (1896, 1291). When I asked elders in Ta K'Thwee Duh to help me get a better impression of Indigenous/Thoo Hkoh histories of these highlands, they were prone to telling one of two types of tales: those of events within living memory, such as World War II and the end of colonialism, which some of the eldest villagers had lived through, or those of cosmogony, on how the universe came into being. As noted earlier, these histories were continually coming unstuck and being reshaped in the face of decades of armed conflict. What follows is an abbreviated version of the way Hpee Thoo, one of oldest women in Ta K'Thwee Duh, narrated this tale to me:

> In the beginning there was only wind, sky, and water. In the water there lived one fish, and in the sky one bird, a *htoe hklu* (a Drongo bird of the Dicrurus genus). On the water there was a tiny clod of earth the size of a large seed. Out of this clod of earth grew a banyan tree, forming a tiny island.
>
> On this island lived Mu Khah with her daughter (who is never named).[7] However, because neither of them had the ability to create anything new, the world remained in this state for a long time, just wind, sky, and water. This and the inhabitants of this tiny island, one fish and one bird.
>
> But one day, while her daughter was playing by this vast and endless ocean, stirring up the water with her hand, she created eddies that fermented the surface so that it began to foam and bubble. All of a sudden, one of the bubbles burst and a little boy appeared out of it. She took the boy to her mother, who named him Y'wa, meaning "to flow like water."

As this boy grew older, he began to realize that, unlike Mu Khah and her daughter, he was possessed with *ta thoo ta pgho*: the potency or power of creation. This potency allowed him to create new matter, to build on this desolate world. So one day, while Mu Khah and her daughter were distracted,[8] he drafted the bird and the fish to help him smuggle tiny clods of earth from under the banyan tree and transplant them to another area. From these tiny clods, they slowly created the first landmass. [In some iterations there was a termite nest in the Banyan tree and these insects also helped Y'wa with this task.] Eventually, Y'wa, together with these animals, created all the earth that humans, animals, and specters alike reside upon. Later Y'wa folded the earth to create the hills and valleys that form the landscapes of the earth as we now know it. Upon forming the landscape, Y'wa set to work populating it by creating all the other animals and the humans that now exist. The two first humans he fashioned were a woman and a man, Naw Eh Oo and Saw Ah Dah.

After spending some time with his creations, Y'wa eventually decided to leave the earth to reside in Mu Hkoh (the sky, heaven, or firmament), never to be seen or heard from again. Upon leaving, he took most of the *ta thoo ta pgho*, the potency to create new matter, with him. However, he left a few deposits, littered in the landscape, in places he had touched, in a few exceptional beings such as *k'sah* (his "emissaries"), and a tiny fraction in the bodies of all male and female flora and fauna so they might also create new life. He no longer intervenes in earthly affairs, and the *ta thoo ta pgho* he left behind is finite, slowly waning for each generation that passes.

In these tales the history of creation is not abstract but rather embedded in specific contours of the landscape (cf. Hau'ofa 2008). As such, histories are never inert. They continued on in the deposits of *ta thoo ta pgho*, of "potency," that Y'wa left behind in places he had touched (I address these points more thoroughly in chapter 1). Yet this potency, this power of creation, could not be accessed directly. While Y'wa was revered as a kind of demiurge, in day-to-day matters one had to pray to, propitiate, and beseech his *k'loo* (ambassadors or emissaries), the *k'sah*. I delve deeper into who these emissaries are and their effects on everyday life and politics in chapter 3. However, their potency was also waning.

Through this Indigenous lens, the arrival of the white foreigner in the form of missionaries in the early 1800s, and some years later colonialists, was regularly grasped via the tale of a returning *pu dee wah*, or "younger white brother." This tale is perhaps one of the most well-documented Indigenous histories among Pwakanyaw, residing in both Myanmar and Thailand (see Cheesman 2002; Hayami 2004; Marshall 1922; Renard 2003; South 2008). I was regaled with these tales on numerous occasions throughout my stay in these highlands and was regularly referred to as *pu dee wah*.

In broad brushstrokes, these tales detail how, at some undisclosed point after creation, there were three human brothers. These three brothers were to become the main groups of humanity: the oldest brother is the ancestor of all Pwakanyaw (here, in the sense of all Karenic-language speaking groups); the middle brother is the ancestor of all dark-skinned peoples; and the youngest brother, *pu dee wah*, is the ancestor of all light-skinned peoples. When Y'wa came to collect these first humans, the oldest brother, the ancestor of the Pwakanyaw, was away working in his rice field and they left without him. Later he lost his "golden book" of knowledge given to him by Y'wa, or it was stolen by his youngest brother. The oldest brother then found himself orphaned, alone, and with no written language. Eventually, he migrated to the Mutraw highlands along the Salween, being the first human to step foot here, and his progeny are the current Pwakanyaw residents.[9] It is prophesized that *pu dee wah*, the younger white brother, would one day come back and return his older brother's golden book, along with their lost knowledge.

In this framework, *goh la wah*, or white foreigners, be they missionaries or anthropologists, are frequently seen as this returning sibling and spoken of as obligated to help their long-suffering older brother. As one visiting elder insisted to me, the eyes of those *goh la wah* who do not help their older brother will turn *khah* (pale), implying they will become blind. This tale has been the subject of much heated academic debate since the 1970s (Hayami 2004; Keyes [1977] 1995, 2003; Rajah 1990; Renard 2003). Eschewing early missionary notions that these tales add credence to the proposition that Pwakanyaw are "fallen" Christians, these tales are regularly taken to be the result of the machinations of Christianized elites who have rewritten and co-opted histories to entrench their own political dominance. More recently, however, researchers have begun foregrounding the syncretic aspects of these oral histories to argue that they evidence an Indigenous mode of dealing with alterity.

Anthropologist Yoko Hayami argues that these stories illustrate an Indigenous regime of causality and temporality, where events are apprehended ex post facto, after the fact, as a premonition or a prophesy (2004, 29). In this manner, inexplicable events and alterity—whether in the form of pale-faced missionaries preaching the gospel or of visiting anthropologists—are drawn into existing narrative schemes and histories to contextualize them and give them meaning. Events, and indeed history itself, are understood not in a unilineal temporal sequence but rather in a far more circular and ad hoc manner: ex post facto. Histories are constantly reworked in relation to pressing current events.

These oral histories might be best understood as an Indigenous archive of the past, as "contact histories" that are constantly reworked. Indigenous histories are littered with fragments and remains of Christian tales. The names of the first two humans, Naw Eh Oo and Saw Ah Dah, are strikingly similar to that of the biblical figures Eve and Adam, and men who actively defined themselves as Thoo Hkoh or Bah Hpaw (a syncretic form of Buddhism) regularly referred to finding their wife as "getting my rib back." In the next section, I elaborate how we might grasp these pliable and often playful histories and practices.

TOWARD A PLAYFUL MORE-THAN-HUMAN POLITICAL ECOLOGY

When approaching contexts in which people struggle over access and control of their landscapes, it is important to carefully balance political analysis with taking Indigenous cosmologies seriously. On the one hand, if one focuses too intently on Indigenous cosmologies, one risks becoming analytically blinded to the constant multiscalar struggles over power and ownership underpinning them (Bessire and Bond 2014; Hornborg 2017b; Vigh and Sausdal 2014). Such political struggles over possession lie at the very heart of this book. Yet if one focuses too doggedly on political struggles for power and possession, one risks treating the land as a set of extractable resources and eclipsing awareness of the interdependence of human and more-than-human lives (cf. Escobar 1999; Karlsson 2018)—a perspective at the heart of both Indigenous experiments with conservation and my research. In trying to understand politically complex places such as the highlands along the lower Salween River, and practices such as those of possessed landscapes, this fine balance can be exceedingly difficult to achieve.

When I began conducting fieldwork in the Mutraw highlands, I was determined to earnestly engage with both politics and Indigenous cosmologies. But I quickly noticed the ways in which the residents themselves were, in certain circumstances, less than deadly serious. People regularly engaged in highly indeterminate, pragmatic, and, at times, playful relations with histories and with the world. Beyond easy binaries, the politics of possession were constantly (re)negotiated in the grip of "worldly" encounters (Tsing 2005, 1). Here, the old missionary translation of the descriptor Thoo Hkoh as "worldly people" and "unbelievers," whether intended or not, becomes immensely apt.

As Cho (2023) stresses is the case in the Christian Pwakanyaw communities she studies, the notion of "belief" cannot be understood independently from the practices/actions that animate it: Belief (*tana*, in Pwakanyaw) and action (*tama*) are intimately entangled. Stretching this understanding a little, I argue that what is at stake has less to do with belief (in the traditional sense of the word) in these more-than-human actors than their "power to work" (James 1907, 58)—their *effect* on the world.

In this manner, I suggest a methodological move toward a more playful more-than-human political ecology that is engaged and critical—taking both cosmologies and politics seriously, while remaining agnostic to both. I deploy the word *playful* here to emphasize the manner in which my interlocutors often spoke and acted: with a certain twinkle in the eye, suggesting both lightheartedness and a willingness to experiment with different roles and practices. Fittingly, Donna Haraway describes the constant oscillation inherent in contact zones between efforts to conserve a relational order and efforts to hash out new modes of relating as a form of play, where "play breaks the rules to make something else happen" (2007, 238). However, this is not to say that such play was frivolous or flippant; rather, it was playing seriously.

Taking Both Cosmologies and Politics Seriously

People's day-to-day practices along the Salween River—particularly, their relations to the environment as possessed by biotic and spectral more-than-human actors, from tigers to ancestors—are usually gathered under the rubric of "animism," or as one specific iteration of the mode of "hierarchical" animism prevalent in Southeast Asia (Århem 2016; see also Sahlins 2014). In this book, however, I do not tackle thorny issues of religion head-on. While I touch on the topic obliquely in chapters 4 and 5, a deep dive into the blisteringly complex and highly vexed nature of religion in southeast Myanmar is beyond the remit of this particular book. There is already a plethora of scholars who do a sterling job of describing and analyzing religion among Karenic-language-speaking groups across Myanmar and Thailand (see Buadaeng 2003; Chambers 2024; Cole 2020; Gravers 2007; Hayami 2004; Horstmann 2011b). Accordingly, I treat practices and cosmologies labeled as Thoo Hkoh/Moh La Pa Lah as "more a sensibility, tendency, or style of engaging with the world and the beings or things that populate it" (Swancutt 2019) and as "orientations" (Bielo 2015). These practices are an aesthetic and a way of being enmeshed with the world.

In previous studies from Myanmar, practices and histories similar to those discussed in this book are regularly categorized under the rubric of *nats*, and their interferences in human lives and politics are grasped as part of "supernatural belief systems" (Leach 1954; Spiro [1967] 1996). Thus, in Burma and beyond, "supernatural beliefs" are commonly understood as, in Edmund Leach's words, "in the last analysis, nothing more than ways of describing the formal relationships that exist between real persons and real groups" (1954, 182)—that is to say, metaphorical representations of real events, which should be properly understood as symbolic (see also Willerslev 2007, 182).

A tendency remains in contemporary political anthropological accounts to pay respect to such "beliefs," insofar as this respect does not undermine the "critical realism" in which scientific writing and politics are grounded (Graeber 2015; Hornborg 2017a, 2017b). A similar critical realism undergirding most forms of political ecology "starts from the premise that the world exists independently of our knowledge of it and that its very independence means that human knowledge is not itself reality, but a representation of it" (Neumann 2005, 9–10). A corollary of this critical realism in both political ecological and many political anthropological accounts alike is that, in the last analysis, tigers, mountains, and most of what we name "nature" more generally should be treated as inert resources to be managed by human political action (Peluso and Watts 2001; Sikor and Lund 2010). In such theoretical schools, spectral persons are reduced to "beliefs"—as opposed to "how the world is, as a matter of empirical fact, constituted" (Good 1993, 9; see also Apter 2017, 293). Implicit in the notion of belief is the tacit premise that, in opposition to "fact," belief is essentially a "logical error" (Favret-Saada 1980, 5n2). But what happens when we do not take a point of departure in the notion of belief?

In this book I join the growing chorus of critical voices who have begun questioning the grounding of both political anthropology and political ecology more generally in a critical realism. Political ecology approaches often translate Indigenous peoples' own histories and practices, hedged in the inextricable entanglement of human and more-than-human, into beliefs or representations of the "actual" struggles over control of natural resources (Escobar 1999; Karlsson 2018, 22; see also Chao 2022; B. R. Middleton 2015, 563).

Perhaps one of the most prominent voices pushing back against such approaches is Marisol de la Cadena, who attempts to bring Indigenous worlds and political accounts together in her work among Quechua people in the Peruvian Andes. She argues that belief does not necessarily mediate the relations between humans and various unseen more-than-humans (2015, 26). It was not so much, as she shows, that people "believe" in what they termed *tirakuna*, or "Earth Beings"—who bear a strong resemblance to the *kaw k'sah* (spectral sovereigns) I discuss in detail in chapter 3—as it was that an Earth Being "*is*, period" (2015, 26), enacted in everyday practices of being/becoming together.

De la Cadena's argument bears a striking resemblance to Benedict Anderson's ideas on power in Java as "concrete, homogeneous, constant in total quality, and without inherent moral implications... Power is" (1990, 22–23). Earth Beings, like power in Java and "potency" in Southeast Asia more generally (Chua et al. 2012; Errington 2012), are not something mediated and cannot be questioned directly but rather are hypostatized as part and parcel of people's everyday reality. De la Cadena strives to "take seriously (perhaps literally) the presence in politics of those actors, which, being other than human, the dominant disciplines assigned either to nature (where they were to be known by science) or to the metaphysical and symbolic fields of knowledge" (2010, 336). In hypostatizing more-than-humans and taking their presence in politics on their own terms, de la Cadena attempts to marry research into Indigenous worlds with political anthropology by evoking Isabelle Stengers's ([1997] 2010) notion of cosmopolitics.

This work follows a growing tradition in anthropology attempting to go beyond merely respecting and representing others' realities and instead to take them seriously. Such a move opens up the possibility for Indigenous concepts and realities to unsettle and challenge our own preconceived suppositions. This approach has been variously described as "theory/practice of the permanent decolonization of thought" (Viveiros de Castro 2014, 40) and a "politics of ontology" (Holbraad et al. 2014). In this move, the political and critical imaginary of anthropology is shifted from investigating struggles over power and ownership toward allowing Indigenous practice to critique our own (theoretical) presuppositions (cf. Hage 2015).

I draw inspiration from these powerful critiques of approaches that would attempt to reduce Indigenous practices and cosmologies to beliefs and subordinate them as representation of paramount ("more real") reality—while keeping in mind important concerns that have been raised toward such modes of critiques as either a continuation of colonialism or as a way of twisting in situ struggles for decolonization into mere metaphor (Todd 2016; Tuck and Yang 2012; see also Mehtta 2022). Along these lines, I attempt to take the ways people related to their environments, and their practices and politics of possession, on their own terms. This move to take Indigenous practices on their own terms, however, bears with it the corresponding threat of flattening social worlds and the politics at play in the shaping of what "is" (Bessire and Bond 2014; Vigh and Sausdal 2014, 63)—which, in turn, threatens to obfuscate people's perpetual indeterminacy as to how to respond to constantly shifting political, economic, and ecological terrains.

Throughout this book I argue that, in the context of chronic armed conflict along the Salween River, Thoo Hkoh (so-called animist) practices were constantly interwoven with interminable cycles of armed violence and upheaval. Between spectral and indeterminate phenomena that may or may not be present and equally unpredictable patterns of insurgency, counterinsurgency, and dispossession, people were left to tinker with different ways of responding to and negotiating with these ever-shifting and unsettled terrains of war (cf. Pedersen 2011, 4–9). War reverberates through the web of both human and more-than-human entanglements, acting as a force capable not only of destroying relational worlds and the practices tied to them but also of generating them anew (Khayyat 2022; Ruiz-Serna 2023). Thus, taking Indigenous practices (overly) seriously, or even literally, threatens to miss the mark and flatten the complexity of people's lives. In response I draw out the persistent sense of indeterminacy and doubt and foreground the distinct playfulness, in the sense of both levity and of experimentation, of people's relations with the world.

Taking Doubt Seriously

To paraphrase de la Cadena's statement on Earth Beings, for the women and men living along the Salween River, more-than-humans such as the *kaw k'sah*, the spectral owners of the area around a village, were—full stop. Unless, of course, they were not.

In the Mutraw District, I learned that sometimes a mountain was the seat of a *kaw k'sah*, and the appearance of a tiger was a harbinger that the *kaw k'sah* had become vexed by human moral transgression. In these instances, the mountain and the tiger were deeply entangled in day-to-day politics. At other times, however, a tiger was just a large cat, and a mountain was just a pile of rocks. Each time a tiger was spotted, it was not immediately taken to be the *kaw k'sah* or its emissary. Rather, only after careful observation and discussion of the effects it had on their lives was its presence discerned or denied.

In chapter 1, I follow Tim Ingold (building on the work of Alfred Irving Hallowell) in showing how, while landscapes always had the potentiality to be animate and to be possessed by unseen more-than-humans, "the crucial test is experience" (Ingold 2000, 96–97), in people's pragmatic engagements with them. Michael Lambek describes this as a "pragmatic dimension" in which, when traversing possessed landscapes, people are less preoccupied with ontological questions as to "which of these spirits exist" than with "which of them has power to influence my life now?" (1996, 247). To this end, histories and practices were not so much ancient as adaptive, often grasped ex post facto (Hayami 2004, 29), after the fact. Like specters, they were indeterminate and constantly negotiated, selectively co-opted according to the situation at hand. It is only through such "worldly encounters" that, for example, a tiger could be known to be the emissary of a *kaw k'sah* or just a tiger. I return to these points in the epilogue to this book.

This pragmatic engagement with the world resonates with Cho's work on Christian Pwakanyaw communities in Myanmar and the Andaman Islands. Pragmatism and ambiguity are, as she notes, a common strategy for survival and progress (2023, 113). Illustratively, in Pwakanyaw the term *tana* (belief) is derived from the verb *na*, which refers to the process of becoming conscious that something is real, while *tama* (actions) is derived from the verb *mar*, referring to "work"—intimating that things only become true though their actions in the world (57–58). Thus, belief among Pwakanyaw communities is "relational, fluid and constantly shifting" (59). In a similar vein, among Thoo Hkoh communities in the Mutraw highlands, when they talked of spectral persons, they tended to speak of their relations to them in terms of *tana*.

Tellingly, while *tana* can be rendered as "belief," it has closer connotations with "faith, confidence, trust" in something or someone (Wade 1896, 716). People used the word *tama* when talking not only of their faith or confidence in the potency of unseen more-than-humans to have effects on their lives, but also of the political efficacy of their political leaders in the KNU. In everyday conversations it was often opined that people felt a lack of *tana*, as in faith or confidence in certain political leaders, on account of experiencing them as corrupt or ineffective. In this way, *tana*, bound as it is to action, bears little resemblance to the way belief has come to be known through enlightenment thinking (Apter 2017; Good 1993). Lacking *tana* in their leaders implied less that they doubted their existence than that they did not hold trust or confidence in the leaders' capacity to have an effect on their lives. From this perspective one can assess the effectiveness (or lack thereof) of a particular entity without having to believe in it, in the sense of taking a stance on its ontological status.

Consequently, in my analysis I am less concerned with uncovering whether a particular phenomenon actually exists than with observing its "power to work"—that is to say, understanding its practical effects on people's lives. As such, reality is constantly in the making, born through lived experiences with the world. This pragmatic and worldly approach is akin to the more phenomenological work of both Ingold (2000, 2006, 2011) and Michael Jackson. As Jackson states, "The world is never something finished . . . the world is always in the making" (1996, 4) and never quite settled. What is true, I found, is often what works in any given situation, what emerges in practical engagements and encounters with the world.

Taking a cue from multispecies studies, this book aims to "hold open a question of who—and what—is taken to exist and of how certain modes of existence are (and are not) made to count" (Dooren et al. 2016, 16). In this manner, a space is left for the possibility of unseen more-than-humans to have political effects on human lives. When such practices played out in constantly shifting political landscapes, they sometimes introduced more, not less, indeterminacy into the picture; spectral interventions led to a great deal of speculation *"precisely because"* they themselves generated indeterminacy in previously settled explanations and meanings (Bubandt 2014, 42).

Following these lines, throughout this book I strive toward a more-than-human political ecology: a method that is deeply inspired by the indeterminate, pragmatic, and playful manner in which the residents of these highlands constantly juggled and negotiated both the cosmological and political (ecological) entailments of living in possessed landscapes. This method gestures toward a way of conducting fieldwork that takes politics and cosmologies seriously and maintains a playful relation to both while also taking doubt into account. I attempt to turn method into play—and always to play seriously across the possessed landscapes of southeast Myanmar.

PART I

Possession

ONE

Possessed Landscapes

Negotiating Histories and Specters

Many years ago, my father decided to dig up a hillock that is said to be the burial mound of the queen of the K'wa [a group of people who resided in this area in the past but now live in Thailand]. They say she was interred here together with her fabulous riches. To access this treasure, my father had to first ask for permission from the hillock's *k'sah* [owner], the specter of the queen herself. My father conducted a *su hta gah hta* [divination] that involved scattering sand around the small hill and leaving it overnight. The footprints he found the next day would indicate what kind of offering he would have to make to gain her permission. Footprints of a pig, for instance, would indicate that the queen requested a pig to be offered. When he returned in the morning, however, he found the sand peppered with the footprints of a small child. After this he got really scared and abandoned his plans. Nobody dares to excavate the hillock. Its *k'sah* is too *hsoo* [strong], and the price to access it is too high.

—DEE NAY, SPEAKING IN MAY 2017 IN TA K'THWEE DUH

IN this chapter, I delve deeper into the differing ways in which landscapes were possessed up in the highlands along the Salween River. I demonstrate how, while things, animals, and (historically) people could and often were owned, the landscape itself could never be fully held in human possession. As the above quote illustrates, the current residents of these highlands understood themselves as far from the first settlers of these lands; it was already owned by others. As a consequence, they spoke of the landscapes they lived and farmed on as *hee loh*, meaning "borrowed," from the spectral presences with whom they coexisted. This emic term implies a mode of ownership that comes closer to custodianship.

To capture this perspective, I describe these highlands as *possessed landscapes*, deploying the word *possessed* in its dual and entangled senses. In this manner, I aim to tease out the ways landscapes were at once already occupied or haunted by spectral presences or persons such as ghosts, ancestors, and territorial spirits and also, ultimately, owned by these specters. I attempt to hold in focus both the cosmological sense of *possessed* as occupied or haunted and the political-ecological sense of the word as referring to multiscalar conflicts over control and ownership. To this end, the notion of possessed landscapes delineates alternative modes of ownership (that I explore further in chapter 2). I show how people's relations to their landscapes were oriented less toward control and management of resources, instead demonstrating deep "contact histories" of co-presence and highly asymmetrical relations of power, as well as improvisation and negotiation between the human and the spectral realm—to varying degrees of success. What is more, as I touch on in the introduction to this book, landscapes act as starting points that "usher us into exuberantly more-than-human lifeworlds that are constituted and composed of heterogeneous rhythms" of life and of war (Khayyat 2022, 28). Landscapes, as I conceive them, are made up of the entangled lives of humans, other species, histories, and specters, each with conflicting claims on the earth.

I begin this chapter by showing how histories of the region are neither abstract nor inert. Remnants from the past continued to enact their ruination on the present, like revenants. Certain objects were possessed by, and extended the legacy of, violent histories. Moreover, histories were wedded to the landscapes in which they unfolded—landscapes that people traversed on a daily basis—as traces or "footsteps" left behind.

REMNANTS/REVENANTS

While I was initially concerned that the villagers might feel uncomfortable when I photographed and filmed them, it quickly became apparent that many relished the opportunity for a photoshoot, endlessly posing for the camera. Each time I returned to the village, my small house would soon become inundated with people wanting to see, comment on, and take home the latest photographs I had printed out for them. Some insisted that I print out photos with me in them, "to remember" as my elderly neighbor Hpu Gay put it.

On one occasion, when my intrepid partner at that time was visiting the village, Hpu Gay came by and asked us to visit his home for a photoshoot.

With a severe stoop, and a rattling cough from decades of smoking hand-rolled cheroots, he walked straight through the door, sat down on the floor, soon after asking that we "take a photo together, so I have something to remember you by." He had laid out some of their finest Pwakanyaw clothes he wanted us to pose in for the photo. As I rummaged through the intricately hand-woven tunics and sarongs, my fingers fell upon a pair of black trousers with a texture quite different from the coarse cotton of the others. They had the undeniable feel of silk. When I asked Hpu Gay what they were made of, I found that neither he nor my field assistant Naw Paw knew what silk was, even after my rather crude explanation of it as a thread that comes out of a certain worm's bottom. After some back and forth, we ascertained that these trousers were hewn from a parachute left behind from one of the many airdrops the British Royal Air Force made over these hills during World War II. These airdrops involved soldiers, guns, and (according to all the elders I met who still remember the taste) rather stale rice and rancid meat. Indeed, those old enough to remember these times talked incessantly about the airdrops, with all the drama and intrigue they entailed—lighting signal fires and dodging Japanese soldiers. These trousers and tales of provisions falling from the sky, like the photographs I took, helped people "to remember"—in this case to remember violent colonial pasts and bold acts of resistance. Simultaneously, these tales led many to ponder aloud how it could be that all the grand promises made to them by the representatives of the British Empire, that after the war they would be granted autonomy and prosperity, had come to naught. I, too, was left to ponder: What would future generations make of the photographs I gifted the villagers?

Once I started noticing how certain objects were wedded to deep histories of contact, violence, colonialism, and broken promises, I discovered that the village and surrounding areas were awash with remnants from the past. Some days later, in Hpu Gay's oldest son's hut beside their family's paddy field, he brought out a British rifle he had stashed away in the rafters to show me. Perhaps coming from one of the airdrops or a colonial soldier, it had been gifted to him by his maternal aunt. The bullets, he explained, were very hard to come by and prohibitively expensive, so the rifle was quite useless to them. He hoped to sell it but had no idea who would want to buy it.

While this British rifle just so happened to be the only intact one left, countless others that had been reworked and recycled circulated in these highlands. One sunny afternoon, for example, I found one of the village elders, Hpu Waw, in front of his home repairing his own hunting rifle, which had once belonged to a Japanese soldier. Squinting in the morning sunlight, his grave face in stark juxtaposition to the pink tartan hoody and yellow

T-shirt with kissing penguins he wore that day, he explained that "usually the barrel is the only part of the original weapon that remains intact." Like most others in the village, he had carved a new stock out of fresh wood and added a firing mechanism fashioned out of bits of metal and elastic bands to make an improvised matchlock musket. To shoot it, the barrel had to first be filled with homemade black powder and lead shot bought in the local market, then tamped down. Hpu Waw and others use these firearms for hunting all types of game, from small birds to muntjac and wild boar. These were also the only weapons they had at hand to defend themselves should the Myanmar Army return again.

Helmets left by Japanese soldiers as they beat a hasty retreat in 1945 also continued to litter the Mutraw highlands. Most people had reworked the remains of these army helmets, much like they did with British and Japanese rifles, adapting them to very practical means, while some people kept them intact in hopes of future profit. The former became particularly apparent one rainy morning when I visited the oldest woman in the area, Hpee Thoo. She was one of the few who could still remember how bad the British airdropped rice tasted. Upon arriving at her house in a satellite hamlet of Ta K'Thwee Duh, I found her outside feeding her chickens with a rather peculiar-looking receptacle. When I inquired as to what she was using to scatter the feed, she chirpily replied, with a surprised chuckle, "What this? Oh, it once belonged to a Japanese soldier" (see figure 2). Her father, Gwa Nee, from the founding lineage of the village and the first Christian convert, had joined the British to fight the Japanese. During this time, he had taken the helmet from an emaciated Japanese soldier as he fled across the border. When the tide of the war turned, the Japanese forces were scattered. Their soldiers were left to flee through unhospitable forests in these highlands for many weeks, discarding their arms and uniforms, eating pig swill to survive, and were repeatedly chased off by grandmothers brandishing brooms, as many of the elders gleefully recalled.

Remnants such as these were not treated as artifacts, preserved for posterity like museum pieces. Rather, they were constantly negotiated and reworked, turned into something useful to the present predicament. Hpee Thoo's father's Japanese army helmet, part of long histories of highly masculinized armed conflict, oppression, and resistance had been turned upside down, literally and symbolically, so that it could be used in the deeply feminized routine activity of rearing and nurturing chickens. As this vignette suggests, histories of contact and violence were not abstract stories but tangible, often strongly tied to everyday objects such as trousers, guns, and helmets. Through these remnants, the past continually returned to haunt the

FIGURE 2.
Hpee Thoo with a Japanese helmet/bird feeder.

present, like a revenant, threatening to break into the future. Such histories possessed not only objects but also parts of the landscape itself.

These remnants of the past are akin to what Ann Stoler (2008, 2013) calls "imperial debris." While reworked to become part of people's everyday lives, through them imperial formations persist in material form, demonstrating "unfinished histories, not of a victimized past but of consequential histories of differential futures" (Stoler 2013, 11). As such they "occupy multiple historical tenses" and "selectively permeate the present" (Stoler 2008, 194–95). The remains of a British parachute, repurposed into a pair of trousers, were not only part of latent violent pasts but also part of potential futures, laden with peace and prosperity. In conversations around these repurposed objects, I was regularly struck by how many of the villagers would add that they sometimes wished the British would return and recolonize the area again.[1] Histories up along the Mutraw highlands were always ongoing, entangled, and interdependent with multiple (potential) pasts and futures.

Many thinkers have sought to grasp the ways in which physical remnants can "occupy multiple historical tenses." Jacques Derrida (1994) invokes the first line of *The Communist Manifesto*, "a spectre is haunting Europe—the spectre of communism" (Marx and Engels [1848] 2008, 31), to exemplify how histories constantly haunt the present, bearing with them the latent potentiality to (violently) refigure the future. Following this provocation, other scholars have invoked metaphors of haunting and ghosts as a way to grasp the "uncanny" fashion in which "ruins of empire," from bombed-out pagodas in Vietnam to unexploded ordinance in Laos, continue to trouble the present and point to possible futures (Schwenkel 2017; Stoler 2008; Zani 2019). It is fitting that the literal meaning of a revenant is "one who returns" (Derrida 1994, 2) since, through remnants such as the objects discussed above, these (often violent) pasts have a reiterative tendency.

However, as Heonik Kwon points out, Derrida's ghosts are general and allegorical: abstract "collective phantoms" like communism (2008, 15). In this way, they remain steeped in dualistic metaphysical traditions, inherited from the enlightenment thinkers, that draw a sharp line between a narrowly defined "empirical" reality and constructions of the mind or imagination. For thinkers such as Derrida, ghosts are always disembodied, disjointed, and untimely—descriptively useful but belonging to the realm of allegory rather than "reality." Kwon, by contrast, stresses how in Vietnam (as was the case in the Mutraw highlands) ghosts, "although belonging to a past era, [are] believed to continue to the present time in an empirical, rather than allegorical, way" (2008, 2). Ghosts are part of the patchwork of everyday life, intrinsic to people's being and becoming in the world. Not unlike imperial debris, ghosts are always tangled up in humans' quotidian existence; thus, they must be constantly negotiated with—a process Kwon describes as "transforming" them (103–32).

With this key distinction in mind, I argue that the remnants of colonialism and violent conflict in these highlands were far from abstract and free-floating "collective phantoms." Rather, ghosts were the very real manifestation of violent histories, which needed to be continually wrestled with and transformed. Histories were commonly tied to specific objects such as guns, helmets, and clothes. It was through these "possessed" objects that the past continually returned to haunt the present and presage the future. Furthermore, histories possessed not only objects but also parcels of the land itself. This became most apparent in the ghostly presence of landmines in the landscape.

Landscapes Littered with Landmines

Both the Tatmadaw and the Karen National Union have extensively used landmines throughout the counterinsurgency, leaving the borderlands between Myanmar and Thailand in the 2010s as potentially one of the most landmine-littered places on earth (KHRG 2012; Landmine and Cluster Munition Monitor 2013). Sustained armed conflict and military occupation, however, seemed to constantly skirt around Ta K'Thwee Duh village itself.[2]

Speaking to people who had lived through the conflict, which had slowly abated since the ceasefire in 2012, I learned that despite many false alarms, Tatmadaw soldiers had only ever passed through the area around the village on a handful of occasions. Each time, these soldiers were en route to strategically more important areas. Despite this, there were still areas in which people dared not tread, due to a fear of landmines.

One such area was a swidden field, just on the border to the nearby area of Htee Khu Duh Kaw, beside the road, shortly before it branches off to the Salween River in the east and the administrative capital in the west. As many of the villagers—including the surprisingly unfazed current cultivator Wee Daw, the gentleman with the four-letter word embossed on his cap we met in the introduction—explained, the KNU had given chase to a small group of Tatmadaw soldiers through this area after sustained fighting close to the Salween River. As these soldiers fled, they laid around three landmines on and beside the path in this area to perturb their pursuers. One had seriously injured a KNU soldier pursuing them—a local boy who moved to the camps and is now in the United States—while the other scared the living daylights out of a villager some years later when it detonated as he was burning this swidden field. As Wee Daw rather casually reminded me, "that leaves one landmine unaccounted for to this day," lurking somewhere under the earth there.

Landscapes littered with landmines, much like helmets and guns left over from colonial times, are also remnants of ongoing histories of counterinsurgency and imperialism. Landmines are very much an empirical entity yet also hold a particularly haunting quality. Each time the rains come, the earth becomes mud, unpredictably relocating these explosive devices. The remaining landmine could be anywhere or nowhere at all. Mines originate in violent pasts and persist unseen into the present—constantly threatening to, quite literally, cut the ground from under people's feet in the present, portending terrible potential futures in indeterminate ways. However, as Eleana Kim shows is the case in the demilitarized zone between North and South Korea, while mines can act as "area-denial weapons," people are "loath to let perfectly good land remain uncultivated" and often carry about their day-to-day livelihood activities regardless (Kim 2016, 177–78). In a war zone, as Khayyat reminds us, "navigation, habitation and domestication are creative everyday acts that reclaim a place" (2022, 127). As imperial debris, landmined landscapes are more than mere reminders, cues that jog memories of the past; they are part of people's quotidian life, obstacles they must navigate on a daily basis (see also Arensen 2022; Zani 2019).

This landmine's potential presence haunted, and indeed possessed, a large swath of land beside the road along the Bu Thoe ridge. It was not, however, only objects of violent pasts, of colonialism and counterinsurgency, that haunted the present landscapes. Nearly all histories and the spectral presences tied to them were embedded in the land and water. As Epeli Hauʻofa argues, "We cannot read our histories without knowing how to read our landscape" (2008, 73). Oral histories are inextricably entangled with the landscape they unfold in "right there . . . in front of our very eyes" such that in traversing the terrain, "familiar features of our landscapes keep reminding us that the past is alive" (73). Landscapes are always layered, thick, and sometimes viscous with history. This was especially the case in stories surrounding the demiurge figure of Y'wa.

"Y'wa's Deadfall Trap Rocks"

Very early on in my fieldwork I found that some the most vivid and captivating oral histories recounted to me were those elicited as we traversed particular landscapes. One of the first, and perhaps most recurrent and elaborated, oral histories I was told related to a chain of five prominent mountain peaks that abruptly jut skyward out of the forest floor. These five rock faces demarcate Ta K'Thwee Duh Kaw not only from two of its neighboring *kaw*—that is to say, "customary territories" (I define *kaw* in more detail in chapter 2)—but also from the locally defined climatic zones. On the west side was Ta K'Thwee Duh Kaw and *k'nuh htee*, or temperate montane evergreen forest, and the eastern front that faces the Salween was *kaw bway hkoh*, or warm mixed deciduous teak forest (Trakansuphakon 2006, 36). The first time my attention was called to this distinct mountain chain was by the headmaster of the local school and grandson of Gwa Nee (and thus Hpee Thoo's nephew).

While walking north from the village, we stopped to catch our breath, drink some water, and smoke a cheroot. The headmaster pointed eastward to a set of jagged peaks, crowned with forests a deep shade of emerald, characteristic of primary forest. His face cracking into a knowing grin under a meticulously maintained mustache, he explained, "that formation is called Y'wa Ma Htu Lay." Naw Paw, my field assistant, translated this for me as "Y'wa's trap," but the full translation of this place-name comes closer to "Y'wa's Deadfall Trap Rocks." In his characteristically engaged manner of storytelling, the headmaster then went on to explain that the name comes from how, in an undated, presumably mythical time, Y'wa created these five *lay* (steep rock faces). "After folding the landscape to create all the hills and valleys, Y'wa began building a trap big enough to capture a giant white elephant, to stop it from following him and stay among the humans in this area," the headmaster told us. This trap's design was a hugely scaled-up version of a type of (*ma*) *htu*, or deadfall trap. People place these traps at regular intervals along fences they build around their rice fields to protect them from marauding rats and even wild boar. Tracing the contours of the mountain chain with his fingers, the headmaster showed how each peak was to act like the bamboo pillars of the deadfall traps they use in their fields. With these traps, a third weighted length of bamboo is suspended between the pillars so when the trap is triggered, it falls on the animal, crushing or capturing it.

The headmaster continued, "Before Y'wa could complete his work, he was tempted away by Loo Seh Buh [i.e., Lucifer]," who is also known as Mu Kaw Lee, the great trickster. "Loo Seh Buh fooled Y'wa into believing that his mother was deadly sick and that he must attend to her immediately, before he could finish the fifth and final peak that would make the trap impassable. When the white elephant arrived in this area, it found it could simply walk around the uncompleted deadfall." Upon grasping that Y'wa had attempted to trap it, the headmaster explained, the elephant flew into a rage, and traces of its anger can still be seen today. At one bend of the Bleh Mah Loh River that flows unhurriedly along the foot of this mountain, there are still two deep indents in the otherwise shallow riverbed. These deep pools are the elephant's footprints, from when it stomped in fury. He then looked up and beamingly pronounced that because of this footprint, we know how big the elephant was. "Its foot was this big," he exclaimed, stretching his arms out as far as they would go, before joining them together to form a large circle. Near the top of one of the peaks there are also two large holes in the rock, made by the white elephant's tusks as it continued its rampage.

* * *

These five peaks were one of the various spots in the landscape that continued to be possessed with *ta thoo ta pgho*, with the potency or power left over from creation (as explained in the introduction). *Ta thoo ta pgho* was used interchangeably with *hsoo* (locally pronounced as *choo*), meaning "strong," and indicated an area that could not be cleared for cultivation and exploitation (the K'wa queen's burial mound was among these) or, in particularly "strong" areas, that people ought not pass through unless unavoidable. These "footprints" were continual traces of the divine forces of Y'wa that maintained a historical link with creation, imbuing places with their strength/potency. In this way, histories carried on into the present and possessed the surrounding landscapes.

On additional walks with people out and about around the village, I found that vast swaths of the landscape were possessed with potency. Y'wa

Ma Htu Lay was, in fact, one of the few places that bore Y'wa's name and held clear ties to stories of creation. Others, such as "the forest where Y'wa hid the teak trees," an incongruous coppice of teak trees surrounded by evergreen forest toward the Yunzalin River in the west, and "where Y'wa wrestled," a flat open pasture on the northern border of the *kaw*, evoked less elaborate and well-known stories. Areas such as Y'wa Ma Htu Lay were considered strong/potent on account of the past lying embedded as "footprints," the tracks and traces that have survived into the present (cf. Gan et al. 2017, g5–g6). Countless other landscapes were strong (*hsoo*) due to being possessed not only by traces, ghosts of the past, but also by various other unseen but felt spectral persons. People in the Mutraw hills lived in landscapes possessed not only by the ghosts of histories that continued into the present but also by unseen spectral persons that did not always have such deep histories. Here the line between haunting stories and these empirical entities became messy and blurred. While some specters closely resembled the way (colonial and violent) histories continued on into the present, other presences came closer to what might be defined as people. As such, I think of them as neither ghosts nor spirits but rather as spectral presences or persons (a point I come back to later). Another such *hsoo* place was Hpu Noh Noh Deh: the name of a small path, the surrounding forest, and the spectral presence or person that possessed the area.

"THE PATH THAT DRINKS YOUR BLOOD"

The first time I heard the name Hpu Noh Noh Deh uttered was by my neighbor Naw Htoo, a woman my age, when she was visiting Naw Paw and me one dark night and we exchanged ghost stories. Naw Paw joked that she already looked the part, dressed as she was in the long formless white tunic of unmarried women, her raven black hair loose, and the burning embers of the small pipe she constantly tugged on intermittently illuminating her face. She began with the warning, "You should avoid traveling down this small path to the west of the village if possible. This place is *hsoo* and it can be dangerous to walk here, especially at night. It is Hpu Noh Noh Deh's path." She continued the story by telling us that the path is "the place" of a powerful *ta mu khah* (a genus of spectral persons) and, as Naw Paw hesitatingly translated, "he will drink your blood." I learned that this blood drinking was commonly spoken of as *aw loh*, meaning to snatch and to consume a person's *k'la*, her "soul or spirit" (each person possesses seven *k'la*, of which all but one are detachable and can periodically leave the body). When a person loses their *k'la*, they become weak and are susceptible to illness—if it is not returned, they may even die. This was especially dangerous for people who were already weak, such as those who were sick or pregnant.

When I asked Naw Htoo if she had experienced anything spooky along this path, she emphasized that, while others do walk there, she tried to avoid it whenever possible. My interest piqued, I inquired as to where this path was, to which she replied that it was close to several fallow fields belonging to a rather outspoken elder named Hpu Hkee. She went on to tell us how, once, when this elder was walking along the path carrying a bag of paddy home from his field, just as the dusk was gathering, he stopped to rest a while. Just then he heard a sound of chains jangling and the heavy footfall of an elephant. But no matter how much he strained his eyes, there was no elephant in sight. As the sounds edged closer, he slipped his heavy burden and ran all the way home. Indeed, as Naw Htoo elaborated, many people heard sounds in the treetops, or footsteps on the ground, but no matter how hard they looked, they saw nothing.

After hearing this tale, I wanted to experience for myself how it might feel to be in a *hsoo* area such as this. Alas, neither the villagers nor Naw Paw were willing to accompany me to this area when I was eventually able to pinpoint its exact location, close to the village. Later, as the agricultural season picked up again following the short winter hiatus, I learned that the quickest route to Hpu Hkee's paddy field was along this very path. And as we grew closer, he invited us to accompany him to visit his field, taking the fastest route through Hpu Noh Noh Deh Kleh (*kleh* meaning "path").

Hiking this path for the first time with Hpu Hkee, I was struck by the deepness of the greens in the forest we passed through, many of the trees towering over the forest floor (see figure 3). Hpu Hkee explained as we walked at a brisk pace that the forest was so rich there because nobody dared to clear it. Long ago, a young and vigorous man, not yet married, decided to clear a patch here, certain that due to his youth, strength, and lack of family he would not be affected. Soon after he had cleared the land, however, he fell ill and died. Hpu Hkee explained that many attempts had been made to placate this *ta mu khah* and urge it to move on, but all had ultimately failed. Like the specter of the K'wa queen, it was simply too strong. However, one enterprising villager began planting cardamom seeds there some sixty years ago. When he did not fall ill, many households followed suit, carefully planting this spice in the understory of the forest and then harvesting it as a cash crop, while leaving the trees for Hpu Noh Noh Deh. In this way, they created their own vibrant agro-forestry area.

From the tale of this particular *ta mu khah*, we see how this spectral presence or person was strongly felt though never quite perceived by human

FIGURE 3. "The path that drinks your blood."

eyes. So strongly was its presence sensed that Hpu Noh Noh Deh was spoken of as possessing the path and the forest surrounding it, in the multiple senses of the English word *possessing*: both in the ways the spectral presence continued to haunt and control the earth and in the ways the path was spoken of as also belonging to the spectral presence. Hpu Noh Noh Deh was the *k'sah*, or "owner," of the path and the surrounding forest, which was "his place."

This is similar to the way another genus of spectral presence or persons, known variously as *ta yoh* or *ta wee ta nah*, could take up temporary residence in and afflict a human body, continually returning. Classically, these types of phenomena have been grasped as examples of "spirit possession," in which a spectral person temporarily occupies and controls a human's body (Brac de la Perrière 2015; Spiro [1967] 1996, 157–63; see also Bourguignon 1976, 5–7; Lambek 1981), the body becoming a site of interaction between the human and spectral realms (Lambek 1981, 9). Yet, as more recent studies have pointed out, the etymological origin of the word *possess* describes the occupation of a particular place, from the Latin *potis*, "power," and *sedere*, "to sit in" (Crosson 2019, 546). This is also the main sense in which I have been using the word *possessed* thus far: to refer to the way in which a particular history or specter can "sit in," haunt, or control a particular place.

As Naw Htoo explained, however, "it is Hpu Noh Noh Deh's path," and the whole area belonged to this specter. The *ta mu khah* residing here did not simply straddle the terrain, as a *ta yoh/ta wee ta nah* takes temporary residence in a body, but held territorial dominion over the landscape. Landscapes, much like bodies, are sites of interaction between the human and spectral realm, as well as their contesting claims over ownership of the earth.

The second sense of *possessed* thus speaks to political-ecological notions of access to and control over land (Peluso and Watts 2001; Sikor and Lund 2010). While histories leave "footsteps" and traces that continue on into the present and haunt the landscape, spectral presences or persons such as Hpu Noh Noh Deh often had blurrier historical moorings and more definite identities, with names and (as I show in chapter 3) biographies. All the same, their stories and their continual effects on human lives also possessed the landscape.

This sense of landscapes being haunted or possessed by unseen presences has historically been grasped as a form of animism (Tylor 1920, 426–29). In Burma/Myanmar, where the vast majority of people are Buddhist, this phenomenon has classically been glossed, at least by Western scholars, as part of a so-called supernaturalism belief system that accompanies Buddhism (Spiro [1967] 1996, 3). To this end, place-based presences such as *ta mu khah*, described variously as tutelary spirits (Aragon 2003, 127) and in Central Burma as *nats*, are commonly addressed as supernatural representations of the "real" natural landscapes (Spiro [1967] 1996; see also Allerton 2009, 236). Yet, as I argue in the introduction to this book, tales such as that of Hpu Noh Noh Deh often trouble and unsettle notions of belief. In grasping these practices as part of a belief system, it is tacitly implied that, in the final instance, they are unfounded due to being empirically unprovable.

Rather than reducing people's practices and cosmologies to a belief system, I attempt to take seriously the significant effects these practices and cosmologies have on people's day-to-day lives and politics—while remaining attentive to their own doubts and skepticism. Accordingly, I treat these practices more as an outlook, an orientation, or a sensibility (Swancutt 2019) through which people engage with and attempt to sense and make sense of their worlds. Moreover, as Daniel Ruiz-Serna stresses in his griping ethnography on armed violence in northeastern Colombia, "it is not only peoples and their cultures that are at stake when war strikes but also the cosmos itself" (2023, 3). Accordingly, I take the ways warfare fundamentally warps and remakes the spectral realm, over and over again, equally seriously.

To begin grappling with the ways such possessive specters played into the everyday lives of these highlanders, I draw on more recent studies that, taking their cue from Tim Ingold (2000, 189–93), trouble sharp distinctions between "cultural" and "natural" landscapes. This newer crop of studies approaches the ways in which lands and waters across Southeast Asia are commonly treated as possessed by a clamor of unseen more-than-human life by describing them as "spiritual" or "potent" landscapes that people traverse and negotiate on a daily basis (Allerton 2009, 2013; Guillou 2017). Rather than seeing them as "sacred" places set apart from the "profane," they are treated as part and parcel of everyday life. Building on these findings, I earnestly engage with the manner in which place-based specters across Southeast Asia are commonly referred to as "owners" (see Forth 1998; Lehman 2003; Pannell 2007), as a way of unsettling and rethinking notions of ownership and the politics of possession.[3]

I further explore differing modes of ownership in the following chapter so shall only touch upon them here. But by spending time in the Mutraw highlands, I came to appreciate how people did not inherit a certain parcel of land used for swidden cultivation itself as much as they inherited usufruct ownership over it. While one particular patch of land might be referred to as so-and-so's field, all the land and waters humans lived on and lived off were spoken of as simply *hee loh* (borrowed): lent from their spectral owners, the *ta mu khah* and *k'sah*, with the ardent promise to return them at a later date (I return to this notion of borrowing in chapter 2).[4]

Moreover, as touched on at the beginning of this chapter, the current inhabitants did not understand themselves as the first people to have settled here. Fragments of pottery and jewelry that people dug up from time to time (as well as tales of buried treasures) acted as constant reminders that when they first came to this area, it was already occupied and possessed. Oral histories tell of how they inherited the landscapes they now dwell in from a semi-mythical group, the K'wa (or Lawa), who were forced to flee across the Salween River many centuries ago, now occupying the area around Mae Sariang (in present-day Thailand; see Kauffmann 1971, 1977). These oral histories tell of how the K'wa, too, did not arrive to terra nullius. They arrived in a landscape that had been folded by Y'wa and was already possessed by a bustling crowd of spectral presences.

Thus, in possessed landscapes, people not only shared the land and water with a whole host of ghosts, territorial spirits, ancestors, and other unseen beings but also constantly negotiated with them to borrow the landscape for cultivation. As I touch on in the introduction, terms such as *ghost* and *spirit* map awkwardly onto how people related to these presences; the human inhabitants of these highlands were constantly engaged in efforts to make and maintain good relations with their spectral counterparts, to be good neighbors. To begin exploring this, I take a closer look at one particular class of spectral person, the *ta mu khah*, such as the one we met along the path in the vignette above.

"The Realm of That Which Is True"

Although Pwakanyaw/Sgaw Karen-English dictionaries tend to define *ta mu khah* as a spirit or a kind of ghost, other classes of spectral presences fit this description far better. *Ta mu khah* come closer to spectral persons, unseen entities with histories and homes whom people engage in social relations with. Take the notion of ghost, for example. Ghosts that arise from bad deaths are commonly referred to in Southeast Asia as "green ghosts" (Gan et al. 2017, 7; Thwe 2003), as opposed to ancestors who died more "natural deaths." In the Mutraw hills, such green ghosts were commonly known as *ta reh t'kah* or *teh preh*. These vengeful revenants of humans continued to haunt the areas near to where they suffered their gruesome demise, such as the river they drowned in or the house in which they were murdered. Stories of how *ta reh t'kah* and *teh preh* cling to these places and "eat" (*aw loh*) the "souls" (*k'la*) of the living who carelessly pass through there abound. These presences were paralleled in remnants and traces in the landscape that extended (often violent) pasts into the present.

Some *ta mu khah*, such as Hpu Noh Noh Deh, resonate strongly with what have been termed as territorial or tutelary spirits and *nats* (Aragon 2003; Spiro [1967] 1996) tied to a specific spot on the landscape. That said, other *ta mu khah* were known, like their human counterparts, to roam far and wide from "their places," throughout these hills. The corridors of thick primary forest that were maintained between each *hku*, or "swidden patch," for example, while acting partly as a firebreak during the burning season, were often referred to as *ta mu khah kleh*, or "the *ta mu khah*'s pathways." As villagers in Ta K'Thwee Duh explained to me, these paths (*kleh*) were maintained to allow spectral people to move easily from forest to forest. In linking different forests together to form vast networks, they allowed *ta mu khah* to roam freely across these highlands. Consequently, humans risked provoking the ire of itinerant *ta mu khah* should they attempt to clear these paths. Doing so may cause the *ta mu khah* to lose their bearing or become trapped in a certain section of the forest, unable to get home. As such, it was *ta du ta htu*, or "taboo/prohibited," to remove the trees and attempt to cultivate in these pathways in any shape or form (cf. Trakansuphakon 2006, 39). As I shall address more thoroughly in chapters 2 and 3, other genus of specters such as *nah htee*, who possessed certain bodies of water, and *k'sah*, or "owners/lords," came closer to the definition of territorial/tutelary spirits or *nats*. Such specters were said to be the *k'sah*, or the "owners," of certain rocks, rivers, ponds, fields, a whole mountain, or even all the earth and water in the area.

Spending more time in these highlands, I heard countless oral histories that spoke of the *ta mu khah*'s origin, not as spirits or ghosts, but as former friends to the human inhabitants who continued to roam the hills, living in their own villages and engaging in some social relations with them. These oral histories told of how *ta mu khah* once lived together with humans and were even enmeshed in mutual aid networks, taking turns caring for each other's children while the other went to work in their fields. These stories went on to expound how often, when it was the humans' turn to care for the *ta mu khah* offspring, the human parents would regularly neglect and mistreat them. Upon learning of how the humans were treating their children, the *ta mu khah* parents responded by making their offspring imperceptible to humans, either by placing a magic leaf upon their faces or slapping them so hard that they became invisible (depending on who is telling the tale). Ever since, the *ta mu khah* have continued to live side by side with humans, with their own villages and their own livestock. Only now, humans can no longer see them. As Andrew Paul found during his research a day's hike north of Ta K'Thwee Duh, *ta mu khah* are "humans' friends and blood brothers" (2018, 76). By some accounts, due to this kinship bond, it was not the *ta mu khah* themselves that afflicted humans, but rather "their animals, such as pigs and dogs that bite humans" when they violated taboos (76). In and around Ta K'Twee Duh, however, while most people agreed that there was a kinship between humans and *ta mu khah*, they replied rather incredulously that, just like other specters, it was them and not their dogs that fed on (*aw loh*) humans.

Ta du ta htu (taboos), especially those connected to *ta mu khah* and other spectral presences, were not to be trifled with. Hpu Hkee, the outspoken elder, had experienced this firsthand. A few times each year, a person from a neighboring village would arrive to Ta K'Thwee Duh in the morning and announce that they had brought with them *ta du ta pluh*, a special taboo day. The following day the villagers would be prohibited from going to their fields, from weaving cotton, and from engaging in any form of work; indeed, the whole village would be forced to rest. Albeit, as one headstrong young mother, Hpa Kha Moh, pointed out to me on one such taboo day as she balanced an infant on each hip, "we women do not get any rest days." When the taboo day passed, one of the villagers would travel to a neighboring village and bring "the *ta du ta pluh* to them." Many years ago, when one of these traveling taboo days was announced in Ta K'Thwee Duh, Hpu

Hkee decided that, since he was strong and healthy, he could simply ignore these *ta du ta htu*. The next morning, he rose early and worked as usual on his field. While Hpu Hkee himself was fit and strong at this time, his wife was heavily pregnant. Tragically, when she gave birth a short time later, the child was born with his anus fully fused together (known in medical terms as imperforate anus). The infant died a few days later. When people ignore the particular set of *ta du ta htu* related to *ta du ta pluh*, I was told, it was common for their children to have birth defects in which one of their bodily orifices was fused together. Here, we see how the person who breached a *ta du ta htu* was often spared and their close family was affected instead. In this manner, the person who breached the *ta du ta htu* may, in many cases, rectify their *k'ma* (mistake), or at least refrain from repeating it a second time. This was certainly the case with Hpu Hkee. He has since studiously observed each and every *ta du ta htu*, even those that seemed to contradict each other. As he saw it, it was better to be safe and give all *ta du ta htu* the same attention than to be sorry again.

Returning to the *ta mu khah*, in all these differing tales, akin to many other places in Southeast Asia, "human life is mirrored in the immanent realm of spirits" (Allerton 2013, 8), with a doubling of both human territoriality and hierarchy (Holt 2009, 44). As I have shown, like humans, *ta mu khah* had their own places, villages, children, and livestock. The specter who possessed the path beside the village was referred to as Hpu, or grandfather, implying that he both had and was kin.

Delving deeper into these tales and experiences from the Mutraw hills, I began noticing resonances with findings from starkly different contexts, among other Indigenous peoples commonly classified as "animist." Among Amerindians in the Amazon basin, for example, both animals and spectral persons are understood as "ex-humans" (Viveiros de Castro 2004a, 465). This was a notion shared by many in the Mutraw hills, where it was only after a process of differentiation that these specters "disguised" themselves, becoming invisible to humans, such as by way of magical leaves or shapeshifting. Their invisibility in no way made them less persons. They maintained their own houses, villages, livestock, and particular proclivities, just like other people. These parallels become even more apparent in light of fragments of stories I heard of how snakes once lived among humans. In each case, after a critical event, these snakes "left the humans," as people put it. Eduardo Viveiros de Castro points to something similar in how animals become "disguised by their ostensibly bestial forms" (2004a, 465). This form of anthropomorphism established a state of affairs in which unseen persons, and to an extent some non-human animals, were treated as conscious subjects, able to communicate with humans. Specters and some animals were addressed as people who were to be engaged in reciprocal relations of respect. In both these contexts, we find that relations with what we in the Euro-American context might call "nature" can take on the quality of what we would term "social relations" (Descola 2013, 8; Kimmerer [2013] 2020; Viveiros de Castro 2004a, 465). The focus was on making and maintaining "good" social relations with landscapes and the specters who possessed them (Govindrajan 2018; TallBear 2019; Wildcat 2013).

Consequently, as touched on earlier, I am reticent to describe specters as spirits. In most circumstances, specters were understood and treated as people—albeit those who could see but could not be seen directly, necessitating particular forms of mediated relation (I return to this point in a moment). Specters resided in an intersecting and imbricated realm to that of humans, known as *ta taw ta loh kaw*, which directly translated means the "land/realm of that which is true." Similarly, one collective (albeit rarely used) name for all these different specters, including the shades of the dead such as ancestors, was simply *ta taw ta loh*, or "that which is true." While living human beings could not perceive *ta taw ta loh*, or their homes and their livestock, *ta taw ta loh* had no issues seeing each other, or seeing humans.

Humans were only afforded brief glimpses of this realm, through the jangle of spectral chains in the dark, through the feeling of one's *k'la* being snatched and consumed, or through metaphor-laden visions, in dreams and during spells of fever/mental illness. In dreams and hallucinations, for example, everything is *hkoh hkee*, or "backward," implying that what they experienced in their visions was the exact opposite of their experiences in waking life. Moreover, as I explore in the final section of this chapter, technologies of divination, such as consulting chicken bones and strips of bamboo, allowed people to peer dimly, and often imperfectly, through the veil separating the spectral realm from our own. Otherwise, humans could only gain this point of view upon shedding their bodies when they die. This spectral asymmetry suggested a hierarchy of sorts, at least in perception, in which humans were only able to engage in lateral perception with the human realm, whereas "those who are true" are able to perceive both realms simultaneously.

I found, therefore, that a whole host of spectral people not only shared these highlands with humans but also possessed them in the double and entangled sense of the word. In the final section of this chapter, I explore how, in their day-to-day lives, people negotiated with these already possessed landscapes, peopled by unseen presences whom they had to first discern before communicating and appeasing them—constantly striving toward making and maintaining good relations.

NEGOTIATING (WITH) POSSESSED LANDSCAPES

While I was out walking with Hpa Htwee, who swiftly appointed himself as my local guide when I began fieldwork in Ta K'Thwee Duh, he gestured to a gnarled and ancient-looking banyan tree, commenting that it has a *k'la*, a spirit. In this way one can say that it has a *k'sah* (spectral owner), he added, who possesses it.[5] Yet, when I asked him whether all trees were possessed by a *k'la*, rather than his usual quickfire manner of responding in a breathless stream of explication, he took a moment to mull it over. Finally, he responded, "No, but you can tell this one has a *k'la* as it has more than six *khaw* [ladders]"—that is to say, prop roots that reach down to the ground.

Hpa Htwee's measured response bears a striking resemblance to ethnographic work among other Indigenous groups, where seemingly "inanimate" and "inert" objects such as stones are grammatically classed as animate. This linguistic quirk did not lead to a state akin to that imagined by vitalists (Bennett 2010) of the whole landscape being infused with life. Rather, as Ingold (drawing on the work of Alfred Irving Hallowell) notes, people often spoken of as "animist" do not "perceive stones in general, as animate, any more than we do. The crucial test is experience. Is there any personal testament available" (Ingold 2000, 96–97). In what follows I explore how, in a similar vein, along the Salween River, while all trees, stones, ponds, and other spots in the landscape had the potential to be animate, this could only be qualified through people's experiences of their animacy. People in these highlands, as I argue in the introduction, engaged in highly indeterminate, pragmatic, and playful relations with the world around them, appearing less concerned with uncovering whether spectral persons actually existed as they were with the effects they had on day-to-day life.

When I asked similar questions to the elders in the village about the animacy of certain spots in the landscape, I received similarly qualified answers. These answers were often to the effect of "it depends." The animacy or personhood of a rock, tree, stream, or any other feature on the terrain could not be given in advance. While each bears the latent potentiality to be alive, or even to be treated as a person, one must look intently for signs that would suggest this to be so. This deeply pragmatic and experience-based notion stands in contrast to more generic notions of potency in Southeast Asia as "manifested in every aspect of the natural world, in stones, trees, clouds and fire" (Errington 1990, 22).

Sometimes the process of discerning whether something was animate or an area was possessed was a quite straightforward affair. As I have shown, for a banyan tree one can often simply enumerate its prop roots. In contrast, to determine the animacy of rice, a rite that mirrored a funeral rite was occasionally conducted when it was harvested. This rite quite concretely tested whether the rice grain, or the cadaver, was still possessed by a *k'la*, or a "soul." The *k'la* was led away to the afterlife, then ritual practitioners checked to make sure the ritual was successful. Threshed paddy was weighed before and after the rite. If it weighed less, it was concluded that the rite had succeeded and the *k'la* of the rice grain had now left. If not, then the rite was repeated and the result weighed again until the practitioners were certain the rice's *k'la* had departed.

As these rites suggest, animacy and indeed personhood were asserted by dint of possessing (and being possessed by) a *k'la* or some form of spectral presence such as *k'sah*, or "owners." However, in most cases, discerning whether rocks, trees, ponds, and other swaths of landscape were possessed and/or possess life was far less straightforward than enumerating roots or weighing rice.

In cases in which there were no preexisting oral histories of the activities of powerful spectral beings, the process for discerning which specific parts of the landscape were possessed was not a given and was a fraught and indeterminate affair. The process often began with a person sensing, through their body, the presence of a specter in a certain area in the landscape. While particularly strong or potent *ta mu khah*, such as the one possessing the path west of the village, made their presence known by sound, most were perceived by humans only through the effects they had on villagers' bodies. After a person had stumbled upon "the place" of one particular spectral person, they often became weak and/or sick, physically or mentally. This was the specters feeding on their *k'la*. The *ta mu khah* of Hpu Noh Noh Deh did just this to the young man who attempted to cultivate there, causing him to become deadly sick. When humans floundered into the specters' "area," it was reasoned that spectral persons could become highly vexed and retaliate by afflicting the body of the interloper by way of *aw loh*, snatching and eating their *k'la*, and making them weak and sick.

The focus of this book, however, while partly phenomenological in its outlook, is less on how it might feel to lose and regain one's soul (as done in exemplary fashion by Desjarlais 1992) than on the effects these encounters had on people's lives and how they negotiated them. Upon experiencing the sensation of their *k'la* being snatched away or fed upon, I found that people attempted to hastily make amends with the offended specter. In understanding the specters as the owners of discrete areas of the landscape, the residents of the Mutraw hills were constantly engaged in efforts to make and maintain good relations with the spectral realm—"to make friends" as they commonly phrased it (I return to this phrase in chapter 5). As a result, people's relations with the world around them was not based on management or mastery, but rather on negotiation with fellow beings who had specific capacities and needs. One clear example of this can be seen in the case of Lee Kyaw Hta's daughter.

* * *

When Lee Kyaw Hta's daughter fell ill, feeling weak and tired, the first thing her family did was to march her down to the small clinic nestled in a valley below the village. Here, they received a rather general diagnosis, a fistful of paracetamol tablets, and doctor's orders that she should rest. Indeed, the tendency for this clinic to simply hand out paracetamols and then send people on their way had earned it the nickname "para-clinic." After some weeks, when she did not recover after resting and taking the tablets, her father decided that her ailment might have a cause that biomedicine could not address.

He then went to consult another kind of expert, Lur Gay's older brother Dee Klee, a slightly built man with a face dominated by a large and bushy mustache. Like his brother, Dee Klee had converted to Catholicism many years ago when he married. Despite this, he was well versed in most Thoo Hkoh rites and had trained under several Pwakanyaw ritual experts in Thailand to hone his skills further. After Dee Klee asked Lee Kyaw Hta a series of questions, it transpired that his daughter had been playing beside a small stream adjacent to the villages that might be possessed by a *nah htee*, a kind of tutelary spirit/*nat*. To make sure, Dee Klee conducted a *su ta gah daw*, a divination. In this case the divination was conducted with chicken thigh bones, but it can also be done with strips of bamboo or the stem of a certain plant. During this form of osteomancy, a question was asked and then the thigh bones were consulted to discern whether the omen was good—that is, a positive answer—or bad. In this manner they were able to quickly confirm that the stream was possessed by a *nah htee*. "The girl must have angered it by carelessly passing by, leading it to *aw loh* her and make her weak and tired," Dee Klee surmised. Through a series of yes/no questions to the oracle, he ascertained that the *nah htee* required a chicken, a bottle of rice wine, cigars, betel nut, and a simple chicken curry dish before it would relinquish its hold over her.

When I caught up with them later, I found them beside the stream hard at work constructing a *ta lu*—literally, a place of nourishing or feeding. The *ta lu* took the form of a spirit house made of bamboo. The chicken Lee Kyaw

Hta had with him in a small bamboo basket was summarily slaughtered, the blood spread over the *ta lu*, and the chicken cooked into a curry. When these preparations were complete, all the other items were placed inside the spirit house, a small plate was provided for the best morsels of chicken curry, and a cup with a straw for the alcohol was laid out. A short prayer was then incanted, with hands pressed together and fingers splayed out, entreating the *nah htee* to relinquish the girl's *k'la*. People and animals passed uninterestedly by as these two men rather unceremoniously carried this out and ate the rest of the curry in silence. The men and the *nah htee* then ate together beside this small stream. Afterward, the *ta lu* was left untouched until it finally rotted or was knocked down by animals. Only time would tell if this would cure the girl, they explained. When I asked Lee Kyaw Hta how his daughter was doing some days later, he explained that the ritual had not worked, so they would try again, in another place, until she recovered. The last time I saw her, she was tearing around the village once more.

* * *

This episode of making contact and negotiating between the human and spectral realms was, in many ways, typical in these highlands. Negotiating possessed landscapes was a fraught business. What becomes apparent here is the "pragmatic dimension" (Lambek 1996, 247) of inhabiting such landscapes: the process of trying to constantly figure out how to maintain good relations with spectral beings. People were less preoccupied with ontological questions as to "which of these spirits exist" than with practical questions like "which of them has power to influence my life now?" (247). Spectral persons' capacity to have an effect on human lives—the *tama* or action/work (Cho 2023) they have on the world, as felt in the body becoming weak and sick—was the paramount concern of the women and men I came to know in the Mutraw highlands. On stumbling upon such a specter, a process of highly mediated negotiation was enacted. Specters were regularly treated as conscious subjects able to communicate with humans and, as such, were addressed as people that could be engaged in reciprocal relations of respect. This was very much in evidence in the case of Lee Kyaw Hta's daughter.

The encounter between the *nah htee* and Lee Kyaw Hta's daughter took place in a more-than-human contact zone, involving both asymmetrical power relations, improvisation, and constant negotiation (Haraway 2007; Isaacs and Otruba 2019). Encounters with the landscape were characterized less by control or management of scarce "resources" than by an open-ended asymmetrical grappling and negotiation between the human and the spectral realms. In the case of Lee Kyaw Hta's daughter, for example, the men did not attempt to turn the specter to their own needs, to co-opt it, or to transform it, as Kwon (2008) has shown was the case with ghosts of violent conflict in Vietnam. Instead, what followed was more like a negotiation, by way of propitiation, to attempt to straighten out relations between the human and spectral realms that had become strained as a result of the girl's careless intrusion.

Hpu Waw once described the way in which a certain specter possessing a path or road *aw loh* (eats) a person's *k'la* as "like putting the person's *k'la* in prison." When this happens, the specter demands not only alcohol and food but also some coins, as a fee or even a bribe to release the *k'la* again. This resonates with the ways in which, as Marisol de la Cadena shows, "offerings" among the Runakuna in Peru are locally referred to as a "payment" and echo acts of bribing judges (2015, 95). Following de la Cadena, I prefer to see these acts as relations not of co-option or transformation but of obligation and alliance, resembling what, as I discuss in more detail in chapter 2, Vinciane Despret and Michel Meuret call an "ecology of obligations" (2016, 27). In each instance, *lu ta* involved feeding the spectral person in question to curry their favor. The ravenous spectral person was entreated to come and eat together with the humans. The two men in the vignette above ate together after first giving the best morsels of food to the *nah htee* as a way to "pay back" and to realign relations between the human and spectral realms.

As I argue in this chapter, the Mutraw highlands might best be described as a possessed landscape, where the lands and waters are not only haunted by spectral persons but also ultimately owned by them. A corollary of this was that people carefully negotiated landscapes, mindful that they might at any time disturb the "area" of a certain unseen, more-than-human person and constantly attempting to realign relations by way of feeding and eating together with them. These findings then illustrate a specific regime of ownership and of sovereignty that prevailed in these highlands. It is toward these alternative modes of ownership and sovereignty that I now turn in the next two chapters. In part 2, I go on to show how these practices and cosmologies were translated and rescaled into the Salween Peace Park.

TWO

Alternating Ownership
Ephemeral, Nesting, and Patchwork Lands

WALKING five minutes up the hill from the bottom of Ta K'Thwee Duh, which is built on a steep incline, past the school hall where the Karen flag flutters in the stiff breeze, and past women and children laden with woven bamboo baskets filled to the brim with firewood and foraged forest products slowly lumbering back home, one eventually comes upon the main road. The villagers referred to it as the *kleh doh* (big road) or the *kah kleh* (car road)—despite the fact that vehicles larger than a motorbike were only able to traverse this "car road" in the dry season, some five months of each year. This road, built by the Karen National Union, wended its way along the very top of the Bu Thoe ridge that demarcates the Salween and the Yunzalin River basins as they run side by side along this stretch. A three-meter-wide strip of stamped-down earth was carved out of this mountaintop by bulldozers and earthmovers some five years earlier and has to be harrowed out anew after each monsoon season, due to erosion. To the north, this ever-shifting dirt road drew the village into connection with a slightly larger village and a Karen National Liberation Army base and connected to a warren of motorbike trails leading to the rest of the district. Traveling south, it soon bifurcated, connecting the village to a tiny market town on the banks of the Salween in the east and to the regional center to the west.

The original main objective for building this road was tactical: to string together the various KNLA bases along the ridge and facilitate their resupply. This was the first, and to date only, large infrastructure project in the area, and, especially among the elders, it continued to generate a considerable amount of anxiety. The project began generating more than its fair share of contentions even before a single meter of earth had been cleared and stamped down. When the villagers were first informed about the construction plan, many held grave concerns upon learning that the road was projected to cut right through their *kaw*. The *kaw* is the village land or realm, often translated as their "ancestral" or "customary territories" (see map 1 in the introduction).

People realized that the construction threatened to segment their *hku* (swidden patches), to which the rights to cultivate are inherited. It was also projected to carve up an area that had been heavily planted with cardamom, a popular cash crop. Thus, the villagers grew increasingly anxious that the road might lead to conflicts over the control of land. One way they hoped to alleviate this was for the road constructors, contracted and led by the KNU, to buy them a large pig for the whole village to share together. They hoped a collective feast might dissipate some of the growing anxieties. It is not clear who actually forwarded this request to the road foreman, as the ritual leader, the *hee hkoh htee*, declined all such duties and neither he nor the headman of the village were vested in the necessary de facto political power to take such an action. Either way, the villagers were rather curtly informed by the road foreman that there were no funds for such frivolous things. Work on the road would progress as planned.

As this disquiet was building, and as road constructions began in earnest farther south, some of the villagers from Ta K'Thwee Duh went to labor on the road. Here they learned that it was projected to cut straight through a mountain in their *kaw* named Ta Bu Kyoh. This mountain, 1,300 meters above sea level, was known to be the seat of, or perhaps *is*, Naw Ghoo Hsaw: the *kaw k'sah*, "the owner of the earth" or "owner of the -*kaw*." As such, this mountain was ritually and politically central to day-to-day life. Any disturbance of this area would surely illicit the wrath of the *kaw k'sah*, which could potentially be catastrophic—not only to the humans but also to all animals, plants, lands, and waters under her dominion. While people fretted greatly about what would happen, they lacked an apparent village leader who could convey their concerns to the relevant authorities in the KNU.

This incident came to a head when a young woman, Naw Ghaw, dreamt that a spring at the top of Ta Bu Kyoh overflowed, inundating the whole area. When she recalled this dream to her fellow villagers, they interpreted it as a terrible and foreboding omen. Following this, her father, Hpu Hkee, possessed with an idiosyncratically quavering yet booming voice, marched over to the road constructors to explain that the road could not be built there. But, once again, he was curtly told that it was too costly to redirect the road. With neither the authority nor the power to demand that the KNU desist, and with few other recourses left open to them, Hpu Hkee and several other elders turned to the *kaw k'sah*. They ascended Ta Bu Kyoh, as their ancestors had done before them, and entreated Naw Ghoo Hsaw that, should she agree that a road run through there, to let nothing bad happen. But, if she did not agree, then to let terrible misfortune befall all those who conspire to build this road through "her place." Following on from this, they returned home and left it at that. "Nothing more could be done," they told their fellow villagers; "we have put it in the hands of the *kaw k'sah*." Many of them then returned to labor on the road as it slowly made its way north toward them.

Some unspecified time later, the foreman, who had repeatedly ignored the villagers' requests, suddenly and mysteriously fell ill. Shortly afterward, he keeled over and died. Following these events, his replacement came to pay a personal visit to the village to hear their grievances; consequently, the road was redirected around Ta Bu Kyoh (see figure 4). Moreover, as each teller of this tale was eager to stress, the new foreman even asked the villagers what other demands they had. The elders in the villages told him that they also needed a pig to share with the village, but it need not be so large. As long as every villager could take one bite, it would suffice. A week later, they received a huge barrow that was more than ample to feed every single person in the village. A taut triumphant smile slowly crept over Hpu Hkee's deeply wrinkled face each time he told this part. While there were numerous variations on this story, each narrator came to the same conclusion: It was through the intervention of the *kaw k'sah* that they had finally succeeded in their demands. The mountain had intervened in the realm of human life.

The furor elicited by the construction of the road along the Bu Thoe ridge brings several issues of possession and ownership, addressed in the previous chapter, into sharper relief. In this chapter, I further unpack these concepts and the relationship between them. I begin by digging into Indigenous notions of *kaw* and *hku* and explore why the villagers were so afraid that they would be segmented by the road. This exploration leads away from notions of common property, pushing me to instead consider alternative and alternating modes of ownership. I show that while people were regularly spoken of as the *k'sah*, or "owner," of a certain patch of ground, this is perhaps best understood as a form of ephemeral ownership (cf. Empson and Bonilla 2019; Viegas 2016). When a person stopped cultivating a swidden patch and the jungle began reclaiming it, their rights to the lands waned. Rather than returning to undifferentiated jungle, ownership of a patch of land returned to the person or kin group who had first cleared this land, as its original owner. Pushing further, I describe how the human "owner" was spoken of locally in terms of *hee loh* (borrowing) the land from its true

FIGURE 4. The *kah kleh*, or "car road."

spectral owners, such as *ta mu khah* and *kaw k'sah*, who possessed it (in the twinned and entwined senses). To grasp these kinds of complex relations, I draw on notions of nesting hierarchies (Allen and Starr 1982; Simpson 2014; Volk 1995, 125–51) to demonstrate how one layer of ownership was often nesting in broader and more encompassing layers of ownership. I speak of "nesting," rather than nested, hierarchies here to capture how ownership in the highlands along the Salween River was highly indeterminate and unsettled, subject to ongoing negotiations.

I then delve into the ways in which ephemeral ownership was increasingly stretched, almost to breaking point, by newer forms of agriculture. The relative permanence of orchards and wet rice cultivation was slowly transforming Indigenous practices, replacing them with individual ownership. The road, then, was one of a growing number of threats to these alternative and alternating modes of ownership. Returning to the notion of commons, I close by exploring the ways in which *kaw* were patchworks, where many different categories of land were stitched together to form a largely autonomous area, becoming itself a "patch" (Tsing, Mathews, and Bubandt 2019).

KAW AND ALTERNATING REGIMES OF OWNERSHIP

In the events that unfolded following the construction of a "car road," we are introduced to the terms *hku*, denoting the parcels of land used for swidden cultivation, and *kaw*, which I have until now followed local activists in translating as "customary territories." These terms took center stage as tensions mounted around the roadbuilding project.

The villagers in Ta K'Thwee Duh fretted that as the road plowed through their *kaw*, it might potentially segment and throw into disarray the intricate system of inherited *hku* (swidden patches) and carefully negotiated patches of cash crops held by the different households, provoking conflicts over the use and control of land. As I shall show, notions of *hku* and *kaw* and the *kaw k'sah* were integral to the organization of day-to-day social life in these highlands and were intimately bound up with Indigenous regimes of possession. As the road drew closer, people were forced to renegotiate ownership and, as I show in chapter 3, sovereignty not only with the KNU but also with the spectral realm.

The suffix *-kaw* added to a place or group name in Pwakanyaw usually denotes a "delineated space or area," such as a country (Wade 1896, 259). Burma/Myanmar, for example, is known as Kaw P'Yaw, "the land/territory of the Burmese."[1] In these highlands the suffix *-kaw* also connotes the collectively held lands around each named village cluster (or, in one exceptional case, a cluster of different villages).[2] The area where I conducted the lion's share of my fieldwork was commonly referred to as Ta K'Thwee Duh Kaw, or the lands/territory of Misty Village. Each *kaw* is made up of *hku* patches belonging to the people living there and is integral to day-to-day affairs.

When I first arrived, people initially seemed to confirm my preconceived notions that all the *kaw* lands around the villages were a form of commons or "common property" (Robbins 2012, 51–54), that the land could not be individually owned, and that everyone had the right to cultivate. For example, Hpa Htwee—my unofficial guide and regular walking companion, who always wore a bomber jacket and baseball cap no matter the weather—would regularly comment that, if I were to settle down there, it would be no problem for me to find a patch of land I could clear in order to begin to farm and feed myself. As he often insisted, "it is no problem to get land from the people here." These theoretical biases were encouraged further when I asked Naw Daw, one of the most prolific rice wine brewers in the village, if people or households could hold individual ownership of *hku* in this area.[3] Her voice suddenly drained of its usual levity and her eyes fixed on mine, she replied pointedly, "There are some people who like to think they can, but this is not so." Spending more time in this area, however, I found that, while it was indeed comparatively easy for people to find land to cultivate, this state of affairs was underpinned by highly complex and constantly negotiated ownership regimes.

Ephemeral and Nested Ownership

Upon closer inspection I found that the land and water in these highlands was held and controlled in far more intricate and complex ways than would be expected in accordance with "common property" theory. Indeed, rather than an absence of individual ownership, the region featured a blooming, buzzling coexistence of "alternative regimes of ownership" (Brightman et al. 2016; see also Huard 2020). As I demonstrate in chapter 1, this point became clearer to me as I traversed these highlands together with the villagers.

Once, while out walking along the "car road" with Naw Htoo, who was accompanying Naw Paw and I on this occasion, she brought our attention to the land that lay adjacent to both Hpu Noh Noh Deh ("the path that drinks your blood") and the road. Turning to point, using the pipe tightly clenched between her teeth, to a rough and slightly overgrown patch of land, she told us, "These are Hpu Hkee's *hku*"—his swidden patches, now in fallow. "The *hku* people feared would be divided by the road are in this area," she continued. Upon asking her to elaborate what she meant when she spoke of these fallow fields as belonging to Hpu Hkee, she reiterated that "he is the *k'sah* [owner] of several swidden patches here." My curiosity piqued, I asked her how this squared with Naw Daw's statement that some "like to think" they own land, intimating that it does not really belong to them. To this Naw Htoo replied that, "while a patch of land may belong to one person, others are free to borrow it. To cultivate a particular *hku* that does not belong to you, you just have to ask the *hku k'sah* [swidden patch owner] first if you can borrow it." She continued that, "If the owner is not using the land, and does not have any plans to use it this season, then they nearly always let others *hee loh* [borrow] it." During this time, she added, the primary *k'sah*/owner forfeits all claims over the land, demanding neither rent nor any other form of recognition of ownership. The person borrowing the land, however, "cannot keep using it forever," she made clear. Soon after they have finished cultivating the land, ownership reverts back to its primary "owner."

An intricate, but far from unique, pattern of ownership and cultivation emerges here, in which the person actively cultivating the land becomes known as the *k'sah*, or owner, and the land is treated, in every practical sense, as his (cf. Huard 2020, in Central Myanmar; Karlsson 2011, 127–65, in Northeast India; and Viegas 2016, in the Brazilian Amazonas). I use the pronoun *his* here since only men were permitted to initiate the process of clearing an overgrown swidden patch. This was commonly explained to me as due to how "only men have the *ta du ta htu*," the associated practices and prohibitions, inherited from their fathers, to clear land. As I demonstrate in chapter 1, *ta du ta htu* (taboos) were not to be taken lightly. Breaching them could have devastating consequences, both for oneself and one's close kin.

When a man cleared a certain *hku* for rice cultivation, this land was thereafter spoken of as belonging to him. The sense of belonging implicated here was akin to what is usually described as usufruct ownership (Empson and Bonilla 2019): temporarily granting a person both access to land and the right to utilize what is grown on it (its "fruits") while it remains, ultimately, owned by someone else. When all the rice was harvested and safely stored, cultivation switched to less soil- and water-intensive crops, such as chilies and aubergines (eggplant), for an additional two- to three-year period. However, as the shrubs and trees began to grow back and the vegetation became too dense to tend to and to harvest these secondary crops, the patch was left to return to forest again. In this manner, as traces of cultivation disappeared and the patch became overgrown, the former cultivator's status as the owner likewise gradually ebbed away. This was similar to findings among other people practicing shifting cultivation/swidden farming, in which ownership has a temporal dimension, subject to forgetting. After a certain amount of time has elapsed, land eventually returns to the forest again, only to be cultivated later by someone else, in a cyclical manner (Butt Colson 1973; Viegas 2016). Similarly, in densely populated areas of Southeast Asia such as Singapore, a veritable army of people is conscripted to continually fight back against the creeping return of overgrowth, forests, and the onset of forgetting, so that the current human occupants can continue possessing this land (Comaroff and Ong 2016).

I grasp this as a mode of ephemeral ownership, resembling copyrights and patents in how it was "designated to expire" after a certain time (M. Brown 2004; see also Brightman et al. 2016, 23). In the Mutraw hills, however, while *hku* (swidden patches) appeared to return to the forest, they did not become undifferentiated and revert to commons. Rather, as they fell back into fallow, tenure defaulted to the primary usufruct owner once more. This ephemeral mode of ownership existed within other modes or layers of ownership, what Audra Simpson describes in a different context as "nested and embedded" (2014, 10–12).

Along these highlands ownership was layered upon ownership, where the ephemeral ownership of the current cultivator of a particular swidden patch was nesting in and subordinate to the encompassing tenure of the person they borrowed the patch from: tenure organized by "layer stacked upon stabilizing layer" (Volk 1995, 127). I grasp this relation by drawing on systems ecologist Tim Allen's notion of a "nested hierarchy" (Allen and Starr 1982, 100) to capture the way each layer of ownership was nested in a higher order—not unlike Russian matryoshka or nesting dolls, or an image of concentric circles. Yet, as I have stressed throughout this book, relations in the Mutraw hills were indeterminate, unsettled, and constantly negotiated, partly as a vestige of intractable conflict. Accordingly, I follow Signe Howell (2002) in deploying the active verb form of *nesting*, rather than *nested*, to describe a constantly jostling hierarchical arrangement of ownership. A person's tenure of a *hku* was always nesting in other modes of ownership. When ephemeral ownership waned following the harvest, as the primary jungle grew back, primary ownership rights waxed, dynamically. This raises the question of how a person attains the rights of primary ownership in the first place—that is to say, the person who one must seek out to ask permission to cultivate a particular patch of swidden, spoken of as hers or his.

While helping my neighbor, and Naw Htoo's brother-in-law, Hpa Dee Pa to plant his *hku* (swidden field) on the startling steep hillside below Y'wa Ma Htu Lay, I constantly stumbled over the enormous stumps and fallen trees that remained scattered around this field. When I grumbled about this to Hpa Dee Pa after nearly falling for the umpteenth time, he explained to me that when they cleared this area, around a month ago, some of the trees that grew there were so massive that it had been exceedingly hard work. Being the only household (at this time) that owned a chainsaw, they were able to fell these towering trees. But soon after they found it impossible to either remove them by hand or burn them away. We were left to simply plant around them. When I, rather naively, inquired as to why the trees there had been so much larger than in any other *hku* I had visited, he explained that his family was the first, at least in living memory, to open this particular parcel of forest land for cultivation. As he let the warm sun soften his aching body—almost fully adorned with protective tattoos from his time as a soldier—in a break between planting, Hpa Dee Pa elaborated that, as the first person to clear this parcel of forest for cultivation, he had become its *k'sah*/owner.

At first glance, the hard work involved in opening up a parcel of forest for cultivation appeared to generate ownership, resonating with Lockean notions in which a person "mixes" a part of themselves with the land through their labor to turn it into their property (Locke [1689] 2003). Taking a step back, it becomes clearer that such processes are a common feature in Indigenous tenure systems not only in Myanmar but across South and

Southeast Asia (Huard 2019, 2020; Karlsson 2011; Li 2014a). Yet, as Hpa Dee Pa hastened to add, this patch did not then become his individual property. Rather, it granted him primary usufruct ownership of this patch. That is to say, his labors allowed him and his kin to be first in line to clear this patch of secondary jungle, to grow crops on it and harvest them. Anyone wanting to use this land would have to get his family's permission first.

Primary usufruct ownership was generated by dint of being the first human to make contact and create a covenant with the spectral owners of a place. To this end, tenure of any given swath of land remained ephemeral. Time and time again, I was told that human "owners" were in fact simply *hee loh*, or "borrowing" the land for a short time before giving it back to its paramount, spectral owner, and that there would be terrible consequences for anyone who attempted to keep it for themselves. In this manner, tenure systems in the Mutraw hills resembled those in other parts of the country.

In Central Myanmar, for example, while people can claim temporary ownership over a parcel of land, due to the persistent uncertainty as to who will own it in the future, people regularly assert that in fact "nobody owns the land" (Huard 2020). Thus, as Stéphen Huard concludes, "ownership is but momentary," and the idea of stewardship (taking care, being in charge of) is tantamount to understanding land relations in Myanmar, rooted in moral and social obligations to others (2020, 110). Yet, while Huard focuses on the centrality of human kinship obligations, the ways in which people related to *k'sah* (spectral owners) in the Mutraw hills push us to accept that who/what obligates stretches far beyond other living humans (Despret and Meuret 2016).

While Hpa Dee Pa was reticent to divulge too many details as to how he actually went about making this covenant (remembering that the rites to do this were inherited *ta du ta htu*, i.e., taboos), he explained how there was no great difference from the rites to clear any other *hku*. He *lu ta* (fed/nourished) the spectral owners of this area with offerings of rice, curry, and betel nut, encouraging them to eat together while he beseeched them that he may borrow the land so he could feed his family, swearing to return it as soon as cultivation was over. That is to say, he exercised his obligations to the land's spectral owner(s). Thus, it was through not only his physical labor but also his ritual labor that he now held primary usufruct ownership of this patch: to use and enjoy the fruits of something belonging to another. He owned the rites, passed down from his father, to make these covenants with the spectral realm, and through these he attained primary usufruct.

Primary usufruct ownership was commonly referred to simply as being the *hku k'sah*. Attained by the first person to make contact and make a covenant with the spectral owners of this parcel of land, rather than ownership slowly waning as cultivation ceased and the forest returned, ownership continued on even after the death, inherited by the original covenant-maker's progeny (Hayami 2004, 153; Huard 2020; Lehman 2003). When Hpa Dee Pa eventually passes away, primary usufruct ownership over this patch of land will be passed down to his children. While the first person to clear the land had to be a man, who had inherited the rites involved in contacting and creating a covenant with the spectral owners of an area, inheritance was almost fully cognatic among Pwakanyaw groups in this area (I explore an exception to this in chapter 3). The descendants of the first covenant-maker, both female and male, had first rights of refusal to a given swidden patch, and ownership (in this restricted sense of primary usufruct) reverted back to them when it was not being actively cultivated. There were, however, ways to circumvent the temporal limitations of this ephemeral mode of ownership, such as by cultivating or building something more permanent than dry rice and chili plants.

Transformative Trees and Paddy Fields

Certain cultivated bamboo groves, household gardens, orchards (mostly of areca/betel nut), and even freestanding fruit trees such as the coconut palm that grew between Hpu Gay's and my homes, were referred to in regular speech as belonging to a specific person. While many people hitched their way up the coconut palm to help themselves to its fruit, people continued to talk of it as belonging to Hpa Kha Pa, the man who led efforts to protect the *loh*. Moreover, as these more permanent plants and trees remained in the ground over several seasons, a person's or household's status as the *k'sah* or owner also continued and could be inherited by their descendants. Much of the cardamom planted by an enterprising villager in Hpu Noh Noh Deh Kleh some sixty years ago, for example, was inherited by his sons after his death. Indeed, as in many Indigenous tenure systems, the materiality of the crops that were planted was formative. The (relative) permanence of certain crops or agricultural infrastructure opened the door to more exclusive modes of private ownership (cf. Li 2014a).

While a shift to private land ownership would have far-ranging and potentially catastrophic effects, it was continuously held in check by the encompassing ownership of specters. In most cases, if a person asked for permission from the human *k'sah*, they were permitted to harvest a few coconuts, cut a stem of bamboo, or fill a rolled-up shirt with areca nuts for their families should they not have any themselves. Underlying these practices was a tacit understanding that there were limits to how much a person might borrow and that what they borrowed should not be sold on for a profit. Although spoken of as owned by one person or one household, these groves, gardens, orchards, and trees/palms fell awkwardly somewhere between exclusive private property, on the one hand, and the commons, on the other. While the material permanency of certain plants, palms, and trees allowed people to stretch and negotiate modes of ephemeral ownership, this never quite led to the alienation of the earth from its spectral owners.

The ephemeral ownership of a person cultivating a patch of land rested in the encompassing ownership of the direct descendant of the man who first made contact and made a covenant with the specter who possesses the area. In turn, this form of human ownership was nesting in and subordinate to encompassing spectral ownership. These various layers of ownership sketch out a nesting hierarchy that was in constant motion. Modes of ephemeral and nesting ownership had, however, slowly begun to shift over the last eight years with the growing popularity of terraced wet rice cultivation. The first blushes of these gradual changes could be discerned in the advent of exchanges of land that often preceded the establishment of terraced wet rice/paddy fields. Hpu Hka Hsoo—an elder, ritual expert, frequent wanderer, and Hpa Kha Pa's father, who always sported a well-waxed mustache—was one of the first people in the area to adopt this form of agriculture, and his experiences were instructive of these transformations.

* * *

Seven or eight years ago, Hpu Hka Hsoo decided he would attempt to establish a paddy field, "like the ones I saw in my travels across Thailand," as he put it. By his own estimate, he had inherited usufruct ownership rights over at least fifteen *hku* (swidden) patches in Ta K'Thwee Duh Kaw from his parents. Yet, when he began searching for a suitable spot to establish a paddy field, he discovered that none of the *hku* he inherited were particularly well situated to this task. "They were either too far away from a water source, or on a slope that made it difficult to get water up to the top of the field." As he continued to search for a suitable area, he found one *hku* that was perfect, nestled along the Bleh Mah Loh stream that runs along the foot of Y'wa Mah Htu Lay. "The problem was," he told me, "this *hku* was not mine; nor did any of my kin own it." But, not easily disheartened, Hpu Hka Hsoo hit upon a novel plan. With a glint in his eye, he explained that, "while there are strict *ta du ta htu* [taboos] against selling the rights to a *hku*, in the past people have swapped land, like for like." Thus, he sought out the owner of

FIGURE 5. Hpu Kee and his paddy field.

this particular swidden patch along the Bleh Mah Loh stream and proposed a swap, exchanging the rights over this patch with the rights he held over a patch in another area of Ta K'Thwee Duh Kaw. After a little persuading, the exchange was completed, and he was given access to the parcel of land along the Bleh Mah Loh stream. The back-breaking labor of carving the characteristic steps of a terraced wet rice field (see figure 5) and the channels to redirect water from the Bleh Mah Loh stream could begin.

Much like the material permanency of areca palms, the drastic reshaping of the earth entailed in the establishing of a field—in which rice could be cultivated year after year without a fallow period—produced a concurrent permanence in rights over this land. Planting trees and establishing a paddy field had the similar effect of stretching how long a single person or household could hold on to a certain parcel of land. Moreover, the growing influence of the KNU and of official documents lent this stretched form of ephemeral ownership an added sense of individuality and persistence.

Upon establishing a paddy field and beginning to actively use it to cultivate wet rice, the Kawthoolei Agricultural Department (KAD) of the KNU required a person to register this land, often via the village tract leader, and to apply for a land title. This KNU land title requires that one specific person be registered as the official owner of the field, effectively making it private property. As I explore in more depth in chapter 4, this was a tactic commonly deployed by the KNU state to make this area "assessable," "legible," and, importantly, taxable (cf. Scott 1998). Yet one corollary of this individualized land title was that it also made it possible, on paper at least, for land to be bought and sold.

Following Hpu Hka Hsoo's initial success in establishing a paddy field along this stream, several other people set to work establishing their own terraced wet rice fields beside it. During my time in Ta K'Thwee Duh, by my reckoning, there were four paddy fields along this stream and another four to the west of the village (and two more that, due to a lack of funds, remained incomplete). In one of the paddy fields along the Bleh Mah Loh stream, the elderly man who held the land title over this field had recently moved to the regional center to be closer to his son who lived there. Since he moved, he rented out the field to Hpa Htwee, ostensibly to cover the taxes he was obligated to pay to the KNU for the land, whether he used it or not. However, at least as Hpa Htwee tells it, the title holder of this land only intended to rent out his paddy field in the short term. His long-term goal was to find someone who would be willing to buy the land from him—that is to say, buy the KNU land title, relieving him of the tax burden. Following this, Hpa Htwee visited me on several occasions to not so subtly suggest that I buy this field. I would then have somewhere to grow food and support myself when I returned, he reasoned. Moreover, out of brotherly love and not the obvious side benefits to him, of course, he promised to take care of it by cultivating the field while I was away.

While it had not quite happened yet, the growing popularity of permanent paddy fields was gradually making it possible to negotiate and in fact stretch and refigure local modes of ownership in ways that bore a closer resemblance to what could be described as private property. It is important to note, however, that the introduction of land titles does not necessarily always lead to the private ownership of land in the strict sense. In Central Myanmar, for instance, while land titling had been common practice since early colonial times, difference between who farms the land, who (momentarily) owns it, and who inherits it in the future continually militated against the adoption of a wholescale private property–based system (Huard 2020, 86). In the final section of this chapter, I shift focus to the other half of common dichotomous models of ownership: the commons.

UNCOMMON COMMONS AND *KAW* AS PATCHWORKS

The closest one came to a form of commons in these highlands was a handful of *hku* where usufruct ownership could not be handed on to the next generation and patches of land that were either unsuitable or too dangerous to cultivate, such as rocky outcrops, ponds, and *ta thoo ta pgho/hsoo*, or "potent/strong" places.

In rare cases in which a person died without direct kin to whom they could pass down the *hku* they held primary usufruct ownership of, these parcels of land were turned over to the commons. All people residing in Ta K'Thwee Duh Kaw had the right to cultivate these lands. Much like other swidden patches, the person/family who cultivated it for a season could only hold it in the ephemeral mode, losing all claims as the land fell back into fallow/forest. In addition, there were several areas in the *kaw* that could not be cleared and cultivated due to the terrain, such as Way Pgha, a rocky and wild forest populated by a whole host of animals, such as tigers, sun bears, and hornbills (see chapter 5). Along with these areas, uncultivable due to the terrain, were the swaths of land that, as I demonstrate in chapter 1, could not be cultivated due to being already possessed, in both the political and cosmological senses. These lands were already possessed either by *hsoo* (powerful) specters, such as Hpu Noh Noh Deh, or by *ta thoo ta pgho* (the "potency of creation")—such as the crest of peaks that make up Y'wa Ma Htu Lay. In a sense, these lands resembled what have been described as "common property" (Robbins 2012, 51–54); all residents of the *kaw* were free to collect firewood, forage, hunt, and even, as was the case in Hpu Noh Noh Deh, plant certain crops such as cardamom in these areas. Delving deeper, however, I found that the very status of this land as common to all humans residing in the vicinity was predicated on this land being, ultimately, possessed and owned by spectral persons.

Two modes of human ownership emerged here, both of which described a person as the *k'sah*, or "the owner," of a certain demarcated area. One mode of human ownership was that of primary usufruct, and the other was that of ephemeral ownership, with the latter nesting in and subsumed under the former. As ephemeral ownership waned, the encompassing ownership of primary usufruct waxed. Both these modes of human ownership were, in turn, nesting in wider hierarchical relationships to the encompassing ownership of various spectral persons, who possessed and were the true owners of the landscapes along this stretch of the lower Salween River, acting as sovereigns over their own domains. I explore the implications of this form of ownership on sovereignty and politics more in chapter 3. Furthermore, the notion of spectral ownership points to what Vinciane Despret and Michel Meuret call an "ecology of obligations" that makes people "capable of being better obligated to and obligated by other beings," be they human or otherwise (2016, 27). Relations of obligation between humans were always enmeshed in their wider relations and obligations to the spectral persons they shared their landscapes with.

In light of what I have shown thus far, on one scale each *kaw* was a patchwork of different types of land, roughly stitched together. *Kaw* were patchworks composed of lands with identifiable human *k'sah* (in the sense of usufruct ownership), such as swidden patches, paddy fields, household plots, gardens, orchards, groves, and some trees; areas with identifiable spectral owners, such as those spoken of as *hsoo* ("strongly" possessed) or *ta thoo ta pgho* ("potent" places); and lands understood more diffusely as possessed by a whole host of indeterminate spectral persons, such as the surrounding forests, lakes, and rivers, which were often unsuitable for cultivation. In turn, at a larger scale, landscapes across the Mutraw hills were made up of a patchwork of *kaw* lands, themselves sewn together by mutual obligations of kinship, friendship, and exchange.

Kaw were thus not quite "units" of local governance, which suggests a certain uniformity, interchangeability, and scalability (Tsing 2012). Instead, they came closer to what Anna Lowenhaupt Tsing, Andrew Mathews, and Nils Bubandt (2019), borrowing and modifying ecological terminology, describe as "patches." In this line of thinking, landscapes are composed of heterogeneous patches with a "uniqueness [that] is generated by [their] historical-ecological relations to other patches" (Bubandt et al. 2023, 19). Each *kaw* formed a patch that, while composed of heterogeneous elements, formed a delineated space with rather definite boundaries, implying notions of an inside and an outside (cf. Tsing, Deger et al. 2024, 35–38). This last point became clearer when conversation turned to questions as to who belonged to a specific *kaw*, hedged in notions of *htoo lee hpoe*, or "Indigenous."

I found that certain people were understood to be (*pgha*) *htoo lee hpoe*. The activists based in Chiang Mai consistently translated *htoo lee hpoe* as synonymous with "Indigenous," yet locally this term was used in the very restrictive sense of belonging to a particular *kaw*. Only a person who was *htoo lee hpoe* could hold and inherit swidden patches and be permitted to gather food/fuel and hunt there. Delving deeper, I learned that both a person and their parents/ancestors must be born within a particular *kaw* and continue to reside there to be considered *htoo lee hpoe*. Should a person move to another *kaw* after their birth, such as through marriage, they forfeited both the rights to "own" and to inherit land and had to request permission to cultivate in the *kaw* of their birth. A non–*htoo lee hpoe* person, who has married into the *kaw* (sometimes pejoratively called *hsaw mee*, or "wild jungle fowl"), much like a person who lives in a neighboring *kaw*, has to ask for permission to borrow a certain *hku*. Non–*htoo lee hpoe* people could only hold land in the sense of ephemeral ownership. The temporal constraints on this kind of human ownership allowed land to be shared with neighboring areas while arresting attempts to permanently annex a patch to make it their property, or part of their *kaw*. It was in this sense that Hpa Htwee could say that it would be easy for me to find land to cultivate should I move to Ta K'Thwee Duh Kaw (also, as I later learned, hinting that I should marry a local woman, such as his daughter).

Each *kaw* formed a patch that was clearly demarcated, albeit verbally rather than by conventional maps. A particular rise in the path or prominent stone was used to mark their borders. Nearly all members of the community, young and old alike, could recognize these physical boundary markers. When in doubt one could always consult the village elders or a small scrap of paper kept at the headman's house that, in lieu of a map, was a transcription of several of the village elders' verbal demarcations. To this end, Ta K'Thwee Duh Kaw shared continuous borders with its neighboring *kaw*, forming part of a sprawling patchwork of heterogeneous yet interlinked lands, which spread over much of the Mutraw District of southeast Myanmar.

Each *kaw* acted as a largely autonomous patch of political organization both transcending and binding together the different households, families, and even villages and sub-villages while remaining deeply connected to other scales of political organization. Each *kaw* had its own sets of *ta du ta htu* (taboos) that people were required to follow. All those residing in a specific *kaw* were woven tightly together by their shared status as *pgha htoo lee hpoe* and/or as people sharing a particular swath of agricultural, foraging, and hunting land. In effect, *kaw* were actually existing pockets of autonomy. I return to these points around patches and scale in chapter 6, where I take a closer look at the ways the Salween Peace Park was translating and rescaling these practices, tapping into this de facto autonomy.

Returning to the roadbuilding incident that opens this chapter, it becomes clear that many of the villagers' concerns arose from understandable fears that, as the road scythed its way through the middle of the *kaw*, it might subdivide and complicate this delicate pattern of nesting ownership. Should one part of a *hku* be split off from the rest, bitter disputes over ownership would surely ensue. Tearing the fabric of these patchworks, in turn, threatened the integrity of this particular scale of political organization—that is to say, the *kaw* and its autonomy. As such, land possession practices related to *kaw* implied alternating modes of not only ownership but also sovereignty. Shifting focus from ownership to sovereignty elicits a battery of new questions: Who acts as the head of each *kaw*, organizing the division of lands such as *hku* among inhabitants? Who are the sovereigns of each *kaw*? Commonly, especially in political ecology (which, in part, guides this book), one attempts to answer such questions by looking for the key actors involved in political processes (Karlsson 2011; Li 2014a; Robbins 2012). However, as the vignette of the "car road" suggests, along the Bu Thoe ridge this was far from a straightforward matter.

THREE

Spectral Sovereignty

Negotiations of State, Power, and Politics

RETURNING to the opening vignette of chapter 2, this chapter delves deeper into the implication of the roadbuilding project on politics and sovereignty. Since longer than anyone can remember, the Myanmar state has remained distant in the Mutraw hills. While the Karen National Union acted as the de facto state, it, too, struggled to extend its influence there, becoming threadbare along the Bu Thoe ridge. This road was the KNU's first large infrastructure project to reach this elevation. In people's day-to-day lives, the state was only felt faintly. What is more, there was a dearth of local human actors and institutions vested with the de facto power and authority to push back against the KNU state, who were building this road.

These highlands, however, did not quite fit the descriptor of "non-state spaces" or pockets of anarchy, as similar small-scale societies at the edges of states in Southeast Asia tend to be described (Gibson and Sillander 2011; Scott 2009). The term *anarchy*, derived from the Greek word *an-arkhos*, is commonly approximated to "no ruler" (Morris 2014, 62) or "without government" (Barclay 1998, 8–10). Yet, along the Bu Thoe ridge, rulers and sovereignty at large were not so much absent as they were spectral. As opposed to the Myanmar and KNU (revolutionary) states, the spectral world regularly intervened in human affairs, having palpable, yet unseen, effects on local politics, rooted in people's past embodied experiences of living in possessed landscapes (cf. Govindrajan 2022; Thomas and Masco 2023).

I speak of this mode of politics as *spectral sovereignty*. Strikingly egalitarian relations between villagers were hedged in wider notions of the paramount political authority and sovereignty of spectral presences. Residual local political sway was largely derived from negotiating power—that is to say, the power to negotiate and the negotiation of the power of distant others. I end this chapter by exploring how these Indigenous practices and cosmologies unsettle many hegemonic notions of sovereignty, gesturing toward alternate modes of politics that, as I explore further in subsequent chapters, other movements were tapping into.

AT THE FRAYED EDGES OF STATE SOVEREIGNTY

One striking facet of the tale of road construction along the Bu Thoe ridge was that, as has long been the case in these highlands, the Myanmar state remained largely distant. As noted in the introduction, the period in which I conducted my fieldwork, from 2016 to 2017, was bookended geographically and temporally by conflicts arising from the Tatmadaw-led roadbuilding projects. To the southeast, in September 2016, just months before I began my fieldwork, conflict flared up around an access road to the contested Hatgyi hydroelectric dam (Bright 2019, 79–80; Karen Rivers Watch 2016). Then, from March 2018, sporadic armed clashes erupted around the construction of a road that also aimed to concatenate military bases (albeit Tatmadaw ones), to the northwest in Ler Mu Plaw, a day's hike away (Moo and O'Connor 2018; Nyein 2020). The construction of the "car road" along the Bu Thoe ridge seven years prior to my arrival, described in chapter 2, was however a purely KNU project. The Tatmadaw and the Myanmar state were only implicated in its construction insofar as the road was a part of the KNU's defense strategy to keep them at bay.

The relative absence of the Myanmar state followed the pattern I have illustrated previously, of conflict and state conquest tending to simply pass through these wind-swept uplands, on the way to more strategically significant areas. This pattern, in turn, followed deep histories of the wider Salween District. The Mutraw hills were treated by precolonial and colonial government alike as a frontier area, under indirect rule through strategic alliances with local "tribal chieftains," never brought fully under centralized state control (Furnivall 1960, 12; Jolliffe 2016, 9). During my fieldwork I found that, in much the same way, the greatest presence of the Myanmar state in the areas around Ta K'Thwee Duh was a Tatmadaw military encampment some two- or three-hours' hike away, down along the banks of the Salween River. In people's day-to-day lives, especially since the ceasefire in 2012, the Tatmadaw's presence was largely only felt in the patchy military-owned Myanma Posts and Telecommunications mobile network coverage that emanated from this base, which could be caught at a few spots along the ridge (when the wind was not blowing too strongly). Indeed, nearly all trade was conducted in Thai baht; Myanmar kyat notes were either refused outright or accepted begrudgingly at unfavorable exchange rates. Moreover, the vast majority of items sold in the small tea shops along the Bu Thoe ridge were imported from Thailand by the fleet of long-tail boats that plied the Salween day and night, then freighted up the mountainside along the span of the "car road" and beyond by motorbikes. The cars and motorbikes negotiating this crumbling and constantly shifting road also drove or rode on the lefthand side. "It's just like Thailand," people would exclaim each time I veered over to the righthand side of the road when I rode a motorbike up there. One consequence of the protracted armed conflict was that there were few passable roads to the markets inside Myanmar, constraining the flow not only of goods but also of people coming from Central Myanmar. Burmese-speaking people who were not Tatmadaw soldiers only made it up there on a handful of occasions that people could recall. When they did, they were often met with considerable trepidation, suspicion, and sometimes outright violence.

Consequently, people felt the sovereignty of the Myanmar state largely through its faint effects: in rumors of the movements of Tatmadaw troops on the ground, the roar of fighter planes and helicopters overhead, and the traces left in its wake, of scorched earth and landmines underfoot—and patchy mobile coverage. However, as the events following the KNU attempts to construct a road along the Bu Thoe ridge demonstrated, where the sovereignty of the Myanmar state contracted, rather than pockets of non-state space opening up in its stead (Scott 2009, 60–61; see also Rajah 1990, 120; South 2008, 38–39), the sovereignty of the KNU expanded.

From its very formation as the Karen National Association in 1881, this so-called non-state armed group (NSAG), much like its sister movements such as the Kachin Independence Organisation in the north and the New Mon State Party in the south, not only struggled against the Burmese state but also struggled to attain greater self-determination. The KNU has long strived to establish the autonomous Karen State of Kawthoolei. To this end, in many of the so-called liberated areas under its control along these highlands, the KNU acted as the local state. This was not, however, without a significant degree of overlapping and contestation (Harrisson 2021; Harrisson and Kyed 2019; South 2018). The presence of the KNU was most profoundly felt in the larger villages in the foothills and valleys, such as the administrative center of the Mutraw District, Deh Bu Noh, and the seat of the local village tract close to the Salween River. Here, the KNU had not only cornered the "markets of protection" (Shah 2013, 489), in the form of the Karen National Liberation Army and police force (as many violent groups, from mafias to "rebels," excel at); they were also often the sole providers of care, education, justice, and transportation in these areas. The KNU had its own schools, clinics, and courthouses, with state departments dedicated to forestry, mining, and education—along with all the accompanying bureaucracy. As one young judge in Deh Bu Noh explained to me, they even have a special "witchcraft law" governing the use of magic and would soon have their own prisons. The road itself was commissioned by the Department of Transportation and Communication of the KNU, and all motorbikes that traversed it were required to pay road tax each year—proof of which must be clearly displayed at all times and subject to inspection at each checkpoint along the road.

In this light, the KNU is commonly described as a NSAG (Kyed and Gravers 2014) and its control over its liberated areas as an example of so-called rebel governance (Brenner 2019; Loong 2025). Grasping the KNU as "rebels" helps foreground how they not only seek to create new socio-political orders by use of, or threat of, armed violence but also provide vital services such as health, education, and justice systems (Kasfir 2015; Mampilly 2011). I would argue, however, that "rebel governance" fails to capture the full extent of what the KNU have attained in their liberated areas. The KNU governance apparatus is modeled, at least in part, on the former colonial system and has its own flag (that flew above the school at Ta K'Thwee Duh), national anthem (which the school children sang each morning), and complex governance structures. In its liberated areas, the KNU has accrued most of the accoutrements of what would usually be associated with a modern nation-state. Mutraw and the other liberated areas form Kawthoolei, the territorialized nation-state that the KNU has struggled to attain for over seventy years. Moreover, and pivotal here, people working for the KNU and its affiliates strongly rejected the labels of "rebels" and "insurgents," preferring to see themselves as revolutionaries (for more on this, see chapter 6). Accordingly, I refer to the KNU as a (revolutionary) state. After all, for the past seventy years, they were the closest that most people in the Mutraw hills had come to experiencing a state.

The process of building a road along the Bu Thoe ridge, however, brought to light how the highlands were themselves divided into hills and valleys. And, much like its historical predecessors, the KNU state also struggled to expand into the higher elevations of the Mutraw hills. Much like in other upland areas of the Southeast Asian massif, this difficulty could, in part, be accounted for by the "friction of terrain" of the steep slopes and dense forests of this area and KNU's lack of "distance-demolishing" technologies to surmount this friction (Scott 2009). While the villagers had planted the KNU's rising sun flag in the soil at the top of the village, the large infrastructural project to build the road was the first time the KNU had managed to establish themselves firmly along this ridge, beyond small outcrops of basic military infrastructure. As one Indigenous activist lamented to me, capital from development and infrastructural projects, be they KNU or NGO led, had a habit of "jumping over the mountain" and ending up on either side in the lower elevations. Consequently, the majority of the primary schools and clinics along this ridge were funded by a spattering of cross-border, often Christian faith-based, organizations with only loose ties to the Karen Education and Culture Department and Karen Department of Health and Welfare branches of the KNU government. Their main offices and activities remained in the settlements at lower altitudes.

In this light, the KNU state resembles Indigenous modes of governance that Stanley Tambiah (1976) describes as *galactic polities*, possessing a mandala-like cosmological topography (see also South 2008, 2, 38–39). Akin to the precolonial Burmese and Thai states that once ruled over this area, the KNU's sovereignty radiated outward from its centers of power at lower elevations, slowly losing strength toward the periphery. Tambiah describes this as analogous to a "field of radiation of light or heat from a source," modulated by pulsating alliances (1976, 123; see also Anderson 1990). This description resonates with Thongchai Winichakul's (1994) observation that "premodern" states in Southeast Asia lacked defined boundaries and that sovereignties overlapped prior to colonialism. In view of this it becomes clear that villages such as Ta K'Thwee Duh sat at the interstices between the KNU and the Myanmar/Thai state where, rather than a power vacuum, a space opened: a contact zone for continual encounters with and negotiation of power and sovereignty.

Most villagers living along the Bu Thoe ridge whom I had a chance to talk with spoke warmly about this *kah kleh*, or "car road." Indeed, a large proportion of them, including Hpu Hkee, had helped with its construction. While many protested the particular route it was projected to take, few disagreed with the road itself in principle.[1] Far from attempting to constantly evade the state, on the whole people desired and welcomed more KNU involvement in their area, despite holding deep reservations. Many hoped that a closer connection with the KNU would allow them to make claims on it and "construct [more] desirable forms" of dependency (Ferguson, "Declarations," 2013, 237). This aligns with Penny Harvey and Hannah Knox's (2015, 1–17) work, in which they show how roads as "public works" come to matter: provoking conflicts and negotiations over ownership as well as becoming entangled with desires for connectivity and prosperity. In this manner, struggles over the path of this particular road were indicative not of wholescale rejection of the KNU's sovereignty but rather part and parcel of people's processes of negotiating with it. Where the KNU's influence became threadbare not only did alternating modes of ownership emerge but also of sovereignty. In the following pages, I take a closer look at the key human actors and institutions involved in the political process in and around Ta K'Thwee Duh—the *kaw*, the headman, the ceremonial leader, and the elders, as well as the role of moral sentiments—before moving on to demonstrate the central role of the sovereignty of the spectral realm in day-to-day life.

KAW POLITICS: NEGOTIATING POWER

Throughout upland southeast Myanmar, as touched on in chapter 2, the basic unit, or perhaps more precisely patch, of political governance (with a few exceptions) was the *kaw* (which were clearly demarcated; see figure 6). Each main village in a *kaw* elected a person to represent them, known as the *tha waw tha pgha*, or the "old heart of the village." In English this person is more commonly referred to as the headman. The headman and vice-headman were elected by popular vote once every four years in a meeting that gathered all the inhabitants of this area to cast their vote by a show of hands. In Ta K'Thwee Duh, the headman had always been a man, and the holder during my research there, during most of 2017, was a Baptist man called Hpa Thoo.[2] In Ta K'Twee Duh Kaw the largest sub-village/hamlet also had its own sub-headman, while the elected headman and vice-headman of the main village remained the key figures in most political matters.

The "Old Heart of the Village"

Initially I was convinced that the headman was a key political actor and that the headman office played a central role in the delegation of land within each *kaw*. During the period between January and February, when people select which swidden patch (*hku*) they will cultivate for the coming agricultural season, the villagers regularly visit the headman to discuss it with him. Talking to Naw Ghaw (the woman who dreamt of an overflowing spring at the top of Ta Bu Kyoh) one chilly February morning, I learned that her husband had just returned from paying a visit to the headman of a neighboring *kaw*. She explained that, since he was considering cultivating there this agricultural season, his first port of call had been the headman's house, to broach the subject of borrowing land in their *kaw*.

To learn more about the role of the headman in the division of land, I began spending time with Ta K'Thwee Duh's headman, Hpa Thoo, a reserved and laconic man who usually only opened his mouth (especially

FIGURE 6. The boundaries of Ta K'Thwee Duh Kaw as illustrated by Dee Klee (right).

after his tongue had been loosened by a little rice wine) to playfully tease people. Through our stilted conversations I learned that, while people often came to him when they were deciding which land they would cultivate that season, in his words, "I have no authority to make decisions or give orders in such matters." He was, however, required by the KNU to keep a ledger of where each person farmed each year to facilitate the collection of taxes, which was also conducted in this lull in agricultural activities. The reason people visited the village headman's home during this period was not to obtain his permission but rather to take a look at the ledger (or get someone who could read to look for them). The ledger helped people get both a better overview as to where others were planning on cultivating this season and to whom they must ask for permission to clear a certain fallow over which they did not hold primary usufruct ownership. Thus, while people consulted him for information, the headman had little if any influence on how land was actually cultivated and shared. In a way, he and his home acted more as a hub from which negotiations over land use could begin. As he so pointedly put it, "People just discuss it between themselves and decide like that." As I came to understand, in most cases, the headman's political power stretched little beyond his authority to call the villagers to meetings on certain subjects and make decisions via consensus.

Inevitably, the headman called meetings, to be held in his house, at the behest of others. At these meetings, the people in attendance discussed the matter brought forward between themselves, listening to different sides of the subject at hand, before there was a show of hands to attempt to come to a consensus decision. If no consensus could be reached, in most cases, no action was taken. The headman and his house, in many ways, acted as a forum for facilitating negotiations. Spending more time with Hpa Thoo, I learned that his elected role as headman largely revolved around administrative duties such as calling meetings, helping people find out where they should go to request permission to cultivate a certain area, or relaying orders from the KNU (cf. Boutry et al. 2017, 64; Huard 2019, in Upper Burma; Karlsson 2011, 242–43, in Northeast India). He also acted as the village representative at KNU and Salween Peace Park meetings, returning home to report back what he had been told. Indeed, much of the headman's duties centered on him acting as an intermediary between the KNU and his fellow villagers.

Official orders from the KNU and their armed wing, the KNLA, were usually conveyed to the village in the form of a written request addressed to the village headman, delivered by motorcycle courier. In most cases, this was a signed letter from the commander of the local KNLA encampment formally requesting that the villagers provide corvée labor. The headman's job was to collect villagers for such labor, which during peace time largely consisted of portering supplies between KNLA camps (less often now that the camps were connected by road) and assisting with the rebuilding of KNLA bases after the monsoon season. At times of heightened conflict, villagers were occasionally drafted into serving as guides and even to bear arms.

The collection of taxes to the KNU also went through the headman's house, collected each February, after the harvest, by the village tract leader (again, always a man in this area) and his entourage. The amount of land each household cultivated the previous year was recorded in the ledger in the headman's home and tax paid per acre, as either a portion of the rice harvested or a cash equivalent. Those few households with paddy fields were levied an additional fixed amount each year, regardless of whether or not they had actually cultivated this field the previous season. On his yearly visit to collect taxes, the KNU village tract leader and his entourage, including the captain in charge of the KNLA detachment for this village tract, also collected new conscripts. As villagers (often ruefully) explained to me, each household was obliged to "give one son to the KNLA" as a soldier who would serve "for life" and one child to serve for just one year.

As these examples illustrated, while these villagers had relatively warm relations with the KNU, contact was both sporadic—KNU officials rarely visiting and communicating largely through letters—and entrenched in hierarchy. Once again, the headman's political position was mainly that of an intermediary between the villagers and the KNU. As Stéphen Huard notes is the case in Central Myanmar, "Being a village headman was a matter of craftsmanship and political navigation" (2019, 20). The headman's job consisted largely of hosting KNU officials each February, showing them the ledger, and calling a meeting when taxes were collected. As Hpu Gay, who served as headman for over ten years, explained, if a household was not able or willing to pay, the headman often acted as an arbitrator between them and KNU/KNLA officials to attempt to resolve such impasses. The headman himself was thus neither vested with the authority to demand that the villagers carry out an order, nor did he have the capacity to coerce them to do so. As such, while relations outward, toward the KNU, could at times be strikingly hierarchical, relations inward between villagers remained largely horizontal.

The role of headman is, in part, a vestige of colonial rule. Maxime Boutry et al. (2017, 52–53) show that the figure of the village headman, as we see him today, emerged through the Village Act (1887), shortly after colonization. This law aimed to break up former administrative structures by emphasizing the village (rather than the *kaw*) as a political territorial unit and by tying the headman to the collection of a "household tax" (Taylor 2009, 82; see also Huard 2019, 173–87). In many ways, it appears that the KNU inherited this administrative system in which the village acted as the smallest unit of governance in the KNU system, at least up until their new land law was passed in 2015 (re)introducing the *kaw* system (see chapter 6).

These yearly visits from the village tract leader, the local KNLA captain, and their entourages to collect taxes and soldiers were, as I have shown, some of the few times villagers felt the KNU state on their skin. The village tract leader would rarely be seen again until the time of the next harvest, unless some unforeseen event drew him back. I found that, up along the Bu Thoe ridge, the KNU and even the KNLA had surprisingly little presence in people's day-to-day lives. Soldiers would occasionally visit the village but, more often than not, arrived in civilian clothes for weddings and other ceremonies, to chat, drink, and sometimes flirt (largely unsuccessfully) with the local single women. As I show in the next section, while the KNU's lowland-based governance and judiciary branch were often invoked as a threat to people suspected of theft and the like, they were rarely, if ever, actually drawn upon in everyday governance. The headman kept out of most day-to-day affairs and held little political clout beyond his ability to negotiate with the distant powers of the KNU. This could be discerned most clearly in the roadbuilding project that opens chapter 2, for which he only played a bit part, simply collecting labor from the villagers to help build the road.

Given these rather unenviable tasks—assisting the collection of taxes, conscripts, and labor—few villagers relished the prospect of becoming the headman. Hpu Gay told me how the current headman had attempted to quit on three separate occasions, and the village elders had been drafted in each time to persuade him to stay on. The other villagers told me how, in a myriad of subtle ways, they had attempted to evade being chosen each time there was an election for a new headman. However, most accepted that, once this decision was made, there was nothing they could do about it; at some point it would be "my turn," they reasoned. Albeit, as Hpa Kha Pa confided in me, when his turn came around six years ago, his formidable wife was furious and did not speak to him for two days.

The "Owner of the Water and Land"

In addition to the headman, the *htee hpoe kaw k'sah/hee hkoh htee*, the hereditary "owner" of each *kaw*, was the only other political office I was able to identify in my time along this stretch of the lower Salween River. If the headman was the head of the village, then the *htee hpoe kaw k'sah* was the head of the *kaw*. However, much like the headman, also always a man, his political authority was largely rooted in his ability to negotiate, in his case with the surrounding spectral powers. His power was ceremonial in both senses of the word.

The title of *htee hpoe kaw k'sah* (literally, the owner of the water and land) was passed down patrilineally from the founding lineage, descended from the first family that settled in this area. As was the case in the process of establishing primary usufruct ownership over swidden patches (*hku*), the *htee hpoe kaw k'sah*'s ancestors were the first humans to make a covenant with the spectral owners of the area around Ta K'Thwee Duh. This ancestor made a pact not only with the local spectral persons but also directly with the *kaw k'sah*, "the owner of the earth"—that is to say, the owner/lord (*k'sah*) of this entire *kaw*. It was in this sense that this living descendant was known as the hereditary "owner of the water and land" (*htee hpoe kaw k'sah*) of this *kaw*, having inherited usufruct ownership over this entire delineated area from its overall spectral owner. This relation is commonly known as a "founder's cult" and is a widespread phenomenon across Southeast Asia. In this covenant with the spectral owners of the earth, "in return for regular offering, the spirit/s ensure the fertility of the land in the form of bountiful crops" (Kammerer and Tannenbaum 2003, 3). As a result of this relation, the position of *htee hpoe kaw k'sah* implied that he was charged with leading negotiations with the spectral owner of this area.³

The *htee hpoe kaw k'sah* of Ta K'Thwee Duh, however, also patiently explained to me that he had little de facto power or authority. His father, a middle child, inherited the title only after his older brother, the only child instructed by their father in all the correct rites and practices, had suddenly absconded to Thailand. As a result, the "generation had been lost" and much of the knowledge of how to execute the duties of a *htee hpoe kaw k'sah* had been lost with him. "I cannot do anything," he repeatedly replied to my questions. Indeed, as Hpu Waw, the village elder with a repurposed Japanese rifle, told me, people tend to refer to him as *hee hkoh htee*, meaning the house or village head. Hpu Waw emphasized that calling him the *htee hpoe kaw k'sah* might be construed as mocking his lack of abilities as a hereditary leader. That said, most referred to the *hee hkoh htee* simply by his teknonym Hpaw Htoo Pa: as the father (*pa*) of Hpaw Htoo (his first-born child). Hpu Waw continued that the reasons the villagers encouraged Hpaw Htoo Pa to continue as *hee hkoh htee* were mostly practical. They noticed that as long as there was a *hee hkoh htee* holding the generation, they received considerably more baskets of rice come harvest time. As such, his main duties, like his ancestors before him, revolved around being the first to conduct the *lu ta* (offering, but literally, feeding) to the spectral owners of the fields, which were connected to each agricultural cycle. For example, it was prohibited to begin propitiating the spectral owners of one's swidden patch before the *hee hkoh htee*. It was his duty as the direct descendant of the first settlers to open and facilitate smooth communication and negotiations with the local spectral population of the *kaw*.

Conversely, in neighboring Pa Nuh Duh Kaw, the *htee hpoe kaw k'sah* had been effectively driven out for being too demanding, despite having similarly diminished duties. Speaking to the brother of Pa Nuh Duh Kaw's former *htee hpoe kaw k'sah*, I learned that the amount of rice villagers harvest each season stands in direct relation to how little the *htee hpoe kaw k'sah* harvests. Therefore, as the villagers in Pa Nuh Duh Kaw received bumper crops year after year, and *htee hpoe kaw k'sah*'s household eked out a meager existence, it was expected that the villagers would share a small portion of their bounty with the *htee hpoe kaw k'sah*'s family to compensate for their necessary losses. This rice was given in recognition of his position in the village, with none of the usual reciprocal bonds attached. And yet, his brother explained with a sigh, "people in Pa Nuh Duh grew complacent, complaining increasingly loudly." Often in the presence of *htee hpoe kaw k'sah* or his family, they would grumble that "they should spend more time working their fields and not beg for rice from the other households each season," his brother remembers. The *htee hpoe kaw k'sah* tried to explain the situation, that this was how it has always worked, but these laments were ignored. So eventually he also left for Thailand in shame. Soon after his departure, the village suffered one of the worst harvests in living memory. The villagers reasoned that this must be due to the displeasure of the spectral owners of the *kaw* that their intermediary had been driven out. But alas, by this point it was too late to call him back. If a *htee hpoe kaw k'sah* leaves the *kaw* for a prolonged period, the brother explained, "he is forbidden from returning."

As I traveled through the area, I found this tale from Pa Nuh Duh was indicative of the status of *htee hpoe kaw k'sah/hee hkoh htee* all along this stretch of the lower Salween River. Whether this was the result of the protracted conflict, the creeping proselytizing of Christian and Buddhist missionaries, or common tropes that things were always better/more powerful in the past was difficult to ascertain. But there was a clear tendency, even in areas that still had a full *htee hpoe kaw k'sah*, for this ceremonial leader to lack de facto power, political or otherwise, and to regularly be disparaged by the people. It seems that, while it was widely accepted that the specters had broad powers over the human realm, and asymmetrical/hierarchical relations to them were taken as a given, humans who made similar demands of food in return for bountiful harvest were treated with a great deal of disdain.

Just as the headman acted as an intermediary between the villagers and the (distant) KNU, the *hee hkoh htee* acted as an intermediary between the villagers and the (largely unseen) spectral realm, charged with making and maintaining good relations. Indeed, upon closer inspection, both the headman and *hee hkoh htee/htee hpoe kaw k'sah* bear a striking resemblance to the notion of a "powerless chief" (Clastres 1987, 29), with little de facto power and authority and very unwilling to take on more. In most situations, political responsibility was spread reasonably evenly among the residents of these highlands. Relations between villagers remained largely symmetrical and egalitarian, albeit strongly gendered. I found that quotidian life, in lieu of specific leader figures or institutions, was guided by a strong sense of morality and obligation, mediated through the village elders.

Sharp Teeth, Rough Tongues, and Moral Hearts

The KNU state judiciary system was highly elaborate and, from what I could ascertain, reasonably effective in the lowlands. Yet, as I have stressed, it became threadbare at higher elevations, struggling to have enduring effects on and be felt in the day-to-day lives of people in out-of-the-way places such as Ta K'Thwee Duh. The few political positions that existed were largely ceremonial, and the little de facto political power they possessed was derived from their virtuosity in negotiating with powerful external forces. This led me to ponder: What happens when a person does something that is considered morally reprehensible or socially unacceptable?

When I posed this question to villagers in Ta K'Thwee Duh, time and time again, they replied that they try to deal with social, political, and moral problems in situ. Despite threats that a certain person would be reported to the KNU judiciary, the police, or the KNLA should it not be possible to solve an impasse in the village, I was unable to uncover a single account of this actually happening in practice. The inhabitants here repeatedly and actively attempted to avoid the interference of the KNU justice division.

Much of the research on the political workings of everyday justice in pockets of Myanmar where the central state remains distant tends to foreground the plurality or hybridity of forms of governance and justice, highlighting how the rule of the central state, armed groups such as the KNU, and "customary" practices are imbricated (Harrisson 2021; Kyed 2020; McConnachie 2014; South 2018). However, while certainly the case in the lowland areas along the Salween and Yunzalin Rivers, up on the Bu Thoe ridge I found that justice commonly began and ended within the limits of each *kaw*. When an accusation was made, such as of petty theft, if it could not be resolved through the mediation of fellow villagers, more often than not it was left to fester or peter out by itself. This became particularly evident when I began discussing such matters with one of the female elders, Hpee Luh, who had served as the local representative for the Karen Women's Organisation (KWO) for many years. Having lost numerous children during childbirth, a husband who was rarely home, and a large extended family to support, she was intimately acquainted with the struggles many women face.

The KWO is an important arm of the KNU state and has been working to attain gender equality in Karen communities since its formation in 1949, the same year the KNU was founded. When I asked Hpee Luh what the role of the local KWO representative entailed, however, she quickly retorted that it entailed very little indeed. As she stressed, "It mostly involves regularly going to meetings held in [the regional center] and not a lot more." But these days she was getting too old to walk so far, and besides, as she noted, "being the KWO representative doesn't count for much in the village." She went on to detail how, while this position did not allow her to call meetings and open discussions, like the headman, she was still regularly called upon to help mediate certain problems. These problems ranged from incest to gender-based violence to petty theft and everything in between. As such, she often worked in parallel with the headman, as a more informal channel.

Gently patting the bottom of one of the many grandchildren she shared her household with, until he fell sound asleep curled up on her lap, Hpee Luh went on to explain that, when a large problem arose in the village or *kaw* area, the headman was quickly consulted and a meeting called in his house. In broad brushstrokes: in the case of theft, for example, at this meeting the accused was compelled to confess their guilt to the aggrieved parties, with the other assembled villagers acting as witnesses. If the person confessed, with no stipulation made for an apology, the case was considered resolved. Should the accused either refuse to admit their guilt, but have no way to unequivocally prove their innocence, and/or continue to steal after the meeting, the usual practice was to systematically ostracize them and sometimes evoke the threat of exile. One concrete example Hpee Luh gave to demonstrate how these processes worked pertained to a young woman I knew well, Naw Maw Htaw.

Some years earlier, Naw Maw Htaw made a *k'ma* (a mistake)—specifically, she engaged in sex with a man outside of wedlock—which was a grave offense in this area. As touched on in the introduction, a tiger usually appeared or was heard roaring near the village following such an act of impropriety. The tiger was widely interpreted as a sign that the *kaw k'sah*, the spectral "owner of the *kaw*," had been angered by this "mistake." Steps were then quickly taken to placate and propitiate the *kaw k'sah* before her anger overflowed, inflicting disaster on the village, by attempting to make amends and repair the relationships between humans and specters (I return to this in the next section). However, in this particular case, Hpee Luh told me, "a tiger was neither seen nor heard afterward." The man involved took this as a sign that he had done no wrong and refused to accept responsibility by marrying Naw Maw Htaw. This led to an impasse and was the cause of much concern in the village. Despite Hpee Luh's repeated attempts to broker a compromise, the man would not budge, and, in the end, both were labeled *pgha mee hoo*, which translates as "people with a name heard/known," meaning people of ill repute. Yet, while the man had little trouble finding a wife a few years later, Naw Maw Htaw had incredible difficulty finding a suitor in the village. So difficult, in fact, that she and her mother beseeched me several times to help her find a *goh lah wa*, or "white foreigner" husband. In the end, she met a man living in Karenni State, several days' hike away, who was unaware of the poor status of her name in Ta K'Thwee Duh.

Elders such as Hpee Luh were often called upon to help resolve these kinds of issues, leading them to sometimes be known as *pgha meh ay play thweh*, or "people with sharp teeth and rough tongues." It was said that the ability of elders to *deh* (speak) with sharp teeth and tough tongues—that is to say, their accrued experiences and adroit speech—on many occasions positioned them as mediators, much like the headman and the ceremonial leader (cf. de la Cadena 2015, 45–46; Clastres 1987, 151–55). This was part of their negotiating power.

When the intercession of the elders did not have the desired effect, forms of a public shaming acted both as a punishment and a deterrent—albeit often directed more at controlling women's bodies than perturbing would-be thieves. In part, they resembled what has been defined as "moral coercion" (Clastres 1987, 22–23; see also Radcliffe-Brown 1952), which stands in contrast to the physical coercion relied upon by states, through violence and threats thereof. Morality is commonly used to explain such so-called anarchic solidarity among small-scale societies with subsistence economies across Southeast Asia (Gibson and Sillander 2011). The highly egalitarian practices of the Batek of Malaysia, for example, have been grasped as a consequence of their strong sense of "moral community" (Endicott 2011). While this was far from the whole picture, morality as a form of non-coercive power figured centrally in the day-to-day lives of many of the women and men living along the Bu Thoe ridge. This became particularly evident in the way that social life was often patterned by mutual aid. One example of this aid could be seen in the building and maintaining of houses.

Once every two to three years, each household had to replace the roof of their house. Commonly at these elevations along the lower Salween River, roofing tiles were made of a kind of palm leaf, known locally as *loh lah*. Since this was far too big of a job to be undertaken within the household alone, rice wine and beer were brewed, predominantly by women of the household, before kin and neighbors were invited over to drink, eat, and help replace the tiles. People then worked, drank, chatted, and joked until the roof was complete and/or the food and alcohol were exhausted. This labor was deeply gendered, the men perching in the rafters of the house and affixing the tiles with moistened thin strips of bamboo while the women remained on the ground handing the tiles up to them. Each time I joined in, I was inevitably placed with the women, as they feared I might fall. A similar pattern repeated itself when it was time to build a house, plant/transplant rice, and harvest it. Each instance was initiated by the hosting household who invited people to come to the area where the house would be built, or to their field where the rice needed to be (trans)planted or harvested, to help them with tasks too large to complete alone. All those invited had a strong obligation to attend; sometimes nearly the whole village joined in to help out on a particularly large field. The host, in turn, was obligated to feed the helpers, once or twice depending on the task, and keep their cups brimming with alcohol. As such, before a house could be built, a field planted, or the rice harvested, the hosting household—that is to say, the women of the household—had to brew a large batch of alcohol and prepare enough food to feed all those who came to help.

While the food and drink provided was often talked of as a form of payment for the services rendered, such assistance always incurred *k'mah*, or a debt. While I was attempting to help Hpa Kha Pa (Hpee Luh's son) plant his *hku* (swidden field) with rice, he explained to me that, "if one of the other households sends three members for a day to help me plant my *hku*, I have to send three members of my household to help when it is their turn to plant." Failing to reciprocate incurs a *k'ma* that one must pay back later. Indeed, as he added, another term for a person of ill repute is *pgha mee k'mah*, or "a person whose name has incurred a debt." As David Graeber noted is the case globally, there was a deeply ingrained moral sense that "one has to pay one's debts," and a heavy feeling of shame and distrust haunted those who did not (2012, 2–19). These continual reciprocal acts of mutual aid between households bound them more tightly together, acting like "the movement of the hook that serves to bind together the various sections of the straw roofing so as to make one single roof" (Mauss [1925] 2002, 27), as so evocatively phrased in a New Caledonian saying.

All along the Bu Thoe ridge, I found that the Myanmar state and, to an extent, the KNU state struggled to have a substantial effect on people's everyday lives and make their presence felt. In their stead, relations between the people were remarkably horizontal. There were few political offices or institutions, and those that existed were vested with little de facto political power. Day-to-day affairs were often shaped by mutual aid, and notions of shame, morality, and debt were mediated by the elders. However, as the events surrounding the construction of the "car road" indicated, while day-to-day relations between the residents of these highlands were overwhelmingly horizontal, this never quite added up to a form of anarchy in the sense discussed above of "no ruler." The ruler was not absent but spectral. While rarely if ever seen, spectral sovereigns were commonly felt in and had a significant effect on people's bodies and their everyday lives—often to a greater extent than their this-worldly counterparts.

KINGS AND QUEENS, UNSEEN

Throughout this book I have argued that landscapes in the Mutraw hills were teeming with unseen persons, many of whom were spoken of as the *k'sah*, or "owners," of particular parcels of land. In this final section, I take a step back to explore how these "owners" acted as kings and queens, unseen: spectral sovereigns. By focusing on one of the most revered and potent of all specters, the *kaw k'sah*, the overall owner of each *kaw*, I examine some of the ways Indigenous understandings and practices can unsettle hegemonic concepts of ownership and sovereignty.

Looping back to the furor surrounding the initial construction of the "car road," in much the same manner as when a person falls ill, the villagers' first reaction to the encroachment of the road onto village lands was to appeal to human forms of expertise, power, and authority. Their knee-jerk reaction was to appeal directly to the relevant KNU representatives to plead their case and to entreat them to adjust the path of the road, away from the seat of the *kaw k'sah*. The villagers only relented upon reaching the limits of the authority of their human institutions to affect the path of the road. Rather than giving up or leaving it to fate, as the highly charismatic elder Hpu Hkee phrased it, they "put it in the hands of the *kaw k'sah*," leaving it up to the spectral, and ultimate, owner of the *kaw* to decide. The *kaw k'sah* then intervened, affecting the body of the road's foreman, making him deadly ill. This interruption and intervention in turn effected political change. Its intervention led the road to be rerouted and spurred efforts to cool tensions between the villages by sharing a large pig: repairing relationships between humans and between the human and spectral realms.

The *kaw k'sah* acted as the sovereign of this particular *kaw*. Or, more precisely, the sovereignty of the *kaw k'sah* over Ta K'Thwee Duh Kaw continually interrupted and encompassed human forms of sovereignty. In contrast to the sporadic, and oftentimes incoherent, sovereignty of the KNU state, the *kaw k'sah* had powerfully felt effects on people's everyday lives. While talking to the elder and my close neighbor Hpu Gay about how the *kaw k'sah* has intervened in the road construction, he replied that "this is why we sometimes call her our *naw pa mu* [queen]." Delving deeper still, I learned that the *kaw k'sah* of Ta Bu Kyoh, the owner of the entirety of this particular *kaw*, was a spectral person known as Naw Ghoo Hsaw; oral histories spoke of her as an unmarried woman who always wore the white tunic of young maidens and spinsters, with a patch over one eye.

Each *kaw* was the dominion of a different *k'sah*, each with their own "queen" or "king" with their own biographies. In Thoo K'Bee Duh, the other side of

Y'wa Ma Htu Lay, toward the Salween River, for example, the *kaw k'sah* was a female specter who was said to be very tightfisted. Tales described how she rode on the backs of wild boar, which were her domestic animals, and swept into the villagers' rice fields at night to take their grain. As it transpired, certain animals such as the tigers and wild boar in each *kaw* were directly owned by the *kaw k'sah*, who kept them as her or his domestic animals. Hunters often commented that the wild boar they shot and wounded regularly fled toward the top of Ta Bu Kyoh, never to be found again. This led some to speculate that the *kaw k'sah* had a *ta hsah hee* (hospital) up there to heal her animals.

Similarly, as I touched upon earlier, in most cases in which a couple made a *k'ma*, a "mistake," by engaging in premarital sex, it was the *kaw k'sah* who intervened, forcing them to rectify the situation. In situations where justice is absent or deferred, as Radhika Govindrajan notes, it is often experienced as a prolonged haunting such that "the pursuit of justice is a spectral project" (2022, 39). Accordingly, justice in the Mutraw hills could often only be achieved through the intercession of the spectral rulers of the land who, like the revenant of a beloved cow Govindrajan discusses, were felt with a certainty "rooted in past embodied experiences of haunting" (46). For people in these highlands, the felt immediacy of regular interventions by the *kaw k'sah* was deeply rooted in their day-to-day experiences of negotiating possessed landscapes.

The *kaw k'sah* first announced a *k'ma* to the other villagers by sending a tiger—or perhaps by herself taking the form of a tiger—and making its presence known by roaring distantly or by appearing close to the village. Soon after the arrival of the tiger, if nothing was done to address this *k'ma*, it was said that the earth became *koh* (hot, having a high temperature). As Hpu Gay explained to me, this growing warmth was not the *kaw k'sah* becoming angry, but rather the earth becoming gripped by a fever, causing the humans and their livestock and crops to be susceptible to illness (both physical and mental) and even death if not treated quickly. The only way to break the fever and rectify the situation was for the couple to marry and make *ta hku*, meaning an offering or reparation but literally connoting a "cooling" (Hayami 1993; Paul 2018, 69), directly to the *kaw k'sah*. Justice was substantiated through the straightening out and repairing of relationships not only between people but also with the spectral realm (cf. Govindrajan 2022).

In Ta K'Thwee Duh the *kaw k'sah* only accepted a *ta hku* of a mature buffalo, killed and butchered at the top of the village so the blood "cooled" the earth as it trickled down the hill past all the houses. The buffalo meat was first shared with the *kaw k'sah*, then with all the villagers not directly related to the couple, to also "cool" relations between the human inhabitants, not unlike the pig shared by the villagers following the KNU agreeing to redirect the road around Ta Bu Kyoh. In most other *kaw*, the *kaw k'sah* demanded the offering of buffalo, but some preferred a large pig or even a brace of chickens. Different *kaw* had different *ta du ta htu*, or "taboos," as their spectral sovereigns had different tastes and appetites.

In cases where other significant *ta du ta htu* were breached, it was inevitably the local *kaw k'sah* who intervened and forced people to rectify the "mistake" or face terrible consequences. This intervention usually involved the *kaw k'sah* making people temporarily lose their minds, causing catastrophic crop failures, or sending its wild boars and tigers to plague the area. In one tale, of a man in a neighboring village who had repeatedly fornicated with a goat, the *kaw k'sah* became so enraged that the whole mountain, which was its domain, began to tilt. The mountain then threatened to collapse, wiping out the entire village. Only after the goat copulator (and possibly also the goat) was exiled far from the village did the mountain cease tilting; disaster was averted. To this day, this particular mountain top remains crooked, and the village was eventually relocated to a safer location. In a tale from another neighboring *kaw*, one man attempted to expand his own swidden patch by claiming the land of several of his fellow villagers. The *kaw k'sah* then unleashed floods and devastation in response to this man's refusal to respect strict *ta du ta htu* against taking land without permission and to his fellow villagers' inability to intervene and make sufficient reparations, mirroring Naw Ghaw and other villagers' dreams as the "car road" inched closer.

As such, while the Myanmar and KNU states remained distant in day-to-day life, in many real senses, the *kaw k'sah* acted as otherworldly rulers. They dictated laws and meted out punishment to those living under their dominion who did not abide by them, acting as unseen queens and kings. As opposed to the state, their sovereignty was acutely felt on people's skin and deeply marked local politics.

Unsettling Sovereignty

Tales of specters acting as sovereigns are by no means new. Spectral persons referred to as "owners" can be found all across Southeast Asia, from Central Myanmar in the north to the Maluku Islands of Indonesia in the far south (Århem 2016; Kammerer and Tannenbaum 2003; Pannell 2007). In F. K. Lehman's words, specters are regularly grasped as "the original and ultimate owners having dominion over the face of the land" (2003, 16). Likewise, *kaw k'sah* and other spectral persons among Pwakanyaw groups in both Myanmar and Thailand are consistently rendered as "lords" in English. Resisting the pernicious impulse to reduce such cosmologies, practices, and indeed the felt immediacies of spectral ownership and sovereignty to mere "cultural beliefs," in this book I move to take them seriously, as de facto alternative modes of politics that can unsettle seemingly neutral academic descriptors of governance such as sovereignty.

When studying Indigenous practices, researchers tend to look "for 'culture,' instead of sovereignty," as if their sovereignty had already been extinguished, as Audra Simpson (2014, 20) argues is the case in studies of the Indigenous peoples of North America. Likewise, academic work on sovereignty regularly foregrounds what it *looks* like, doggedly fixated on the nation-state and notions of control, obscuring the ways it is actually lived and enacted in everyday practice, or what sovereignty *feels* like (Masco and Thomas 2023). In part, this is predicated on hegemonic understandings of sovereignty as the preserve of the nation-state, and before that of human kings and queens (Agamben 1998; Hobbes 1651; see also Bishara 2017; Hansen and Stepputat 2006). The effects of such academic practices can be seen clearly in how communities located at the interstices between nation-states are consistently defined negatively, by what they are not: as "zones of no sovereignty" (Scott 2009, 60–61), or the sovereignty that emerges in these spaces as somehow "fractured" or "mutated" forms of state sovereignty (Hansen 2006; Ong, *Neoliberalism*, 2006)—as though sovereignty in its pure, undiluted, and unbroken sense without a prefix is the preserve of the nation-state alone (Ong, *Stalemate*, 2023, 8).

Taking Indigenous modes of sovereignty seriously allows for what Yarimar Bonilla (2017) describes as the "unsettling" of hegemonic notions of sovereignty, not so much sweeping them away as bringing them fundamentally into question and exploring their alternatives. The workings of the spectral sovereigns were "acts of productive disruption" that "call on people to reimagine an alternative present and future" (Govindrajan 2022, 39). Thus, I follow Simpson in arguing that these tales of unseen queens and kings suggest that "there is more than one political show in town" (2014, 10–11). Peering closer, we often find that sovereignty exists within sovereignty, like ownership, in nesting forms (Simpson 2014).

Up in the Mutraw hills, however, it was not so much that Indigenous sovereignty was nesting in the KNU state's patchy, intermittently felt sovereignty over this area. Rather, sovereignty was ultimately held "in the hands of the *kaw k'sah*," who regularly intervened in political life. Such non-state spectral rulers "have a grip over ordinary life" all across Asia (Mehtta 2022, 590). Megnaa Mehtta shows how, even among the seemingly most egalitarian societies one can imagine, everyday life is, in the final instance, ruled over and nesting in the hands of what, following Marshall Sahlins, she terms "cosmic polities." As Sahlins himself shrewdly remarks, "there are kingly beings in heaven even where there are no chiefs on earth" (2017, 91). Similarly, largely symmetrical and egalitarian relations between people living in Ta K'Thwee Duh—where few if any persons or institutions were vested with de facto power or authority—rested in and were dependent upon encompassing relations to the spectral sovereigns.

People's relations to the spectral realm were highly hierarchical, with the *kaw k'sah* often treated as queens and kings of the realm. This asymmetry points to the manner in which humans remain dependent upon the life-giving power of the spectral realm. As I show in the introduction to this book, Indigenous histories tell of how, when the great creator Y'wa departed from the human realm, he left the remaining and waning *ta thoo tha pgho*— that is, the potency of creation—in the hands of his emissaries, the *k'sah*. Humans were thus left to constantly negotiate with the spectral realm over the land they live on and live off, which they can never hope to own fully. Once again, these highlands might be best grasped as more-than-human contact zones, where different modes of sovereignty meet and grapple with one another.

Marcel Mauss pointed out already in the 1920s that "one of the first groups of beings with which men had to enter into contract, and who, by definition, were there to make a contract with them, were above all the spirits of the dead and of the gods. Indeed, it is they who are the true owners of the things and possessions of this world" ([1925] 2002, 20). I return to these points in later chapters, where I argue that spectral sovereignty gestures toward an alternative mode of politics, or "alter-politics" (Hage 2015), and unsettles many established notions of sovereignty and politics at large. In part 2 of this book, I shift focus back across the border to Thailand to explore how burgeoning ensembles of farmers and activists, such as those behind the Salween Peace Park, were starting to translate and rescale these Indigenous modes of ownership and sovereignty to push back against dispossession and to continue the struggle for greater autonomy in southeast Myanmar.

PART II

Dispossession/Repossession

FOUR

Countermovements

Dispossession, Repossession, and Translation

In November 2016, I caught up with a general from the hawkish wing of the Karen National Union in Chiang Mai, Thailand's second city. During our conversation he put it to me that, "since the KNU signed the NCA [National Ceasefire Agreement] in 2015, our leaders are in the Burmese's pocket." This statement was very much of a piece with those made by other so-called hard-liners. Along the border and in the diaspora, the political elite I met regularly peppered their speeches with accusations of corruption leveled at the current KNU leadership and claims the ceasefire was exacerbating dispossession in southeast Myanmar.¹ Hard-liners like the general had long opposed any rapprochement with the Tatmadaw, speaking of ceasefire as tantamount to surrender. Beyond these jingoistic and saber-rattling discourses, however, I found that this skepticism toward the ceasefire echoed all the way up into the Mutraw hills, resonating in villages such as Ta K'Thwee Duh, among people far removed from these hard-liners. This became particularly evident when speaking to the headmaster in Ta K'Thwee Duh.

Possessed by a sense of great purpose, the headmaster of the local primary school came through the door to my little house, at the bottom of the village, as I sat catching up on gossip with Naw Paw, my field assistant, and Naw Lee Paw (Hpu Hkee's oldest daughter). He sat silently on the floor beside us in his navy blue football jersey from the refugee camps. His usual knowing smile, stained almost jet black by his interminable chewing of betel nut and lime, and the familiar glint in his eye signaling he had a humorous story to share were replaced with grave seriousness. Upon noticing this change of countenance, our conversation quickly ground to a halt. We all turned to face him, waiting to hear what he had to say. After a short silence, he explained, speaking slowly in a voice muffled by the copious amount of betel nut he had stuffed in his mouth, that he had just returned from a meeting for all residents of the Pa Heh village tract, which encompassed Ta K'Thwee Duh. At this meeting, the local Karen National Liberation Army commanders had forbidden the villagers from taking me along to *hpeh hku*—the laborious clearing of trees in a *pgha*, or "mature/old," fallow field with machetes—nor were they to take me anywhere with a steep incline. Apparently, these military leaders feared that I might get injured or even die should I take part in these activities and ominously warned the villagers of dire consequences should this happen.[2] Rather than spelling out what the consequences might be, the leaders quickly changed the topic to politics.

The headmaster continued that the local KNLA explained how, "although the *ta du ta yah koh* [literally, hot conflict] may be over, for the time being," they now face a new and growing threat: the threat of *ta du ta yah hku* (cool/peaceful conflict), currently taking place under the guise of the ceasefire. They went on to detail how the Tatmadaw had continued its counterinsurgency against the villagers in these highlands, only now it was visited upon them by other means. The *koh* (hot) means of guns, mortars, and attack helicopters was slowly being replaced by *hku* (cool/er) means of temples and pagodas—that is to say, by way of propagating religion but also, as I shall illustrate, by building mines and hydroelectric dams. According to these KNLA commanders, this new "cooler" counterinsurgency unfolded in a series of steps: first they (it was unclear who "they" were here) assisted the local Buddhist population in constructing a local pagoda or temple; when it was completed, these Buddhist structures started drawing in Burman Buddhist monks and laypeople from far and wide to make pilgrimages and donations; with time, these areas slowly became inundated with non-Pwakanyaw people and capital, including, increasingly, Tatmadaw soldiers; and finally, the Tatmadaw swept in to secure these religious spots and the (Burman) people who had moved there, assuming control of the surrounding area and dispossessing the original (Pwakanyaw) inhabitants in the process.

When the headmaster finished this tale, I asked him whether he, and his fellow villagers, also considered such insidious new forms of warfare to be a serious concern, or whether this was their leaders overreacting—not unlike their excessive fears for my safety. Before answering, he took a long drag of one of the green Burmese cheroots I had placed between us, letting the silence swell around him. "These worries that the building of Buddhist structures may bring back the Myanmar Army," he told me between puffs, "are something most people in this area share, despite us having many Buddhist neighbors and kin."

In this chapter, I take a step back to trace continued patterns of militarization and dispossession during the ceasefire period (2012–21). I go on to explore burgeoning social movements that experimented with translating Indigenous modes of possession into their ongoing struggles to reterritorialize and repossess landscapes in southeast Myanmar, creating small interstitial spaces of autonomy. These highlands were pockmarked with Tatmadaw army bases and lacerated by military roads. Despite the faltering ceasefire agreements and attempts to build a lasting peace, the Mutraw hills (and indeed many other areas of the Karen State) remained deeply militarized. Bringing Indigenous analyses of cool/peaceful forms of counterinsurgency together with academic work on the ways states continue territorializing land during peacetime, I describe how processes and technologies of dispossession, including recent land laws, might be grasped more widely as a form of ceasefire territorialization. I then go on to shine a light on budding experiments by ensembles of Indigenous and ecological activists, students, and Indigenous peoples, who worked tirelessly to push back against this ceasefire territorialization. I show how these ensembles played with translating Indigenous land possession practices and cosmologies to turn state-making processes of mapping and legibility on their head: to reterritorialize and repossess landscapes, in budding countermovements.

THE "COOL" COUNTERINSURGENCY: PROSPECTING, PAGODAS, AND BULLDOZERS

The juxtaposition of hot and cold, drawn on when evoking the notion of a new *ta du ta yah hku* (cool/peaceful conflict), aligned with common practices found among Pwakanyaw communities across Myanmar and Thailand (Hayami 1993; Paul 2018, 69–70). In chapter 3, I demonstrate how people often opposed a sense of *hku* (coolness)—understood as intercommunal peace and harmony—to a sense of *koh* (hotness), of conflict and moral misconduct. Human moral misconduct and conflict often led the *kaw k'sah*, the owner of the *kaw*, to become vexed and to punish not only those responsible but also members of their household, their livestock, and/or their crops, by making them sick and feverish and thus "hot." The earth itself became overheated and fever-like, and, if not cooled down again, death and/or crop failure could occur. To rectify this situation, the persons or parties responsible had to, as soon as possible, *lu ta* (feed/propitiate) the *kaw k'sah* in order to make amends and to cool down the situation again, usually with the blood of a chicken or a buffalo. Accordingly, the chicken or buffalo offered to the *kaw k'sah* was referred to as *ta hku* (literally, coolness/that which is cool).

This bears out in the literal translation of the Pwakanyaw word for peace, *ta mu ta hku*, as "happiness and coolness" and trouble and strife as *ta hkoh ta ghaw*, or "hotness and redness" (see also Paul 2018, 69–70). These counterposed notions of hot vs. cold and of peace vs. conflict were thus deeply entangled with Indigenous practices and cosmologies of possessed landscapes and with the sovereignty of spectral owners in the Mutraw highlands.

Military leaders in this area were latching on to these practices/cosmologies to express a situation in which conflict and dispossession persisted in the absence of the usual *koh* (heat) of armed conflict and moral discord. The notion of *ta du ta yah hku* could be rendered, rather oxymoronically, as "cool/peaceful conflict." To exemplify the coherence between what these KNLA commanders were saying and people's local understandings and experiences, the headmaster told us a story (as was his penchant).

During the period prior to the ceasefire, around 2006 to 2007, the headmaster began, there was a market-hamlet-cum-KNLA-base in the neighboring *kaw* called Thee Mu Hta that lay along the Salween. "The [predominantly] Buddhist residents of this hamlet," he went on, "decided that, since there was no place nearby to worship, they should build their own small pagoda here." They then sought out the help of a highly revered local Pwakanyaw monk from Myaing Gyi Ngu (in Burmese; Khaw Hta in Pwakanyaw). The monk willingly assisted, declaring that "he hoped the building of a pagoda here would help bring peace to warring factions of the KNU" that, as the headmaster reminded us, had split in 1994. The pagoda was quickly erected in Thee Mu Hta, to the great rejoicing of the villagers. This joy quickly turned to despair, however, as a steady influx of Burman visitors, including more and more soldiers, began to arrive on the pretext of visiting to pay respects at the pagoda then stayed on. "As the population of Burmans from Central Myanmar and Tatmadaw soldiers steadily grew," the headmaster continued, "a conflict between the Tatmadaw and KNLA over control of this territory broke out, forcing many villagers to flee." The KNLA were eventually defeated and the hamlet transformed into a white zone/peace area: a large Tatmadaw base in the area, located strategically along the Salween and a bustling market town, he concluded.

I heard numerous variations on this story, the narrators regularly evoking it and similar tales as a way to explain their unease toward plans, in both Ta K'Thwee Duh Kaw and in other villages along the Mutraw hills, to construct pagodas. The story was drawn on to emphasize that people's trepidations were not rooted in their ideological opposition to Buddhism itself. Rather, they were simply worried that the raising of such Buddhist monuments might set off a similar chain of events to those in Thee Mu Hta, potentially leading to their dispossession and their homes transformed into a staging post for further Tatmadaw attacks and militarization. Significantly, the fate of this riverside hamlet rehearsed the events leading up to the bitter factional split between the KNU and the Democratic Karen Buddhist Army (DKBA). In 1994, the very same monk, U Thuzana, built a "Peace Pagoda" beside the KNU stronghold Manerplaw, then called all Buddhist soldiers disaffected with the KNU to join him, forming the DKBA. Soon after, the DKBA joined forces with the Tatmadaw and overran Manerplaw, causing thousands of people to flee (South 2008, 57–60).

The story of Thee Mu Hta (and, by association, Manerplaw) acted as a kind of cautionary tale, warning people of the dangers of this new mode of counterinsurgency that was intensifying as the armed conflict slowly cooled. The hard-line KNLA general introduced at the start of this chapter described the situation quite aptly as one of a "peace trap." During our meeting in one of the glistening shopping centers just outside Chiang Mai's old city, he stated that the ceasefire had hamstrung the revolution since their "leaders have made many concessions and have got nothing back. They keep giving and waiting for a return. [Meanwhile], they [the Tatmadaw] have used the peace to gain ground and reinforce their outposts, and the ordinary people have not received any benefits."

Such tales of this "peaceful" iteration of counterinsurgency usually began not with an armed provocation but an offer, a promise, of something that people genuinely desired—such as a place of worship or of "development." These subtle kinds of overtures rarely evoked the villagers' suspicions or the ire of the spectral owners. Both day-to-day decision-making and spectral sovereignty was bypassed. Yet, soon after accepting the offer, people realized that these seemingly earnest gestures, such as technical and physical assistance to build a pagoda, were in fact a kind of bait to lure them in. As soon as they took the bait, the trap was sprung, and before they knew it, the local inhabitants' lands and livelihoods had been seized by the Tatmadaw. By this point it was too late for either humans or specters to intervene to rectify the situation.

These stories served as a warning of an insidious new iteration of the ongoing counterinsurgency. People's growing fears of being dispossessed, however, went beyond fears that the expansion of Burman-dominated Buddhist spheres might perpetuate the intensification of Tatmadaw territorialization, as the KNLA leaders and villagers' narratives might suggest. I often heard people airing their concerns pertaining to the expansion of not only state/military religious spheres but also economic ones—of both the KNU and Myanmar states.

The gravity of these fears of dispossession by economic encroachments became perhaps most apparent when the new vice-head of the village tract, Hpu Wah, paid a visit to Ta K'Thwee Duh. He arrived in the middle of the day, ostensibly with the remit to discuss issues of conscription with some of the villagers. But, as the day progressed, he appeared far more preoccupied with finding out which household provided the best alcohol than which household should next provide a son to serve in the army. He worked his way, house to house, from the top of the village and downward such that, by the time he got to my house at the bottom of the hill, he was rather inebriated. He came stumbling through my door a little after twilight. While sitting slumped against the wall, he promptly produced a crumpled-up letter out of his jacket pocket that he told me was one of the reasons for his visit. This was a letter from his office informing villagers in this area of the imminent arrival of Chinese prospectors, who planned to survey neighboring Yu Wah Duh Kaw. On account of me being a white outsider, he assumed that I must have something to do with these prospectors and wanted to assure me personally that they would make sure everything went smoothly and would assist "us" as much as they could. In the following days, as word spread of the content of this crumpled piece of paper, I heard my neighbors begin to fret about what would happen should these investors find "valuable things,"[3] such as gold, in the ground and should they expand their survey to Ta K'Thwee Duh Kaw.

Much like the cautionary tale of the fall of Thee Mu Hta, the looming arrival of Chinese prospectors retraced the path of older histories of violent resource frontiers. As the ceasefire set in up in these highlands, the revenant of resource frontiers returned once more—where "entrepreneurs and armies" work in concord to "disengage nature from local ecologies and livelihoods, 'freeing up' natural resources" (Tsing 2005, 27–28) in the name of territorial gains and capital. These stories of "peaceful" conflict urge us to examine closer how, as threats of dispossession returned to these highlands, they did not always assume the same spectacular form.

Classically, processes of dispossession are portrayed in terms of *primitive accumulation*—where people are violently separated from their means of subsistence (their land) such that wealth and power is accumulated in the hands of a few landlords and capitalists—which Marx identifies as capitalism's origin story. More recently, the term *accumulation by dispossession* has been used to underline how processes of dispossession are not primitive, part of dark and violent pasts, but rather an integral everyday aspect of capitalism and imperialism, where the state often plays a critical role (D. Harvey 2003, 2004). Both these terms, however, have become exceedingly "busy" and "elastic" in their definitions, their applications, and the claims they make (Bernstein 2014, 1036n6). To rein in such sprawling terms and grasp the specific insidious and often extra-economic manner in which people in the Mutraw hills were steadily being dispossessed under a ceasefire, I zero in on how the liberal peace propagated by the peace process was turning predatory.

NEGATIVE PEACE/PREDATORY PEACE

One way to begin tracing intensifying entanglements between the Mutraw hills, the Myanmar state military, and commercial ventures is to follow how transformations in national politics during various periods of liberalization played into highlands politics.

As the Cold War drew to a close in the late 1980s and the early 1990s, like many formerly (nominally at least) socialist states, Myanmar began to pivot back toward Europe and America. In ever more desperate attempts to woo foreign investors and their capital, the increasingly cash-strapped ruling military junta, the State Law and Order Reconciliation Council (SLORC), began a wave of liberalization. Monique Skidmore (2004, 109–11) points to the spectacle, and spectacular failure, of the "Visit Myanmar Year" in 1996 as one example of SLORC's attempts to attract foreign capital. Consequently, in November the following year, SLORC dropped their rather Orwellian-sounding name in favor of the far catchier State Peace and Development Council and employed a Washington-based PR firm to lobby on their behalf (Lintner 2015, 248).

These overtures to investors, along with gradual liberalizing processes such as large-scale de-nationalizing and the selling of vast swaths of land to multinational corporations, had sweeping effects across Central Myanmar (see especially Rhoads and Wittekind 2018). Chronic armed conflict, however, largely insulated highland areas such as those in Mutraw from many of these sweeping transformations. A similar state of affairs could be seen in the demilitarized zone (DMZ) between the two Koreas, where a vast military buildup militated against potentially destructive developments, protecting the vibrant biodiversity there (Kim 2022). These liberalizing processes had only begun encroaching into the highlands of southeast Myanmar, and having felt effects on day-to-day life, as the war waned.

Liberalization gradually gained ground as decades of revolution and counterinsurgency receded in the wake of the ceasefire and resulting peace process and as relations between powerful local actors such as the KNU and the Myanmar government/Tatmadaw were progressively normalized. It is important to note that the cooling of conflict did lead to many significant betterments in the lives and livelihoods of people residing in these former war zones, allowing them to return to the agricultural rhythms of their ancestral lands (South 2018, 57). Nevertheless, these improvements were often double-edged.

The de-escalation of armed conflict in Myanmar was not accompanied by a significant revaluation of underlying grievances. Sheila Htoo illustrates this vividly by pointing out that there were over sixty clashes between the KNU and the Tatmadaw in 2018 alone, and from 2017 to 2018 the community-based organization Karen Human Rights Group (KHRG) received ninety-one cases of land confiscation in southeast Myanmar (Htoo, n.d., 118–19). As a result, I found that the residents of the Mutraw hills continued to worry that the Tatmadaw could return at any moment (borne out only four years later, in the events following the 2021 coup).

In response to these continued fears, most of the people I met had a chest filled with their most valuable possessions ensconced somewhere in their homes. For my neighbor Hpu Gay, it was filled with all his finest factory-made clothes and his silk trousers sewn from British parachutes. Naw Lee Paw's chest was filled with all the clothes she had diligently woven in preparation for the time that she would marry, even though she was yet to find a suitor. People kept these chests in their homes, ready to take them at a moment's notice when, not if, they were forced to flee again. Moreover, as I learned from villagers who regularly migrated to other parts of Myanmar to work, both sides of the conflict continued to reinforce their military positions. Each time the path of these mostly young male migrants took them past a Tatmadaw camp, they took note of how it looked ever more permanent, new concrete reinforcement cropping up each time.

Following protests in May 2017 by internally displaced people (IDPs) demanding the closure of seventeen of the more controversial Tatmadaw bases in the Mutraw District, a young Karen Environmental and Social Action Network activist snapped a photo while passing one of these bases on the way to Ta K'Thwee Duh. As this photo attested, the soldiers had scrawled the words "we will fight to the death before this base falls" in Burmese on a sign facing the Salween for all passing on boats to read, sending a clear message that they had no intention of demobilizing any time soon.[4]

One consequence of chronic militarization along the Salween was that the situation came closer to that of a ceasefire in its most literal sense. While armed skirmishes between the two sides still occurred, the conflict had largely ceased for the time being, becoming temporarily crystallized into a stalemate: a freeze-frame picture of an ongoing war. Yet, as Andrew Ong shows was the case farther north in the Wa State of Myanmar, while politics during a stalemate appear stalled, they remain ridden by "a fitful process of maneuvers and counterpostures" (2023, xi). The 2012 bilateral ceasefire accords and their ratification into the National Ceasefire Agreement (NCA) in 2015 emerged neither out of hard-won political demands being granted nor by significant changes in the underlying causes of the conflict. Rather, the ceasefire came about more out of a sense of "war fatigue" and the "departure from violence" (Löfving 2007, 51–52; see also Borneman 2002). Since, as Henrik Vigh phrases it, "wars do not start with the first shot or end with the last" (2008, 5), peace must surely amount to something more than the mere absence of armed violence.

In her work on the (former) war zones of southeast Myanmar, Htoo describes the situation following the signing of the peace accords in 2012 as aligned with the "liberal notion of negative peace, intended for capital accumulation and [the] free market" (n.d., 107). While negative peace is simply the "absence of organized, collective violence," Htoo follows Johan Galtung in opposing it to the concept of "positive peace" as "a synonym for all other good things in the world community, particularly cooperation and integration between human groups" (Galtung 1967, 12).

In the negative/liberal conception of peace, violence is posited to be the disorder ailing a society at war, rather than a symptom of deeper systemic issues. Accordingly, the cure for armed conflict, in all places and at all times, is the administering of intensive democratization and marketization processes (Paris 2004, 41). This conception of peace, embraced and aggressively championed by such global giants as the United Nations and the World Bank (Hetherington 2011; Mac Ginty 2008, 144; Richmond and Mac Ginty 2015, 178), places processes of political and economic liberalization at the very heart of all peacebuilding efforts. The rationale underlying this theory, in simplified terms, is that market (i.e., capitalist) democracies rarely go to war against one another; thus, more liberalization must lead directly to less war (Paris 2004, 42). In practice, however, as seen around the world, the push for economic liberalization and neoliberal reforms often lead the charge toward peace, especially for the World Bank and the International Monetary Fund (Hetherington 2011; Klein 2008; Springer 2013).

In this respect, the NCA that the KNU signed in 2015, and the subsequent sessions of the 21st Century Panglong peace conference (2016–20) that followed in its wake, closely shadowed a global blueprint that banks upon economic development as the primary engine of conflict resolution.[5] Consequently, the deep-seated causes of armed conflict were left relatively unaddressed, and a more insidious form of violence, grasped locally as *ta du ta yah hku* (cool/peaceful conflict), continued unchecked. Moreover, as Eleana Kim notes, the intensification of investments and extractivist enterprises that the liberal peace doctrine demands regularly entail "sacrificing" precious ecosystems in the name of economic development (2022, 5).

One incident that laid bare the logic of the negative/liberal peace thesis was an event held at the beginning of 2019 in the still war-torn west of Myanmar, in the wake of the Rohingya crisis. This event ran with the tagline "Rakhine is open for business to the world," and then–State Councillor Aung San Suu Kyi, who presided over the proceedings, stated, "we have to address economic issues in Rakhine, that we may achieve the progress and development needed to sustain stability and prosperity" (Lwin 2019). As this case illustrates, the liberal/negative peace thesis doggedly insists that the best way to settle armed conflict is by liberalizing the economy and encouraging foreign investors to pour capital into the (formerly) war-torn fringes of the Myanmar nation-state. This approach ignores the underlying causes of conflict and that such investments often serve to further inflame them. It was in this context that the freeze-frame picture of the ceasefire along the Salween River emerged.

Notions of a new "cool/peaceful" phase of counterinsurgency, as well as similar formulations from other "post-conflict" societies around the world (Büscher 2013; Löfving 2007; Lund 2018; Vigh 2006), suggest that the liberal peace thesis fails to accurately capture lived realities on the ground. In southeast Myanmar local military leaders and subsistence-farming villagers alike talked incessantly about the ceasefire as, in many respects, a continuation of the state-sponsored counterinsurgency of the "four cuts" (Smith 1999, 258–59). As the *koh* (heat) of armed struggle dissipated, the counterinsurgency had congealed into a new and more insidious form. Following the signing of the bilateral ceasefire in 2012, people were decreasingly dispossessed by force of arms. They now feared that the land they lived on and lived off would be expropriated by far more subtle means, through the creeping expansion of state-dominated religious and economic spheres—through "peace traps," preceded by promises of places of worship and of prosperity.

The building of pagodas and large investment projects, such as plans for the construction of the Hatgyi hydroelectric dam farther downstream, testified to these new creeping forms of counterinsurgency—and the price environments were expected to pay in order to achieve peace. The Hatgyi hydropower project, funded by Sinohydro (China) and EGATi (Thailand), proposed to build a 1,200-megawatt plant with a 33-meter-high dam (Bright 2019, 79; C. Middleton et al. 2019, 33). Located just downstream of the Salween Peace Park, it threatened to inundate vast swaths of land. What is more, while it promised local "development," the dam offered no discernible benefits for the people living in the area around it, as the overwhelming majority of the electricity produced would be transferred directly to Thailand and China (C. Middleton et al. 2019, 36). A memorandum of understanding to begin work was signed between the Thai and Myanmar governments in 1996, but progress was continually stymied by armed clashes in the immediate vicinity of the dam (Bright 2019, 79). Shortly after the ceasefire, as armed hostilities tapered off, the Myanmar government continually attempted to move this project forward, leading to renewed rounds of armed skirmishes in 2016 (Bright 2019, 79–80; Karen Rivers Watch 2016).

I find the notion of "predatory peace," coined by political ecologist Christian Lund (2018), instructive in understanding these new insidious forms of dispossession in (post)conflict settings. Taking his point of departure in Aceh in Indonesia, Lund shows how the end of armed conflict in Aceh was experienced as a rupture that created "an open moment where both opportunity and risks multiply" (2018, 434). However, this rupture also ushered in a new frontier, leading state actors to give concessions to contractors for huge swaths of land, while smallholders' rights were undermined and silenced as they were slowly dispossessed. This was an extreme case of how "old stories" continued on into the present, where new patterns of dispossession rehearsed those from colonial times, peace slowly becoming predatory.

However, whereas smallholders in Aceh were initially more sanguine about the possibilities opened to them following the peace process—that they may finally be able to assert their customary rights over the land—people along the Salween, after so many years of chronic conflict, were considerably more pragmatic, if not out-and-out pessimistic. While they were able to move around more freely, their hopes that the ceasefire might finally allow them to stabilize their livelihoods and maybe even improve on them were constantly tempered by anxieties that the ceasefire would compound the risks of dispossession they already faced. They feared that the ceasefire could at any moment turn out to be a trap, ready to spring.

While tales of Thee Mu Hta were often evoked in the Mutraw hills to explain trepidations about the ceasefire, for the KNLA commanders at least, stories from other parts of Myanmar helped further undergird their pessimism. For both local KNLA officers and many activists, the hard-won lessons of their former allies the Kachin Independence Army (KIA), based on the Chinese borderlands in northern Myanmar, were not easily forgotten. In 2011, the KNU together with KIA founded the United Nationalities Federal Council (UNFC). For a time, the UNFC was the most powerful alliance of non-state armed organizations in Myanmar, formed as a platform to collectively bargain with the Tatmadaw. This alliance was founded largely in response to the KIA's faltering attempts to strike out alone and sign a separate bilateral ceasefire with Tatmadaw. The fragile peace this ceasefire engendered steadily became more predatory over the years.

As the ink was still drying on the ceasefire accords the KIA signed in 1994, the Tatmadaw quickly began allocating land concessions to local elites and Chinese and international conglomerates and redirecting timber trade in these former war zones. This served to both weaken the KIA's sovereignty and create legible, militarized, state territory (Woods 2011, 747; issues of legibility are discussed in the next section). Rather than threatening state sovereignty, granting land concessions to non-state actors actually augmented Myanmar military state-building efforts. Capturing and controlling flows of capital into these resource frontiers had the effect of generating effective Myanmar state authority, sovereignty, and territory in practice (Woods 2011, 749) and, simultaneously, weakening both KIA and smallholders' customary claims to these lands (754). As Thomas Sikor and Christian Lund (2010, 1–3) demonstrate, processes of recognizing claims as property, in a rather circular manner, also work to imbue institutions and states with the recognition of their authority to do so—thereby bolstering state building.

To describe these processes, Kevin Woods (2011) coined the term *ceasefire capitalism*. Through ceasefire capitalism the Tatmadaw were able to achieve what had eluded them throughout the decades of armed counterinsurgency: taking effective control of this contested territory. Woods proceeds to name the actual workings of this collaboration between the Tatmadaw and investors to seize control of contested land "military territorialization" (748–49), which, he persuasively argues, ushered in a new phase of state-sponsored counterinsurgency. Taken together, Indigenous analyses and academic treatments of the ceasefire predicament illuminate the new face of the ongoing state counterinsurgency in Myanmar and beyond and the resulting territorialization and dispossession it dragged in its wake. These new forms and threats of dispossession were, in turn, deeply entangled with the current global rush for viable land, increasingly conducted via legal technologies such as Myanmar state-level land laws.

LAND RUSHES, LAND LAWS, AND CEASEFIRE TERRITORIALIZATION

Stories of creeping dispossession by alliances of state and private actors offer a window on wider political processes. Upland swidden cultivators' livelihood struggles and their current precarious predicaments are deeply entangled with the global food crisis, driven by increased demands for staples, the reorientation of consumption patterns, and the exploding energy demands of more affluent nations. All these factors have led to the interminable hunt for new zones of valorization in ever-evolving land frontiers, enacting colossal processes of enclosures and land grabs, collectively known as the *global land rush* (Makki 2014, 79–80; see also Hong 2017; Li 2014b; Springer 2013).

In Ta K'Thwee Duh and the surrounding area, soldiers and farmers alike were acutely aware that, as the heat of armed conflict slowly dissipated, a growing form of ceasefire capitalism akin to what happened in the Myanmar-Chinese borderlands threatened to ratchet open these highlands to global capital, generating new (violent) frontiers and echoing dark histories of (colonial) extraction. Local people's apprehensions toward the current political situation could perhaps be best summed up by the slogan of the Tarkapaw Youth Group (2015), in response to the building of the Ban Chaung coal mine farther south in the Tanintharyi Region: "We used to fear bullets, now we fear bulldozers."[6]

One way in which the global land rush portended seismic effects on these highlands was through the enacting of the Vacant, Fallow and Virgin Land Management Law, often shortened to VFV Law, first drafted in 2012 (perhaps not coincidentally, the same year the initial bilateral ceasefires were signed). In a report released on March 12, 2019, the day after the slightly amended law came into full force, the KHRG (2019) christened this moment "Day One." The instant the VFV Law entered the legal fold, becoming part of Myanmar state policy, all land unregistered in state ledgers, estimated to be between 45 and 50 million acres, became "vacant, fallow, or virgin." The lion's share, 82 percent, of this unregistered land resided in "ethnic areas" (i.e., areas under the sway of so-called non-state armed groups such as the KNU and KIA), large swaths of which were held in "customary tenure" in Myanmar's highland areas, such as the patchworks of *kaw* lands in the Mutraw hills. Overnight, these vast expanses of land were reclassified as vacant, fallow (i.e., underutilized, see below), or virgin and thus ripe for government reallocation to more "productive" uses such as monocultures for the mass production of food, mineral extraction, and hydroelectric dams for the production of commodities and energy in faraway places.

Laws such as the VFV Law were a continuation of a long history of targeting patches of land involved in swidden cultivation (Ferguson, "Scramble," 2014; Forsyth and Walker 2008; Springate-Baginski 2018). This form of agriculture/agroforestry is regularly cast as inefficient, due to the long fallowing periods it allows for the soil to regenerate. In the eyes of the state, upland swidden cultivation leaves a great deal of potential agricultural land underutilized. Somewhat paradoxically, swidden cultivation is simultaneously seen as degrading the environment and a major cause of deforestation, due to the periodic clearing and burning of small patches of secondary forest it involves (Forsyth and Walker 2008; Springate-Baginski 2018).

The VFV Law and associated laws such as the Farmland Law (also passed to coincide with the ceasefire in 2012) illustrated one particular modality of ceasefire capitalism. Through these laws, Myanmar state/military counterinsurgency was increasingly wedded to the current global hunt for new zones of valorization in ever-new land frontiers. The military and private sector were joining hands to "secure" and territorialize contested lands through legislative technologies such as land laws (Ferguson, "Scramble," 2014). In concert with mapping (discussed in more detail below), land laws are part of states' wider attempts to bring "unorganized" territory—that is to say, land beyond the horizon of their sovereignty—into the legal/legislative fold by making it, as James C. Scott (1998) so productively puts it, "legible."

As legal technologies, the VFV Law and associated land laws simplified and translated intricate, indeterminate, and playful Indigenous modes of possessing the landscapes, tied to swidden cultivation, turning them into a uniform/standardized form of landholding that was legible—that is, into land that could be registered in Myanmar state ledgers (Scott 1998, 2). Once land was made legible, it could be distributed or sold to state and private actors for investment and development. The case in northern Myanmar—where the state generated de facto authority, sovereignty, and territoriality by ceding land to private actors and erasing local claims (Woods 2011, 749; see also Sikor and Lund 2010, 1–3)—illustrated these processes in practice. Land laws attempted to achieve this same goal by similarly flattening or reifying Indigenous modes of ownership, such as the ephemeral and nesting modes of ownership I discuss in chapter 2, where the ownership of parcels of land constantly cycled between human and spectral hands. These legal technologies rendered landscapes legible by drawing on a property regime where each patch of land became a discrete and uniform unit "owned by a legal individual who possesses wide powers of use, inheritance, or sale and whose ownership is represented by uniform deed of title enforced through the judiciary and police institutions of the state" (Scott 1998, 36).[7]

Through land laws, possessed landscapes were simplified and transformed into a uniform grid of landholdings that could be readily represented on cadastral maps, rendering them "readable" and "assessable" by both the Myanmar state and commercial actors. Yet, as I demonstrate in chapter 2, only a tiny fraction of villagers in the Mutraw hills held land title deeds. What is more, the few paddy field land titles that people did hold were awarded by the KNU and thus unlikely to be recognized by the Myanmar state. Alongside legal technologies, then, maps are a "technology of territoriality," as Thongchai Winichakul so powerfully argues (1994, 16). Following the colonization of Southeast Asia, overlapping "galactic polities" (Tambiah 1976) were gradually displaced by modern Westphalian notions of bounded nation-states, each with its own delineated "geo-body" (Winichakul 1994). Maps became the prime technology to "affect, influence or control people, phenomena, and relationships by delimiting and asserting control over geographical area" (16). As such, mapping has long been wedded to military force.

The application of the VFV Law on the ground in the Mutraw hills would have essentially led most, if not all, the land there to be classified as vacant, fallow, or virgin, ripe for redistribution and investment. Moreover, the gridding and mapping implied in the VFV Law threatened to greatly exacerbate the commodification of land, both by state/private actors and "from below" by the villagers themselves (cf. Li 2014a), which we saw stirrings of in the growing trend toward wet rice cultivation. Thus, these land laws and efforts to map the Mutraw hills foreshadowed catastrophic effects for the subsistence farmers residing there, and indeed all across Myanmar, of mass displacements and political/economical upheavals in the near future.

People's continued fears of dispossession were not, however, isolated to their trepidation about new land laws and other forms of intensified state/private partnerships in the shape of ceasefire capitalism. The fall of the riverside hamlet of Thee Mu Hta took the form not of predatory business ventures but of religious encroachments initially welcomed by the inhabitants. For many of the people residing in the adjacent areas, these events exemplified a growing new phase of counterinsurgency and dispossession. And yet these events came before and appeared to presage the coming new threats inherent in ceasefire times.

Ceasefire Territorialization

After the Tatmadaw wrested control of Thee Mu Hta from the KNU, the surrounding area was rescheduled as a so-called peace area. Shortly thereafter, it became a bustling economic hub for cross-border trade, attracting people from all across Myanmar and Thailand—that is, until the KNU surrounded it with landmines and forbade villagers from visiting. While we cannot rule out that the Tatmadaw planned to later grant land concessions in and around this riverside hamlet to external investors to bolster and extend their territorial control, as was the case in Kachin State, it is clear that ceasefire capitalism was but one part of the story. Predatory business ventures partnering with Myanmar state/military actors followed, and depended upon, prior religious and military encroachments. To grasp the wider story of the ongoing counterinsurgency, I delved into older attempts by the Myanmar state at gridding and mapping these highlands to make them legible.

As I touch on in the introduction, long before land laws such as the VFV Law were conceived, one of the Tatmadaw's first attempts at making these highlands legible was through the "four cuts" counterinsurgency program. In this program, landscapes along the lower Salween were mapped, chessboard-like, into three zones: black zones, obscured from the Myanmar state by being fully under the sway of armed "insurgent" groups such as the KNU; brown zones, where territorial control was still disputed; and white zones, which were classified as "free" or "peaceful" on account of being fully under the control of, and transparent to, the Tatmadaw (Smith 1999, 259). This map was then imposed onto the landscape itself. Areas controlled by revolutionary groups were cordoned off into a grid of black zones, each typically 40–50 square miles across; as Winichakul reminds us, "making wars means making maps" (1994, 14). With these areas mapped and gridded, the "four cuts" strategy aimed to turn all zones designated black into white ones. This was achieved by displacing and resettling the rural population residing in black zones into *byu hla jaywa*, or "strategic hamlets" that were under Tatmadaw control, thereby cutting them off from armed revolutionary groups.

As one popular Burmese proverb puts it, the Tatmadaw was trying "to drain the sea, in order to kill the fish" (South and Katsabanis 2007, 57). By severing the links between armed revolutionary groups and their civilian base, the counterinsurgency aimed to stem the flow of food, funds, intelligence, and recruits from the rural population to these uprisings, effectively slowly starving them into submission. With the insurgencies effectively neutralized, the Tatmadaw could then gradually expand its territorial control over the entire map. All pockets of revolution, such as the highlands along the Salween, were slowly turned into white zones/peace areas that were transparent—that is to say, readable and assessable—to the Myanmar state.

Although in practice this counterinsurgency program was almost exclusively carried out through military might—by the violent displacement of civilians, extensive use of landmines, forced labor, and scorched earth tactics (Ferguson, "Scramble," 2014; KHRG 2000; Smith 1999; South and Katsabanis 2007)—its scope far exceeded this. As Martin Smith notes in passing, the "four cuts" strategy was, in theory, the Tatmadaw's own version of a people's war, their attempt to win the war through the hearts and minds of rural villagers (1999, 259, 495n38). In this light, the tale of Thee Mu Hta offers a glimpse of how, long before the ceasefires, so-called hot and cool measures regularly went hand in hand. What is more, the Tatmadaw's war to win rural villagers' hearts and minds was waged with promises both of economic/capitalist development and of building religious structures. These efforts often preceded and laid the groundwork for later armed military incursions aimed toward territorializing black zones and making them legible. Threats of a looming "cool" conflict in the Mutraw hills following the ceasefires were, in fact, a continuation of the long counterinsurgency. As armed conflict abated, this form of "people's war" was in ascendance. The introduction of new land laws the same year as the ceasefire, and the ensuing intensification of commercial/capitalist and religious-led forms of state territorialization, built on and greatly extended this "cool" shadow side of the ongoing counterinsurgency, which long preceded the ceasefires.

To grasp the wider connotations of local articulations of this new phase of counterinsurgency, I amalgamate Woods's (2011) terms *ceasefire capitalism* and *military territorialization* to describe the situation in these highlands, more broadly, as one of ceasefire territorialization. In much of Myanmar, but specifically in the Mutraw hills, under the guise of the ceasefires, battles continued to be waged, land territorialized, and people dispossessed. Military might was increasingly wedded and subordinated to economic and religious expansions/ventures, which were less spectacular and harder to confront directly. This new modality of the counterinsurgency, of ceasefire territorialization waged against the civilian population with economic and religious means, was not, however, met with resignation and acquiescence by all. In several pockets across southeast Myanmar, growing ensembles of local communities, ecological activists, and in some cases armed groups began to face down, push back, and attempt to reterritorialize and repossess their landscapes. This pushback was akin to Karl Polanyi's ([1944] 2001) notion of multiclass protective "countermovements" that arise to resist the disembodying of the economy and the commodification of land.

To shine a light on these burgeoning countermovements, I begin by taking a short excursion to an organic farming foundation just north of Bangkok to meet an ensemble of farmers, students, and ecological activists from the Tanintharyi Region in southern Myanmar who had begun organizing themselves. Here in southern Myanmar, following a massive intensification of counterinsurgency activities from 1997 to the early 2000s, the KNU was significantly weakened and pushed into a thin sliver of land along the Thai border, paving the way for a dramatic influx of international investments.

As one Chiang Mai–based researcher put it, "Tanintharyi district, in many ways, has become the Wild West of Myanmar," through the (re)opening of a frontier.

KNU ACTIVITY, ECONOMIC ACTIVITY, AND GREEN TERRITORIALITY IN TANINTHARYI

The first time I met Saw Jonny was in yet another of Chiang Mai's glittering shopping centers. I found him on the top floor at a small coffee stand, younger and lither than I had expected, smiling broadly as I introduced myself. Saw Jonny was a leading activist in a mushrooming group of community-based environmental and youth activist movements in the Tanintharyi Region of southern Myanmar. Collectively, these community-based groups called themselves the Tenasserim River and Indigenous Peoples' Network, or TRIP NET for short. While Saw Jonny was a professional activist, with many years of working for various organizations under his belt, the vast majority of his fellow activists had day jobs as farmers and students. Accordingly, as I stress throughout this book, the line between activist and farmer/villager was not always clear-cut. Despite his affable disposition, Saw Jonny was quick to point out when I had misunderstood something and gently put me back on track.

When I tried to pitch a collaborative research project comparing the situation in the Mutraw hills to that in the Tanintharyi Region, he initially agreed that this was an important angle but stressed they were two very different contexts. While most of the Mutraw hills were (nominally at least) under KNU jurisdiction, in the south people lived under "dual administrations." The majority of those residing in the Tanintharyi Region paid taxes to and were governed by both the Myanmar and KNU states. What is more, it was only "half true" to say that some areas were under KNU control. He took umbrage at the word *control* since the KNU's sovereignty there was relatively weak. As he put it, it would be more correct to assert that certain areas had a greater or lesser degree of "KNU activity." Moreover, KNU and Myanmar state/military activity was shadowed by a great deal of economic activity by a growing number of national and transnational investors.

A week later, I joined Saw Jonny for one of his "exposure trips" for farmers and youth from Tanintharyi. This trip took them to the Khao Kwan (Thai, meaning "the goddess of rice") Foundation training center for organic farming in Suphanburi, a few hours' drive northwest of Bangkok. At this center, the instructors encouraged the farmers to "not rely only on the market." The organic agricultural practices they taught there aimed to "liberate farmers and not just to make money" by "increas[ing] happiness not richness and improv[ing] the quality of the air and the water." It was a "question of survivability," the Thai founder of this foundation told these youth and farmers through a translator on the first day. (I return to this theme of liberation in response to dispossession in chapter 6.) When, on the second day, I got talking to the farmers and students from Tanintharyi who had gathered here, they described the ways their rights were gradually being chipped away as armed conflict abated. They explained how, following the ceasefire, they were facing threats of dispossession by sprawling palm oil plantations and alluvial gold mining activities (as documented in Woods 2019). As Saw Jonny later explained, the context of hybrid, or what he called "dual administrations," had exacerbated processes of creeping dispossession in the Tanintharyi Region.

For example, a few years ago Saw Jonny was approached by a senior figure in the KNU asking for his help to deal with one particular alluvial gold mining project. This elected official told him that the mine "received approval from neither the Myanmar government nor us [the KNU's highest political body, the Executive Committee]. It is like how food sometimes falls through the gaps between the [flattened bamboo] floorboards of a house." The Chinese conglomerate that set up this gold mine found a "gap" somewhere, most likely with local-level KNLA commanders, allowing them to set up shop in the area. The KNU official admitted that it was technically within his power to stop it but intimated that due to the delicate nature of this slip, involving high-ranking KNLA officers, his hands were effectively tied. Following this unofficial request, Saw Jonny helped those affected by the gold mine as they began organizing and protesting this development over the coming weeks and months. Eventually, their joint efforts paid off and the alluvial gold mining facility was forced to close, with little explicit help from the KNU government.

In these combined efforts, by villagers-cum-activists, to force the gold mining operation to close, we see glimmers of how countermovements were beginning to gather strength and effectively face down new forms of extractivism and ceasefire territorialization. For Karl Polanyi, throughout history there has been a continual "double movement," where unchecked market expansion is met by a protective countermovement, which was "a reaction against a dislocation which attacked the fabric of society" ([1944] 2001, 136). He goes on to argue that such movements are often "spontaneous, undirected by opinion, and actuated by a purely pragmatic spirit" (147).

Countermovements in Tanintharyi were gaining steam, pushing back against dispossession not only by economic enclosures but also by conservation enclosures. Increasingly, the Tatmadaw and the Myanmar government were attempting to territorialize the ground beneath Indigenous peoples' feet through (seemingly) earnest ecological conservation initiatives, in concordance with global environmental organizations (and indeed, in accordance with the UN's Sustainable Development Goals). This phenomenon is commonly spoken of as "fortress conservation" (Brockington 2002) and "green grabbing" (Fairhead et al. 2012).

In Kamoethway, where the vast majority of the participants who attended this "exposure trip" hailed from, a 420,000-acre (1,700 km^2) protected area, the Tanintharyi Nature Reserve Project (TNRP), was slowly being established (RKIPN 2016; Woods 2019, 226). As Saw Jonny pointed out, this nature reserve was first conceived in 1996, through a collaboration between, on the one side, French and Malaysian oil and gas companies Total and PETRONAS and, on the other, the Ministry of Environmental Conservation and Forestry of the Myanmar government. This project was part of the oil companies' corporate responsibility, to offset the damages caused by the Yadana pipeline that runs from off-shore rigs in the Andaman Sea through the width of the Tanintharyi Region and into Thailand (Barbesgaard 2019, 189). The coexistence and complicity between highly destructive extractive industries and this protected area in southeast Myanmar was not, however, a result of a historical quirk or happenstance, but rather archetypical of so-called mainstream/neoliberal conservation practices (Büscher and Fletcher 2020; Milne 2022; West 2006). Big conservation NGOS are, as Sarah Milne (2022) demonstrates in her "insider's ethnography," themselves corporate in nature, with similar business models and requirements to make the field legible (see also West 2006).

However, the Myanmar government were only able to enforce the TNRP as the political terrain began to become more settled, following the bilateral ceasefire between the KNU and the Tatmadaw in 2012, when people and goods began flowing more freely. Up until this point, the TNRP was simply a "paper park" (Woods 2019, 226), a park in name only. Following the ceasefire, state officials began informing residents that the northern section of their customary lands, which few if any of the villagers held Myanmar state-recognized land titles to, were in fact encroaching on the buffer zone of a nature reserve. Overnight, the rice fields and vast swaths of areca/betel nut plantations people had cultivated for generations became illegal occupations on government land. In response, Saw Jonny added, "the community elders tried to talk to these officials, but they have nothing on paper," no land titles to back up their claims to ownership and access. In one fell swoop, great numbers of subsistence farmers were effectively dispossessed of their lands and livelihoods.

Conservation projects thus bear a striking similarity to the previously discussed land laws. In both cases, in situ land possession practices are effectively ignored and effaced. To capture the wider implications of these processes, I follow Woods in arguing that many (seemingly) earnest ecological conservation initiatives in Tanintharyi were one particular manifestation of continuing ceasefire territorialization, which he describes as "green territoriality" (2019, 219). Green territoriality, as Woods so succinctly puts it, acts as a form of "soft counterinsurgency" (220). Conservation in southeast Myanmar, at times, became a kind of counterinsurgency lite.

This soft counterinsurgency, however, was not going unchallenged. As one younger Karen man I met in Khao Kwan accentuated, the Indigenous people of this area were far from sitting idly, waiting for their lands to be expropriated. In his words, "the situation favors the rich man, because he has money and he is close to those who have more power in the government. . . . This is the reason why we people need to get together in order to deal with those who have money and power and those with the authority." Accordingly, they began experimenting their own conservation project, conducting their own mapping, and creating a small pocket of Indigenous autonomy.

COUNTER-MAPPING AND TRANSLATION

Following the arrival of representatives of the Myanmar Forest Department, the villagers in Kamoethway gathered and began playing with Indigenous modes of conservation that turned processes of mapping and dispossession on their head. One wizened elder wearing a light blue T-shirt emblazoned with the logo representing his community in Kamoethway explained how, when their customary lands were designated as illegal occupations on the buffer zone of a nature reserve, they looked to local practices of protecting the environment:

> The way we manage the forest depends on the landscape and the resources that we each have, so we can [for instance] divide it into wildlife sanctuaries, watershed forests and [zones] utilized for farming. We do this to protect the landscape and the different characteristics of the area. In Karen traditions there is a lot about conserving forests and animals. This is according to our ancestors' knowledge. But we have also found evidence. We can prove that our efforts are effective. For example, we have started to teach fish conservation, and we have seen that in one or two years

the fish population is increasing. So, we have evidence so people can see the results of our activities.

Saw Jonny then elaborated on this, elucidating how they went about zoning their lands (see RKIPN 2016). The community went on to discuss how to formulate local regulations on the watershed forest. First, they "discussed what was the purpose of the watershed forest, why did they need it and how should they regulate it." Saw Johnny then asked them, "Ok, so can we cut down trees?" After a little back and forth, one person said, "Well, for charcoal we would have to fell some trees," then another chimed in, "Oh, but we can also just take the old, dead, and dying wood and use them, for making charcoal and building shelters." Then another villager interjected, "But if we remove too much of this deadwood on the forest floor it could destroy the habitat of certain frogs, fish, and other animals." Through such protracted discussion, experimenting with different approaches, they eventually formulated their own rules and regulations for these areas. These areas were then transposed onto a map and the rules written down for each area.

The community went on to collectively define and map nine categories of forest with rules and regulations tied to each, agreed upon by all members of the community and detailed in a report cowritten by them (RKIPN 2016). Saw Jonny expounded gleefully that, when they presented this plan to the Myanmar Forest Department, "They were just silent. . . . Then eventually, the first thing [the Forest Department] said was, 'who funded this?'" To this, one of the quick-witted villagers interjected, "We started this all by ourselves, and now the donors are starting to come to us." A Forest Department official then asked, "How can this be? Before the people would never agree and abide by the rules we set out for the forest, why is it that you follow these rules?" Another villager chimed in: "Now the rules are written by the people, so it is easy for us to follow them."

Fascinatingly, this ensemble of activists, farmers, and students in Tanintharyi faced down the Myanmar state's continued attempts at ceasefire territorialization by playing with the very same mapping and zoning practices that threatened to dispossess them. In effect, they turned state-like attempts to make these lands legible on their head, as a way to counter encroachments on their lands. By (re)mapping their lands, they were attempting to repossess them. Through these conversations with the participants and with Saw Jonny, I learned that, in a parallel fashion to the Myanmar state, the villagers and activists were experimenting with translating jostling Indigenous modes of possessing the earth into a uniform/standardized grid of different categories of land, to make them legible to the Myanmar state, plotted onto a map and creating their own "geo-body" (Winichakul 1994). Mapping is, after all, "an intrinsically political act" (Peluso 1995, 383). The activists-cum-farmers had effectively created their own conservation zone and with it a small patch of autonomous terrain.

These efforts resemble what Nancy Peluso (1995) calls *counter-mapping*. By appropriating state technologies of territoriality, they hoped to bolster the legitimacy of "customary" claims, in the process redefining and reinventing them (Peluso 1995, 384, 400; see also Chao 2022, 51–73). In this manner, Indigenous maps and practices were translated into legible and legalizing counter-maps to establish property rights that were readable and assessable to the Myanmar state, to be used in negotiations. As the wizened elder put it, in these activities "we have evidence so people can see the results of our activities."

These activities were beginning to bear fruit. Myanmar forestry personnel were left speechless when first presented with this map, finally exclaiming, "How can this be?" This counter-mapping marked a startling turn in the protracted armed conflict in southeast Myanmar. In the face of creeping ceasefire territorialization and threats of dispossession, these counter-movements worked to repossess the landscape. Such radical experiments to (re)zone and (re)map forests to make Indigenous land possession practices legible were ongoing, even as war returned to Myanmar following the 2021 coup.

The last time I met Saw Jonny was at the KESAN office in Chiang Mai where he came for a flying visit, with a large rolled-up sheet of paper tucked under his arm. When some of the activists and I asked what he was carrying, Saw Jonny excitedly unrolled it onto the table in front of us to reveal a rough map of Kamoethway valley, crisscrossed with lines to create different areas, each filled in with bright splashes of color. He was there to get help from resident cartography wizard Saw Hpweh to turn this sketch into a fully scaled and digitalized map. They planned to draw on this map when arguing their case to the relevant authorities in the pushback against the Tanintharyi Nature Reserve Project. He explained how, following the discussion to decide how to divide up the landscape into discrete zones, described above, and having agreed upon the rules and regulations for each of these zones, they marked them onto a map in different colors.

After he showed us these different zones, Doh K'Oh, the overworked KESAN activist mentioned in the introduction, leaned in and asked what all the red patches were. "Aha!" exclaimed Saw Jonny, "they are the 'cultural forest' areas." As he turned to us and immediately caught the puzzlement upon our faces, he added, "These are the areas where people practice *hku* or shifting cultivation." Swidden farming, or *taungya* in Burmese, was, as Saw Jonny put it mildly, "not very popular with the Myanmar government," so instead "we call them cultural forests."[8]

In a community report from Kamoethway (RKIPN 2016) published the year prior to this conversation, "cultural forests" was one of several different categories of forestland that the community demarcated to "preserve" and "revive" disappearing Indigenous practices. Other areas marked on the map that Saw Jonny showed us, and described in the community report, included a forest reserved for growing medicinal herbs and an "Umbilical Cord Forest." The latter was rooted in long-lapsed Thoo Hkoh/Moh La Pa Lah (animist/ancestral) practices in this area in which people once hung or buried the umbilical cords of newborns in or under a particular (usually especially vibrant) tree. As I learned from a Pwakanyaw elder from the Thai side of the border, where this practice was still widespread, this tree kept the child's spirits (*k'la*) safe from being "eaten/attacked" (*aw loh*) by spectral presences.[9] These areas were thus deeply entangled with practices of possessed landscapes, where, as I argue in part 1 of this book, landscapes were treated as already owned, and its uses had to constantly be negotiated with its spectral owners. Yet, as he had told me earlier, Saw Jonny was unsure whether any practicing Thoo Hkoh/Moh La Pa Lah were left in the Tanintharyi Region. This last point illustrates the persistent issues such countermovements run against in the process of translation.

Returning to Peluso's notion of counter-maps, it becomes clear that these technologies often "redefine and reinvent" customary claims as new "traditions" in the process (Peluso 1995, 384). Moreover, counter-mapping runs the risk of "fixing" or "freezing" Indigenous practices, robbing them of their flexibility and indeterminacy (Peluso 1995, 400; see also Li 2010). Paige West has long warned that translations, as deeply political acts, can lead to the "generification of culture" whereby "on-the-ground knowledge and practice begins to look like the outside renderings of them" (2005, 633). As the Italian adage goes, "to translate is to betray," to redefine and reinvent.

Following Walter Benjamin, however, the betrayal inherent in translation is often not to the source language but to the destination language (2004, 253–69; see also Hage 2015, 65). Accordingly, by translating Indigenous notions into forms legible to the Myanmar state, these countermovements in southeast Myanmar aimed to deform and subvert state forms. Rather than continuing here by wading into the broad and vexed debate on the practices and politics of translation in anthropology, I want to foreground the pragmatism of these farmers-cum-activists' relations to translation.[10] In many ways the translation process was grasped as a practical way to bolster the legitimacy of their efforts while also deforming and subverting the Myanmar state's attempts to dispossess them. These inventive experiments in translating Indigenous practices and counter-mapping in Tanintharyi were similar to the situation farther north in the Mutraw hills but differed in several important ways.

In contrast to the Mutraw hills, Myanmar's deep south was a highly hybrid and plural context. The ensemble of activists, farmers, and students (these roles often becoming jumbled) in the Tanintharyi Region constantly countered and pushed back on ceasefire territorialization, not only from the Myanmar government and the Tatmadaw but, in part, also from the KNU itself. This was especially the case with the gold mining project, where this ensemble often had to face down "development" projects that had the approval not of the Tatmadaw, but of the KNU government (at the district level at least). In Saw Jonny's telling of this story, when this ensemble of farmers, students, and activists began to organize and protest against the gold mine, and as it became increasingly difficult for the mine to continue business as usual, some KNLA commanders from this area began calling this same KNU government official. They requested he order Saw Jonny and this motley band of activists/farmers to cease and desist immediately.

The KNLA commanders called these actions "civil disorder," claiming that Saw Jonny was training villagers to rebel against the KNU. The senior official did indeed contact Saw Jonny again, but instead of chastising him, told him that he must continue working and urged him to keep up the pressure. This politician then exclaimed that these activist/farmers were "like the mushroom that grows on a termite mound. You know termite mounds, right? They are very hard but somehow the mushroom still manages to grow." Saw Jonny began giggling as he reached this final detail.

In the next chapter, I turn my attention to the area around Ta K'Thwee Duh in the Mutraw hills to explore similar experiments with conservation. Here, where Thoo Hkoh cosmologies and practices were still commonplace, I found that people were not so much reviving or reinventing but repurposing actually existing Indigenous conservation practices. In doing so, they were drawing on alternative modes of sovereignty and politics that were intermittently becoming aligned with KNU's long struggle for greater autonomy: generating a novel kind of alter-politics.

FIVE

Alter-Politics
Revolution, Conservation, and Conviviality

Returning to the Mutraw hills, similar experiments with Indigenous modes of conservation that pushed back against ceasefire territorialization were afoot. These experiments, however, took on a markedly different texture and temper to those enacted in other parts of southeast Myanmar. In these highlands, in the last stronghold of the Karen Revolution, rather than simply opposing the KNU with acts of "civil disorder," people's efforts to resist their dispossession occasionally became aligned with the KNU seventy-year struggle for greater autonomy. The KNU's revolutionary project was constantly haunted by spectral sovereignty, opening up for alternative modes of politics, or alter-politics.

Feeling the predatory Myanmar state gradually encroach upon their lives through the expansion of economic and religious spheres, people's first reaction was to appeal to the authority and sovereignty of the KNU for protection. The KNU in these parts had, as I have illustrated, long warned residents of the Mutraw hills of the dangers of a creeping *ta du ta yah hku* (cool/peaceful conflict) following the ceasefire and had sworn to assist them. Yet despite many concerted attempts by villagers to entreat them, the KNU once more regularly ran up against the limits of their sovereignty, which became threadbare toward the top of the Bu Thoe ridge. The KNU continued to have little palpable effect on local day-to-day politics. Not easily disheartened, the villagers again turned to spectral sovereigns to assist them, experimenting with Indigenous modes of conservation. The specters then intervened, finally protecting these forested highlands from harm—at least for now. In this manner, spectral sovereignty intermittently became interwoven into KNU's own patchy sovereignty, augmenting their hold over these highlands. In creating small pockets of relative autonomy, such Indigenous modes of conservation also became temporarily aligned with KNU's ongoing struggle for self-determination. The Mutraw hills were becoming a space for staging encounters, where different experiments with conservation and autonomy were coming into contact and being negotiated.

PAGODA POLITICS

During the period I stayed in Ta K'Thwee Duh, from January to September 2017, there were only two Buddhist households in the village. To be specific, these households were spoken of not as Buddhist but as Bah Hpaw (literally, flower worshippers, due to the prominent use of flowers in their offering to the specters and the Buddha). *Bah Hpaw* is a syncretic mix of Buddhism and Thoo Hkoh/Moh La Pa Lah (often glossed as animism/ancestral worship). One of these households belonged to Hpee Luh, the de facto representative for the Karen Women's Organisation (KWO), and her husband, Hpu Hka Hsoo, and the other belonged to their eldest daughter. Hpu Hka Hsoo, the elder with a well-waxed handlebar mustache and a paddy field, had first come into contact with monks during his migrations to and peregrinations around Thailand. Like many other people in these highlands, he adapted several Thoo Hkoh practices to better accord with the Buddha's teachings. One such adaption entailed abstaining from agricultural work, eating meat and drinking alcohol, and making offerings of animals to *lu ta* (feed) the spectral owners and ancestors during certain phases of the moon.[1] Such syncretic practices led the two Bah Hpaw households in the village to adopt several highly inventive variations on day-to-day practices oriented toward traversing possessed landscapes: specifically, the constant negotiation with spectral sovereigns, which regularly involved the slaying and eating of animals and the imbuing of copious amounts of alcohol.

When ritually important days such as the wrist-tying ceremony coincided with a full moon, for example, Hpu Hka Hsoo and the other members of his household forwent the usual offerings. Hpu Hka Hsoo invoked the specters to join them in eating a sacrificial meal of store-bought snacks, not the usual pork or chicken, and replaced libations of rice wine with cans of Sprite. This allowed them to avoid killing and consuming alcohol while still respecting their ancestors. Such heady mixes of practices led some of his fellow villagers to level accusations at him and his family that they had "given way to" *ta lay p'saw* (temptations) from Buddhist monks and been corrupted by them. Some villagers even claimed he had become "crazy with religion."

Despite the persistent suspicions and rumors that swirled around this family's practices, many of the villagers sympathized with Hpee Luh's complaints that she had converted to Buddhism for her husband but had never actually met a monk. One of the villagers, who in his younger days had also migrated to Thailand and found work building temples and monasteries, arranged for a monk he knew to visit the village. This monk was Pwakanyaw, hailing from Khoe Kay, a day's hike south of the village along the Myanmar side of the Salween River. He arrived some weeks later and led the two Bah Hpaw households through several rituals. Despite this visit, Hpee Luh still felt frustrated. She continued to complain that there was nowhere nearby where they could worship. Eventually, she decided to take matters into her own hands and contacted this monk again, requesting his assistance to build a small pagoda in the village. As she asked me rhetorically, "the Christians have their schools and their churches, so why can't we have a small place to worship too?" Before long, however, these plans ran into considerable resistance from her fellow villagers.

Hpee Luh herself later confessed that she had not conferred with anyone outside her household about raising a Buddhist monument in the village beforehand—not even with her husband, who was working in Thailand at the time. So, when the Pwakanyaw monk, along with two Thai monk companions, arrived unannounced in the village one cold January afternoon in 2017, it caused quite a stir. The tension around these monks only heightened when the other villagers learned that they, together with Hpee Luh, planned to build a pagoda right beside the primary school at the top of the village. This all came to a head when, following a heated meeting hastily organized at the headman's house, they agreed that they would forbid this religious structure from being erected so close to the village. Subsequently, I learned that some of the villagers at this meeting had argued strongly against the plan to construct a small pagoda by comparing it to the incident at the riverside hamlet of Thee Mu Hta. In this hamlet (as detailed in chapter 4) the construction of a Buddhist place of worship set off a chain of events that led the Tatmadaw to the capture the whole area and dispossess most of the inhabitants. The arrival of these monks became implicated in growing fears of a new *ta du ta yah hku* (cool/peaceful conflict) as the "heat" of armed counterinsurgency dissipated. The presence of a framed photo of U Thuzana, alongside a vase of flowers, in Hpu Hka Hsoo's household shrine (see figure 7) intensified the perceived linkages between the Bah Hpaw households, the visiting monks, and the threat of "cool conflict."[2]

Upon learning that the villagers had banned them from building a pagoda in the village itself, the monks and Hpee Luh decided to instead build it on the highest peak in the area, which just so happened to be Ta Bu Kyoh—the seat of the *kaw k'sah* and thus ritually and politically central to

FIGURE 7. Hpu Kha Hsoo's household shrine.

day-to-day life. While the other villagers initially assented, many even helping the monks and the two Bah Hpaw households carry building materials to the top of the mountain, a growing torrent of discontent soon enveloped this project. Mirroring the events around the construction of the "car road" some five years prior (see chapter 3), the relative dearth of political offices and institutions in these highlands meant there was little the villagers could do to prevent the disturbance of the seat of the *kaw k'sah*. At this point, several people experienced vivid nightmares. They dreamt of giant mudslides engulfing the village, which recalled tales of neighboring villages being inundated when the inhabitants evoked the ire of the *kaw k'sah* by breaking taboos and not making sufficient amends.

The ominous sense of looming disaster that accompanied the arrival of these monks was exacerbated by the sighting of tiger pugmarks on the road close to the village. A villager first noticed these pugmarks the morning after the monks moved from the village to Ta Bu Kyoh. Taken together, these incidents pointed toward the same conclusion: Attempts to construct a pagoda at Naw Ghoo Hsaw's "place," her abode, were a grave *k'ma* (mistake). Consequently, it was surmised that the *kaw k'sah*, the "owner" or "queen," of Ta

K'Thwee Duh village had become terribly vexed by this mistake, and misfortune, disease, and disarray were surely not far behind.

Despite this growing discontent, again echoing the KNU project to construct a "car road," the inhabitants of this area felt powerless to force the monks to desist. They had plainly forbidden them from constructing the small pagoda in the village proper, but this prohibition did not extend to the whole *kaw*. And indeed, the villagers I spoke to were wholly unsure whether, even if they had held a new meeting at the headman's house, the decision made would have the authority to uphold a *kaw*-wide ban on such constructions. The ceremonial leader, the *hee hkoh htee*, remained, as usual, tight-lipped and unwilling or unable to intervene. Once again, they had exhausted the conventional political means at their disposal to effect change.

The situation reached a tipping point a few days after the monks had moved to the top of Ta Bu Kyoh and construction had begun in earnest. One morning, the monks abruptly decamped and returned home to Thailand. When I went to see the area where the pagoda was to be erected, around two or three weeks later, only the faintest traces of the monks' presence remained: a small ramshackle shrine with store-bought snacks and cans of fizzy drink still resting in it and several bags of cement scattered higgledy-piggledy. The jungle had already begun to reclaim this area. Hpee Luh explained later how, when these three monks had attempted to sleep at the top of the mountain, they also had terrible dreams and experienced a series of inexplicable events. On their last night in the area, one of the monks had moved a little closer to the fire to stay warm and his robes had burst into flames, burning his leg. When they discussed their nightmares and the burning robes the following morning, the monks agreed that these were bad omens. If they were to continue, it might cause great problems in the area. Thus, they promptly ceased building the pagoda and left. Hpee Luh insisted that, at this point, none of them had any inkling of the growing discontent in Ta K'Thwee Duh.

The villagers later insisted that these events were clearly the work of Naw Ghoo Hsaw. The *kaw k'sah* herself was deeply displeased by the construction of a pagoda in "her place" and has once more interrupted and intervened, forcing these monks and the Bah Hpaw families to cease construction.

* * *

The events surrounding these thwarted attempts to build a pagoda on Ta Bu Kyoh rehearsed those that followed the KNU roadbuilding project seven years earlier. Once more, the villagers' first reaction was to appeal to conventional political instruments to prevent the construction of the pagoda. In this case they turned to the headman rather than the KNU directly. It swiftly became apparent, however, that the limits of his authority coincided largely with the limits of the village. Once the construction of the pagoda was moved to take place atop Ta Bu Kyoh, all political offices and institutions in Ta K'Thwee Duh were rendered powerless to intervene. These events evoked looming threats, not only of internal strife but also of the return of the violent resource frontiers, armed conflict, and dispossession of times past. At this critical conjuncture, the *kaw k'sah* intervened; her spectral sovereignty interrupted day-to-day politics by affecting the bodies and lives of both the villagers and the monks and effected change.

Through her intervention, the sovereignty of the *kaw k'sah* acted not as a foil for the KNU's sovereignty—as the inverse of and antagonist to the KNU (revolutionary) state—but rather, for a brief instance, it became momentarily aligned with and buttressed the KNU's patchy control of these hills, helping repel threats of creeping ceasefire territorialization. Where the KNU's sovereign effects tapered off, the deeply felt sovereignty of the *kaw k'sah* stepped in.

THE HAUNTING OF REVOLUTIONARY POLITICS

The events described above, involving the monks from Thailand, became increasingly tangled up with a growing feeling that a new *ta du ta yah hku* (cool/peaceful conflict), fought with religious and economic means, was afoot. While the KNU actively attempted to combat this new "soft" phase of the counterinsurgency, much like the case of a gold mining facility in the Tanintharyi Region (discussed in chapter 4), plans to construct a pagoda in Ta K'Thwee Duh Kaw still managed to slip between the considerable "gaps in the floorboards" of the KNU's influence. However, in the interstices between states and nations along the lower Salween River, where the KNU's reach and felt effects weakened, the *kaw k'sah* often flourished and intermittently intervened—in this case, sending the monks packing. The KNU's revolutionary politics in this area were constantly haunted by spectral politics: at times opposing it, at other times patching over the gaps in its sovereignty.

Beyond a general frustration around not being informed beforehand, discontent and trepidation in relation to the pagoda-building project intensified in Ta K'Thwee Duh as it became linked to the cautionary tale of the fall of Thee Mu Hta. The pagoda became implicated in narratives and fears of a new creeping form of counterinsurgency, which I have described as ceasefire territorialization. While these fears of dispossession were also common among the political and military leadership of the KNU, their patchy control over these hills meant that they struggled to effectively deal with them.

Delving deeper, the monks' offer of assistance to build a pagoda in Ta K'Thwee Duh Kaw shared many aspects with the cautionary tale of Thee Mu Hta. Both instances involved the promise of something seemingly benign that people genuinely desired. Albeit overtly, the highly contentious monk U Thuzana was implicated in both cases. As touched on earlier, U Thuzana was also embroiled in the fall of the once-vibrant center of the revolution, Manerplaw, in 1994 to 1995. This event was well known as a watershed in the armed conflict, regularly debated by villagers and generals alike. In a strikingly similar pattern, prior to the fall Manerplaw, U Thuzana built a so-called peace pagoda on a hill beside it. He then invited Buddhist rank-and-file soldiers, largely disaffected with the Christian-dominated leadership of the KNU, to join him there with promises of significant improvements in their lives (Smith 1999, 446–47; South 2008, 58–59). These soldiers went on to form the Democratic Karen Buddhist Army (DKBA) and soon after assisted the Tatmadaw in overrunning Manerplaw. I often heard tales of how Buddhist monks were "tempting" and corrupting people in these highlands, turning them against the KNU and their fellow Pwakanyaw—"brother against brother," as the more Christian-oriented villagers put it.

This was the context in which talk of Hpu Hka Hsoo having "given way to temptations" and having become "crazy with religion" played out. While never uttered explicitly, these pronouncements intimated that Hpu Hka Hsoo had become tangled up with U Thuzana, the DKBA, and by implication the growing *ta du ta yah hku* (cool/peaceful conflict). The unannounced arrival of these three foreign monks, and their plans to build a pagoda in one of the most potent areas of Ta K'Thwee Duh Kaw, then became ensnared in cautionary tales and growing fears that the Tatmadaw was continuing counterinsurgency by expanding religious and economic spheres.

Whether or not these three monks, and perhaps the Bah Hpaw households, were in fact party to an elaborate Tatmadaw complot to capture Ta Bu Kyoh is of less concern here. As I have emphasized from the start, I am more interested in the effects such events had on day-to-day life and politics. My focus is on how the arrival of these monks evoked growing trepidations toward a creeping ceasefire territorialization and how people in the Mutraw hills grappled with it.

As discussed previously, while the KNU made concerted efforts to combat creeping counterinsurgency, these efforts were constantly frustrated by the friction of the physical and political terrain of these highlands. The KNU, for all intents and purposes, acted as the de facto state, but its sovereignty grew threadbare in certain out-of-the-way swaths of the Mutraw District. People often spoke warmly of the KNU state as "our government" and "our leaders," many yearning for it to have more influence in these highlands. Yet, like the states that reigned before them, the KNU continued to struggle in asserting a lasting effect on the day-to-day lives and politics of the people living there. Moreover, local political institutions such as the headman, tied to the KNU governance system, and the ceremonial leader the *hee hkoh htee* were largely powerless to intervene, vested with little tangible authority to effect change. Consequently, when the monks arrived to assist Hpee Luh and her household construct a pagoda, while many of the villagers were ill at ease with the prospect, they felt that the KNU was too distant and spread too thinly to assist them. What is more, local institutions proved to be toothless when plans were moved outside of the village proper.

The *kaw k'sah*'s intervention, which sent these monks packing back to Thailand, suggested a far more complicated relation between the KNU and the spectral realm than one of constant opposition and competition over sovereignty. The *kaw k'sah* had effectively pushed back against and indeed foiled what for many was a very real threat of dispossession. While the *kaw k'sah* effected this change in response to a *k'ma* (mistake) in the area under its dominion, its response simultaneously complemented, and indeed augmented, the KNU's patchy sovereignty over these highlands. To better grasp the relationship between state and spectral politics, I revisit the notion of contact zone as a space of asymmetrical negotiation.

In chapter 1, I draw on recent adaptions of Mary Louise Pratt's (1991, 2008) notion of contact zones to describe these highlands as more-than-human contact zones (Isaacs and Otruba 2019). In contact zones, different human regimes of power as well as more-than-human realms are locked in both asymmetrical clashes and constant negotiation and mutual accommodation. By locating the KNU and the *kaw k'sah* in a contact zone, it becomes clear that, while relations between them were entrenched in vast disparities of power, these relations always also entailed co-presence, playful negotiations, improvisation, and co-option (Clifford 1997; Pratt 2008). They constantly oscillated between relations of opposition and collaboration, where these two heterogeneous modes of sovereignty occasionally became positively related. The KNU's sovereignty was accompanied and, at times, buttressed by its spectral other.

Symbiotic Events and Alter-Politics

In the Mutraw hills, standard revolutionary politics of setting up a state to rival the (predatory) nation-state, which they were locked in conflict with, was perpetually shadowed by spectral sovereignty, which acted as an alternative mode of politics. Such a myriad of coexisting modes of politics is commonly understood in terms of what Isabelle Stengers ([1997] 2010) calls *cosmopolitics*. For Bruno Latour the notion of cosmopolitics widens politics to "embrace, literally, everything—including the vast numbers of nonhuman entities making humans act" (2004, 454). It is not, as he stresses, the case that people can simply "leave their gods on hooks in the cloakroom" when they enter into negotiations; rather, they always bring with them a "freight of gods, attachments, and unruly cosmos" (456–57). As I argue throughout this book, we must take the actions of more-than-humans seriously as alternative modes of sovereignty, ownership, and thus politics at large.

Notions of cosmopolitics, however, tend to give rise to a kind of "war of the worlds" between clashing cosmologies (Latour 2004, 454; see also Latour 2002). By contrast, I prefer to draw on the ideas of more-than-human contact zones. More-than-human contact zones are spaces not only of constant opposition between radically different and indeed incommensurable worlds but also of encounter between different cosmologies, modes of ownership, and sovereignty and between human and more-than-human realms—locked in processes of continual negotiation and mutual accommodation.

The instance of the aborted pagoda construction on Ta Bu Kyoh stands in stark contrast to previous cases, such as the construction of the "car road," where the KNU's state politics constantly clashed with and was frustrated by the spectral sovereignty of the *kaw k'sah*. In this case, these different modes of politics became momentarily complementary. As Pratt points out, in taking a contact perspective, our attention is drawn to "how subjects get constituted in and by relation to one another" (2008, 8).

The KNU's seven-decade-long struggle for autonomy, focused on opposition and resistance to the Tatmadaw and the Myanmar state, can be grasped in terms of what Ghassan Hage (2015) describes as anti-politics. Anti-politics, such as anti-colonialism and anti-capitalism, overwhelmingly focus on the most pertinent task at hand: the overturning of (unjust) political orders. However, in such a singular focus, this mode of politics is less successful in transforming opposition into an alternative to the reality they have overturned (Hage 2015, 2). In anti-colonialist struggles around the world, when colonial leaders are thrown out and replaced by Indigenous ones, the oppressive government apparatus underlying colonial rule often remains intact, leading history to repeat itself.

In southeast Myanmar the KNU has long strived to attain a counter-state, Kawthoolei or Karen-land. This state has been imagined as a space to shelter the persecuted Karen people (San C. Po 1928) and was brought into being through the establishment of parallel forms of governance systems, laws, and bureaucracies. In this manner, the Kawthoolei (revolutionary) state was in many ways a mirror image of its Myanmar counterpart. This became particularly evident in chapter 4, where I explore the stalemate that followed the ceasefire agreements beginning in 2012, between the dueling visions of the nation-state of Myanmar and Kawthoolei. The Kawthoolei state was (and continues to be) highly effective at both protecting people from the predations of the Tatmadaw and providing vital services such as education and health. However, following the ceasefire there was, as Hage argues, a "routinisation of notions of crisis where conflict and war situations were increasingly perceived as states in their own right rather than as transitional towards something else"—such that politics became bogged down in "unproductive and endless oppositions" (2015, 62).

To break out of this impasse of dueling oppositions, I join Hage's call to not abandon anti-politics (and the many successes wrought by them) entirely but rather attempt to (more comprehensively) weave them together with modes of alter-politics that come from outside these endless oppositions. Alter-politics points toward the possibility that "another world is possible" by gesturing toward an "otherwise" that is continually "at odds with dominant and dominating ways of being" (Povinelli 2011; see also Povinelli 2012). Alter-politics are social forces and potentialities that continually "haunt" us with the possibility of other ways of dwelling and being enmeshed in the world, which we must become aware of and animate (Hage 2015, 54–55).

Responding to this call, I attend closely to and take seriously the way the persistent presence of spectral sovereignty haunted the KNU's revolutionary politics. Following the arguments made in part 1, people living in possessed landscapes along the lower Salween River treated the earth beneath their feet less as a set of resources to be managed and extracted than as a place teeming with and already owned by more-than-human life. Landscapes could only ever be borrowed, with the solemn promise to return them to their real spectral owners. Humans were interminably engaged in processes of making and maintaining "good relations" with the spectral realm. Such modes of alter-politics offered a way out of the stalemate of the ceasefire, by pointing toward radically alternative ways of being enmeshed in and relating to the world.

It is important to note here that momentary alignments between the spectral realm and the KNU did not require that their vast differences be bridged by force, compelling them to become the same. Rather, these two heterogeneous modes of politics, through deep histories of encounter, had worked out a relation, a mutual understanding—enabling them to coexist while still following their own interests, akin to the relation between the phasmid (stick insect) and the twig (Nathan 2004, 526–27). This act of working out relations did not require that they recognize and accept each other as such but simply be moved by each other (527).

Such an arrangement resembled what Stengers calls a "symbiotic event" (2011, 60), whereby two heterogeneous terms relate even as they diverge. These events of connection are less about common interest between the two parties than of opportunities in which their "diverging interests now need each other" (60). Spectral sovereignty and the KNU shared deep histories of encounter, such that these heterogeneous modes of politics had hashed out a working relationship. It is doubtful that the KNU and the *kaw k'sah* came together under a common interest, such as a shared desire to resist ceasefire territorialization. When the *kaw k'sah* affected the bodies of the monks, moving them to leave these highlands, the correspondence with KNU's strategic goals was more a case of opportunity. Their diverging interests simply happened to coincide and to need each other. As I have argued throughout, symbiotic events "demand that we do not accept settled ways of life as being given" (Stengers 2011, 61). They come together only to divide again in indeterminate ways.

The arrival of the monks to Ta K'Thwee Duh, and the subsequent intervention of the *kaw k'sah*, was one such "symbiotic event." In the weeks after the monks absconded back to Thailand, this event continued to reverberate, animating KNU state policy. In a meeting held in Pa Heh, the seat of the local village tract, the KNLA commanders, KNU leaders, and the villagers agreed that, following these events, they would prohibit the building of new Buddhist structures unless over thirty households were Buddhist. Since few villages were larger than thirty households, and none fully Buddhist, this prohibition effectively acted as a blanket ban on all new Buddhist structures. In this manner, the sovereignty of the *kaw k'sah* preceded and haunted that of the KNU's sovereignty, provoking them to act. For a fleeting moment, these two modes of politics came together to effect a lasting change, even as they continued to diverge.

"MAKING FRIENDS" IN VIOLENT FRONTIERS

Tracing the history of how villagers in Ta K'Thwee Duh decided to protect two forested areas from overhunting, touched on in the introduction to this book, really drove home for me the ways human and spectral worlds and different modes of politics were becoming aligned. To protect these forests, the villagers had initially and repeatedly appealed to the KNU's Forest Department for a community forest title. Only when these appeals were indefinably deferred and ultimately failed did they decide to take the matter into their own hands. They began experimenting first with Buddhist, then Indigenous modes of conservation, oriented toward *ray daw* (making friends) with more-than-human others and ecologies. In the process, they created small pockets of autonomy in these highlands.

* * *

Villagers regularly voiced deep concerns about a rocky stretch of land on the western border of Ta K'Thwee Duh Kaw known as Way Pgha. In this swath of land, too rough to clear for cultivation, a large and vibrant primary forest flourished. It hosted numerous old-growth trees of impressive proportions and a plethora of animals. People had, for instance, encountered sun bears, which are on the International Union for Conservation of Nature (IUCN) Red List as vulnerable (Scotson et al. 2017), and great hornbills, also categorized as vulnerable (BirdLife International 2018), in Way Pgha. The most impressive old-growth tree that found shelter here was a giant banyan that stood almost exactly in the middle of the forest. When this banyan fruited, it attracted animals from miles around. As Hpee Luh's son Hpa Kha Pa evocatively spoke of it, "When the banyan tree fruits, it is like it is making a *lu ta* [offering]. The banyan makes an offering of fresh fruit, then calls upon animals far and wide to come and share its bounty." Likewise, as Hpa Kha Pa and many others explained, tigers (*Panthera tigris*) listed as endangered (Goodrich et al. 2015) "like these kinds of rocky areas," such as this forest. At least three different tigers had been spotted passing through Way Pgha on regular occasions.

The villagers were especially concerned about an area of Way Pgha with a rock face pockmarked with *pah poo*, the burrows of Asiatic brush-tailed porcupines (*Atherurus macrourus*). The villagers feared that these porcupines were being overhunted, since one could simply sit in front of the entrance of their burrows as dusk approached and pick them off one by one as they emerged. This was indicative of wider concerns, especially among village elders, that, following decades of armed conflict, these highlands were awash with modern firearms (such as AR-15-style rifles used by soldiers), which were increasingly used for hunting. Use of automatic weapons made the killing of animals "a little too easy," as one young soldier who often hunted with his service rifle put it. Most agreed that, if they did not do something quickly, there would be few animals remaining. The ever-loquacious Hpu Hkee put it bluntly that, "if we do not do anything now, then there will be no animals left for my children and grandchildren to kill and to eat." Consequently, the three men I introduce in the introduction, together with Hpu Hkee and the headman, began discussing how to protect their forests from overexploitation and how to keep it in their hands, so it could not be grabbed by the growing number of outside actors coming to these highlands.

To stem the rising tide of concerns around the status of the flora and fauna in Way Pgha, the villagers in Ta K'Thwee Duh attempted to prohibit people from hunting in this area. They began by trying to issue a decree banning hunting in Way Pgha via a meeting held in the headman's house. This decree had much the same effect as the ban on building a Buddhist pagoda in the *kaw*. During this meeting they struggled to come to a consensus as to how they would actually go about prohibiting people from hunting there in practice. They were unsure whether they had the authority to forbid people from hunting in an area so far from the village proper. And even if they did succeed and the residents of Ta K'Thwee Duh completely stopped hunting in Way Pgha, they held little faith that this ban would be respected by people from the surrounding *kaw* and farther afield. What is more, they had no way of enforcing such a prohibition, unless one of the villagers gave up farming to constantly patrol the forest. To address these issues, for several years they tried and failed to secure a community forest land title from the Karen Forestry Department (KFD) as a more robust legal instrument for enforcing this prohibition.

Despite numerous trips to the KFD offices in the administrative center, the villagers in Ta K'Thwee Duh felt no closer to their goal. From KFD officials and KESAN staff I learned that they still lacked the workforce and capability to extend operations to the very top of the Bu Thoe ridge. They could only offer minimal support for local small-scale initiatives to protect forests. Despite these setbacks, the villagers continued to push for an official community forest title. Many felt that holding a land title would best allow them to enforce the protected status of Way Pgha, since official KNU-stamped documents were recognized and respected not only by the local villagers but also by outsiders passing through. What is more, if it were to become an official community forest, the KFD might even employ someone to actually enforce the ban on hunting.

As hope faded that the KNU would be able to help them, in lieu of an officially sanctioned community forest, some villagers attempted to take matters into their own hands. One of the first local attempts to protect this area was led by Hpu Hka Hsoo, who enlisted the help of the very same monks we met in the previous section. He hoped, with the monks' assistance, they could finally protect Way Pgha.

* * *

In these highlands there was a growing awareness that the environment was being depleted and that an increasing number of outside actors were exacerbating the problem. People's reactions to looming environmental degradation followed a similar pattern to their reactions to other forms of disorder, as described in part 1 of this book. After failing to solve the issue locally through the (highly limited) authority of the headman, they appealed to the KNU directly to secure land titles. Akin to the strategies employed farther south (see chapter 4), the KNU's policy of issuing land titles was deeply entangled with their efforts to map these highlands and make them legible, allowing them to assert their sovereignty and counter Tatmadaw attempts to territorialize these landscapes. In this light, KNU's land titles, which mirrored those issued by the Myanmar government, were a form of counter-titling.

Notwithstanding the KNU's and the KFD's encouragements for residents in the Mutraw hills to apply for community forest titles, the KNU's bureaucratic ability to award titles and their sovereignty to enforce them became frayed in the Mutraw hills. In response to this failure to receive help from the KNU, the villagers took matters into their own hands. First, they turned to the encompassing sovereignty of the Buddha. Later, they appealed to the spectral realm. In the process spectral politics sometimes indirectly complemented and extended the KNU's political strivings.

When Trees Become Monks

Another area the residents of Ta K'Thwee Duh were deeply concerned about, touched on in the introduction, was the riparian buffer strip of forest around the *loh*, the forest where the *k'la* (spirits, shades) of the dead resided. On the one hand, a bend in the river in the middle of the *loh*, where the water slowed to a crawl, was a spawning ground for a great number of fish and other aquatic creatures. The villagers feared that people were overfishing the *loh* since the fish were easier to catch here, just as the porcupine in Way Pgha were being overhunted. If nothing was done, they reasoned, there would soon be nothing left to eat in the river. On the other hand, villagers were concerned that outsiders were visiting the *loh* and removing things. As shown, when a person died, items they were fond of—such as their clothes, an old umbrella, or their favorite hunting rifle—were conveyed to this area at the end of the funeral, along with bone fragments and a lock of their hair. Since the dead lived in the *ta taw ta loh kaw* (the spectral realm) where everything was *hkoh hkee*, or "backward," all these items were ritually destroyed by their relatives to become whole again in the *loh*. Villagers feared that outsiders might not understand that such broken items belonged to the dead and be tempted to take them home as souvenirs. These concerns were compounded by tales, such as those told by Hpu Hka Hsoo, of how people regularly heard the sounds of weeping emanating from the *loh* at night. Such stories led some to speculate that the *k'la* of the dead, or *loh k'sah*, the "owner of the *loh*," were upset because people kept taking their things. Such apprehensions were at once political, ecological, and cosmological in nature.

So, when the monk first came to Ta K'Thwee Duh to visit the two Bah Hpaw households, Hpu Hka Hsoo requested that he also help them protect both Way Pgha and the watershed forest along the *loh*. Hpu Hka Hsoo had seen how Thai monks wrapped their robes around trees to protect them from logging and hoped something similar could be done for the forests of Way Pgha and the *loh*. Through this ritual, a forest comes under the encompassing protection of the Buddha. Hpee Luh described how the monk agreed to help and began by ripping up several strips of a saffron-orange monk's robe. He then proceeded to chant a prayer forty times, one time for each of his forty years of life. These robes were given to Hpu Hka Hsoo with strict instructions that he wrap them around trees at the four corners of the *loh*. Because Way Pgha was a much larger area than the *loh*, he instructed Hpu Hka Hsoo to only wrap robes around the trees surrounding the porcupine burrows, to ensure that at least this area was protected. Hpu Hka Hsoo then hung warning signs stating, variously, *pgha tah* (protected/prohibited forest) and *ta hpoe khah t'mee lah lah, aw t'ghay, ma thee t'ghay*, roughly translating to "it is prohibited to eat or kill any living creature."

The ritual was initially a resounding success. Tales circulated among households in the village about another area that the monk had protected in this manner. In this area a man defied the ban on hunting, later falling off the roof of his house and breaking his spine. As a consequence, people in Ta K'Thwee Duh Kaw and the surrounding area dared not kill so much as an insect when walking through the watershed forest around the *loh* and the protected areas of Way Pgha.

Despite the initial success of the monk's protection ritual—finally achieving the common goal of protecting these two heavily forested areas from overexploitation—some villagers became increasingly vocal in their criticism of the initiative. They openly voiced their discomfort with the notion that their forests were now effectively under the protective influence of foreign Buddhist monks and worried about the implications of doing this. The ceremony conducted by the monk with strips of robes is better known as "tree ordination." Through fastening a strip of blessed robe to a tree, it effectively becomes a Buddhist monk. The trees and the area around them are protected since anyone who attempts to cut them down or kill animals near them was now technically assaulting a Buddhist monk, a serious offense.

The chorus of discontent reached fever pitch following the very same monk's failed attempts to build a pagoda at the top of Ta Bu Kyoh a year later. The cautionary tale of Thee Mu Hta, and its association to DKBA's split from the KNU, was increasingly tangled up with these Thai monks' attempts to construct a pagoda. Subsequently, the status of these forested areas under the protection of Buddhist monks—the trees that were now monks—also came into question. Like attempts to build a pagoda, these protected forests became implicated in this new *ta du ta yah hku* (cool/peaceful conflict).

* * *

Attempting to take care of the situation on their own, the villagers once more turned to alternative modes of politics. Having little luck enrolling the local KNU's sovereignty to aid them, they appealed to the sovereignty of the Buddhist monks, and perhaps also the Buddha himself, as a way to protect their environments. Yet, as Nicola Tannenbaum (2000) shows, such tree ordinations draw the people involved into wider religious, social, economic, and political networks across the region. Thus, in the face of a growing panic over the expansion of religious spheres as a form of ceasefire territorialization in the Mutraw highlands, the assistance of these monks was tarred with the same brush. The monks' intervention was viewed as a threat. People worried that, rather than helping to protect these forests, the monks' actions might, knowingly or otherwise, aid and abet the Tatmadaw in territorializing these uplands and dispossessing its inhabitants. In response, a group of young(ish) men from the village sought out alternatives in Thoo Hkoh/Moh La Pa Lah (animist/ancestral) practices, turning to the Ta Htee Ta Daw K'sah, the sovereign of all specters, to provide a more encompassing form of protection (see figure 8).

Making Friends with the Owner of Honesty

While, following the intervention of the monks, most villagers (sometimes begrudgingly) consented to not kill or eat any living being in the watershed forest around the *loh*, this did not extend to people from outside the *kaw*. Moreover, a great deal of disagreement and debate continued to swirl around which parts of Way Pgha they could hunt and fish in. Some people I spoke with insisted the monks' protection only covered the open rock face pockmarked with porcupine burrows or only the porcupines themselves.

FIGURE 8. Placing the forest in the hands of the highest spectral sovereign in the realm.

Others told me it was now prohibited to hunt in the forested area immediately around the burrows. The limits of the protected area remained unclear and open to much interpretation. Most chose an interpretation that best suited their needs. It also remained unclear as to what extent people could still forage and fell trees in this area.

Eventually, a group of men around my age (that is to say, early to mid-thirties at the time) whom I had grown close to and (predictably) the outspoken elder Hpu Hkee decided to nip these debates in the bud. Tired of all the squabbling and backbiting, and with no sign that the KNU would step in any time soon, one evening over several bottles of rice wine they resolved to protect these forests themselves. They agreed to do this by appealing not to monks, nor even to the *kaw k'sah*, as Hpu Hkee had done previously in relation to the "car road." Instead, they decided to "put it in the hands" of the highest spectral authority in the realm. They planned to place the forest under the protection of the Ta Htee Ta Daw K'sah, literally the owner of all honesty, who was the paramount spectral presence in these lands.

The closest I found to a generic name for the specters in their entirety and complexity was (as discussed in chapter 1) *ta taw ta loh* and the realm in which they resided as *ta taw ta loh kaw*. Given that *ta taw ta loh* can be translated as either honesty or "that which is true," a literal rendering of the realm in which they resided is "the realm of that which is true." Thus, the name Ta Htee Ta Daw K'sah translates to the "owner/lord of all that is true," intimating that this specter was the paramount owner/master over all other specters. This rendering was borne out in the way this sovereign of all spectral sovereigns was treated in everyday life.

All along these highlands, before each meal the patriarch of the household placed a small morsel of food, *may koh,* or "first rice," on the highest ledge in the house. He then whispered an invocation entreating the Ta Htee Ta Daw K'sah to join them to eat together and to protect them. The same was the case when people drank rice wine. When the first bottle of a new batch of wine was opened, the first drops—*thee koh,* or "first alcohol"—were poured into a fine bone china cup and given to the oldest man in attendance. He took the cup between his hands, holding it up to his chest and gently letting the alcohol drip onto the floor in front of him, whispering an invocation to the Ta Htee Ta Daw K'sah. He invited this specter to enjoy the first drops of alcohol, together with them, and to look over and protect them. These libations also preceded *lu ta* and other offerings: The Ta Htee Ta Daw K'sah was invited to drink first, followed by the other specters, in order of precedence, and then finally the humans. The Ta Htee Ta Daw K'sah, the elders explained to me, as the most senior and most important presence, always went first. This spectral sovereign, they explained, was akin to Y'wa. However, Y'wa left the human realm to take his place in *moh koh* (heaven/the firmament), relinquishing his influence over day-to-day life on earth. The Ta Htee Ta Daw K'sah, by contrast, was immanent in all things and saw everything: "It is all around you and in your mind," I was often told.[3] This led elders such as Hpu Gay to describe this spectral sovereign of sovereigns as synonymous with *nay suh,* or nature itself.[4]

Just as with the other spectral persons that inhabited and crowded these possessed landscapes, offerings to the Ta Htee Ta Daw K'sah were a way to *ray daw,* "make friends with" or "work together with" them. As a common adage, regularly recited by elders, went:

> If you want to eat the lizard egg, you must make friends with the termite mound.
> If you want to eat the mushrooms, you must make friends with the fallen log.
> If you want good fortune/good things [*ta ghay ta wa*], you must make friends with the elders.

Hpu Gay elaborated on this adage explaining that, just as one must "make friends" with the environments and elders, one must make and maintain good relations with spectral sovereigns in order to have good health and a good harvest. So "we have to help each other," he concluded. Sharing food and alcohol, as one does with neighbors, engendered a "friendship" that wove people, specters, and ecologies together.

* * *

Such concerted efforts to make friends with these spectral sovereigns, and the landscapes they possessed, bear a family resemblance to Eleana Kim's (2022) notion of "making peace with nature" in the demilitarized zone (DMZ) between the two Koreas. Akin to Kim's work, "making friends" intimated a less anthropocentric and more open-ended approach to peacebuilding, which resonated with cosmopolitical orientations embracing a myriad of political actors, human and otherwise. In this light, it becomes clear that these acts of "making friends" were highly political endeavors of interminable positioning and counter-positioning. Accordingly, what I found most striking in the events described above was the way in which, by "making friends" through making offerings to the Ta Htee Ta Daw K'sah, these highlanders were also effectively maneuvering themselves to be better positioned vis-à-vis this spectral sovereign to make demands upon it.

As described in chapter 3, relations between spectral sovereigns were arranged in an unsettled nesting hierarchy, wherein the Ta Htee Ta Daw K'sah was the most senior. This arrangement allowed for considerable wiggle room for positioning, not only for the more junior spectral sovereigns but also for the humans who propitiated them. As is the case in Myanmar more generally, hierarchical superiority implies not only power over those in subordinate positions but also obligations to them, to protect and provide for them (Keeler 2017, 22). Indeed, across Southeast Asia, sovereignty is commonly rooted in the ruler's responsibility to provide for the other (Tan 2019). Consequently, by positioning themselves within this hierarchy, while at the very bottom rung, people were better able to make demands on their spectral sovereigns: to provide for them, help their crops grow, and offer them protection from harm. From this vantage point, the villagers in Ta K'Thwee Duh could then call upon the Ta Htee Ta Daw K'sah to bring these forests under its sovereignty and thus also its protection.

Putting Environments in Spectral Hands

Following the growing discontent in the village at the prospect that some of their trees had become ordained monks, this group of young(ish) men leaped into action. Rather than calling a meeting at the headman's house, they went door-to-door. At each household they explained that they intended to "put the forests in the hands of the Ta Htee Ta Daw K'sah," as they put it, asking them for their consent. When the villagers overwhelmingly assented to this plan, these men, together with Naw Paw and myself, set out from the village. With two cans of paint and numerous bottles of alcohol clinking in our bags, we made our way to the forests to place them under the sovereignty and protection of the Ta Htee Ta Daw K'sah. We began at the *loh*, which was closest to the village, and completed the process in Way Pgha a week later. On the trip to the *loh*, all the men donned matching red and white Karen shirts since (as noted in the introduction) it was said that the ancestors preferred that people wore "Pwakanyaw clothes." In Way Pgha, however, both Hpa Kha Pa and Hpu Hkee, who joined us for this trip, wore T-shirts with the core ambition of the Salween Peace Park emblazoned on them.

These shirts were handed out at the Salween Peace Park consultation meeting in December 2016. The front bore the words, written in English and Pwakanyaw, "Keeping ancestral territories, nature stewardship, peace and development in Indigenous people's hands." All but one person in this party, like me, had attended the consultation meeting in the regional capital Deh Bu Noh the previous year to learn more about the peace park. At this meeting, KESAN activists and KFD officers had collectively encouraged the villagers to protect their environments. Furthermore, these officers detailed how one way people could do this was by creating community forests in their *kaw*. However, while clearly buoyed by these words, these men continued to express considerable skepticism toward the Salween Peace Park itself; they worried about how its implementation on the ground might affect their day-to-day lives.

Each trip followed a similar sequence of events but was most elaborate in the larger Way Pgha area. Upon arriving at a hut on the edge of Way Pgha, we began by painting new warning signs in gaudy orange paint. Like those hung up by Hpu Hka Hsoo several years earlier, each sign declared "Protected forest: Prohibited to eat or kill any living creature." With the signs painted, we set out into the forests proper, stopping at the border. Here Hpa Kha Pa made a notch, then nailed the first sign to a tree with his machete. After observing our handiwork for a few moments, Naw Paw and the men posed with the other signs, staring gravely down the lens of my camera. When he was not affixing signs to trees, Hpa Kha Pa filmed everything on his mobile phone.

Following the obligatory photoshoot, we all crouched down, facing the same direction. Hpu Hkee explained that we had to face *mu taw* (east) when praying to the Ta Htee Ta Daw K'sah. "*Mu taw* means 'where the sun rises,' and is the place of growing and development. You must always face in this direction if you want *ta ghay ta wah* [good things] to happen," he insisted. Producing two bottles of rice wine from his shoulder bag, Hpa Kha Pa filled two cups, passing one to Hpu Hkee. The two men then began a long invocation and prayer, calling on the names of the Ta Htee Ta Daw K'sah (who was known by many names) to ask for an extension of a special protection to this area of Way Pgha. The others in attendance clasped their hands together, fingers splayed, and eyes firmly shut (although I had to peek to follow their actions). After the libations were completed, the cups were passed around so each of us could take a sip, before they were returned to Hpa Kha Pa and Hpu Hkee. Following this prayer, we drank normally, chatting and joking around. When we had emptied the two bottles, we scrambled down into the forest proper, pushing our way through thickets of double-barbed rattan, trudging through streams and waterfalls, to reach the different spots where Hpu Hka Hsoo had affixed strips of the monk's robe. At each stop a new sign was hung, with great care taken to not disturb the robe itself, and the old signs that had been effaced by the elements were rewritten. Rather than replacing older forms of protection, an additional layer was placed over them.

Each time we affixed a sign to a tree, we gathered again and repeated the round of libations, invocations, and prayers to the Ta Htee Ta Daw K'sah, not leaving until we had drained the bottle of alcohol. We repeated this process six times in total (and four times in the *loh*). This event was a jubilant affair, no doubt facilitated by the copious amounts of alcohol we imbued. We regularly stopped at particularly scenic areas, such as a tiered waterfall, where Hpa Kha Pa and I were instructed to take photographs. Once more, they held up their signs and looked deadly serious, only to burst into fits of laughter as Naw Paw and I struggled valiantly to climb the steep embankments and wade up to our knees in the small stream at the bottom of the forest—tumbling, scrambling, puffing, and panting as we progressed.

When all the signs were hung, the prayers uttered, and the alcohol exhausted, we staggered home again through forests and fields. In the following days and weeks, I found that much of the disagreement and debate around the extent of Way Pgha that was protected had dissipated. With both Way Pgha and the *loh* "in the hands of the Ta Htee Ta Daw K'sah," a broad consensus emerged that it was prohibited to hunt in both these forests and that terrible consequences would hound anyone who attempted to disturb them.

* * *

Through these actions, rather than supplanting one another, these different modes of politics were layered, one over the other. This could be seen in how, when experimenting with Indigenous modes of conservation to protect the two forests, the men took great care not to disturb the monks' robes and the old signs. Rather than removing them, they wrote upon former forms of protection (quite literally in the case of the signs), layering an additional mode of sovereignty on top of the robes and signs. This could also be discerned in how the men wore KESAN T-shirts when protecting Way Pgha. This was less a full-throated endorsement of the Salween Peace Park writ large (especially given their continued reservation) than a way of pragmatically layering or stacking different modes of politics, one upon the other. In this manner, this jumble of divergent forms of sovereignty and politics temporarily became aligned to achieve the same goal. This practice of layering or piling many modes of politics upon one another resembles a palimpsest or pentimento on which new layers are applied, but imprints of earlier versions continue to be discerned underneath (cf. McConnachie 2014; Simpson 2014, 25; Tsing, Deger et al. 2024, 8).

Through these actions, the specters once more intervened and became interwoven with human affairs. For the time being at least, these forests had been successfully protected; the sovereignty of the Ta Htee Ta Daw K'sah had transformed these areas into de facto locally defined community forests—and pockets of autonomy. This was where the story ended for me. I left a few weeks after Way Pgha was placed under the protection of this spectral sovereign. Three years later, the revenant of war returned to these highlands. Only time will tell how these in situ experiments in drawing on spectral sovereignty to protect the environment will play out in the future.

INTERSTITIAL SPACES OF CONVIVIALITY AND AUTONOMY

Much like the case of the KNU-backed road constructed along the Bu Thoe ridge, there was scant evidence of the villagers in Ta K'Thwee Duh "evading" or positioning themselves "against" the state (Clastres 1987; Scott 2009) through their efforts to protect the *loh* and Way Pgha. On the contrary, they repeatedly turned to the KNU state, entreating them for help, and engaged in negotiations with them—just as they did with spectral sovereigns. These highlands were spaces of conviviality, between humans, specters, and the landscapes they possessed and between different modes of politics.

The Mutraw hills were, as I have stressed throughout, located in a contact zone, at the interstices between states, locked in continual asymmetrical negotiations. Contact zones, however, are not only spaces of inherent violence and negotiation. They are also sites of play and experimentation (Haraway 2007) and sites of intimacy and dependency (Faier 2009, 12; Wilson 2019, 715;

Yeoh and Willis 2005): spaces for making friends and good relations. I grasp the intimacy and dependency inherent in such interstitial spaces in terms of conviviality, in the sense of "living-with."

In his definition of *conviviality*, Ivan Illich eschews the common understandings of the word in English that "now seeks the company of tipsy jollyness" ([1973] 1975, 12–13). He favored the more austere meaning of *eutrapelia*, taken from Aristotle and Aquinas, of being skilled in conversation. I, on the contrary, find the sense of "tipsy jollyness" rather befitting here. Bearing in mind that the term *conviviality* in English derives from the Latin word *convivium*, or "a feast," describing practices of *ray daw*, making friends in terms of feasting and drinking together with other humans and spectral persons in a state of "tipsy jollyness" seems rather apt. Conviviality also connotes a sense of cohabitation and interaction that, in its radical openness, offers a measure of distance from identity (Gilroy 2004, xi) while also rejecting divisions between humans and their environments (Büscher and Fletcher 2020, 160–61).

Following Bram Büscher and Robert Fletcher, I grasp conviviality, more specifically, as the ongoing action of the "building of long-lasting, engaging and open-ended relationships with nonhumans and ecologies" (2020, 164). As argued above, the work of creating conviviality does not demand that the different parties must become alike, or even have a common interest, in order to come into relation. This sense of conviviality, or cosmopolitical peace (Kim 2022; Latour 2004), as I have shown, extended beyond brokering convivial and peaceful relation between humans, specters, and ecologies; it also embraced engendering good relations between different modes of politics.

As the civil war wound down toward the end of the 2010s, these highlands were becoming a space for staging encounters with different modes of politics and sovereignties. By experimenting with placing their forest "in the hands of the Ta Htee Ta Daw K'sah" (the sovereign of all spectral sovereigns) to protect them, the people of Ta K'Thwee Duh were also opening up small pockets of autonomy. Much like the sovereignty of the patchworks of *kaw* lands ultimately ruled over by the *kaw k'sah*, the aim of these experiments in Indigenous conservation was neither to set up a counter-state nor to cause the state to wither away but instead to generate what Simon Critchley refers to as an "interstitial distance *within* the state territory" (2007, 92). As I shall explore closer in the epilogue to this book, these practices gestured toward highly relational modes of autonomy (cf. Ong, *Stalemate*, 2023). Such acts of local self-determination, while not their intention, occasionally coincided with and augmented the KNU's over seventy-year struggle for greater autonomy in southeast Myanmar.

In the next and final chapter, I turn my attention to the Salween Peace Park itself to explore how it was purposely building on these fleeting moments of connection between different modes of politics in the Mutraw hills. By tapping into Indigenous practices of possessing landscapes, and these budding experiments in conservation and autonomy, the activists behind the Salween Peace Park were prefiguring radically new modes of conservation and self-determination—what I call liberation conservation.

SIX

Liberation Conservation

Messing with the Scales of Conservation and Revolution

It is not correct to call us rebels; we are not rebellious. However, like our parents before us, we *are* revolutionaries.

—DOH K'OH, AN ACTIVIST WORKING
ON THE SALWEEN PEACE PARK

IN this final chapter, I take a closer look at how Indigenous modes of ownership and sovereignty, and small-scale experiments with conservation and autonomy, were being rescaled into a sprawling (6,747 km²) protected area in the Mutraw highlands known as the Salween Peace Park. Through conversations with the activists behind it, all belonging to the Karen Environmental and Social Action Network, and by analyzing the documents they (co)produced, I explore how the idea of a peace park emerged and how it was enacted in the law and on the ground. In this exploration I show how these activists worked simultaneously bottom-up and top-down. They worked closely with both Indigenous people, rescaling their situated cosmologies and practices to a large-scale conservation zone, and with the Karen National Union, and occasionally Myanmar, state policy makers, lobbying to create a gap in the legal landscape for the Salween Peace Park to flourish. In the process, these activists were messing with the geographic and political scales of conservation and revolution and prefiguring alterative futures that unsettled and subverted established notions of what peace parks and self-determination should look like.

This large-scale experiment in conservation and autonomy worked in concert with the KNU, the Salween Peace Park dovetailing with and extending the KNU's protracted struggle for self-determination. The people working on the Salween Peace Park, such as the activist quoted above, saw themselves as revolutionaries, carrying on the fight of their foremothers and fathers. As the white hot "heat" of armed conflict dissipated during Myanmar's transitional decade, from 2011 to 2021, the struggle for greater self-determination was increasingly enacted by other means. To better capture the revolutionary zeal of the Salween Peace Park, I coin the term *liberation conservation*.

One knock-on effect of bundling conservation together with revolution was that the Salween Peace Park departed markedly from standard models of peace parks, and indeed of large-scale conservation projects in general. Peace parks can be found all across the globe and are generally understood as "transfrontier conservation areas" or "transborder protected areas." Their guiding principle is to cultivate peace between different groups of (warring) people through encouraging them to cooperate in the conservation of an area that straddles a boundary they share (Ali 2007; Büscher 2013; Watson 2014). But the Salween Peace Park straddled no border, and the cooperation it promoted was largely limited to coordination between different departments and townships of the KNU. Rather than seeing this as a grave misunderstanding on the part of KESAN, I show how this mismatch aligned with their pragmatic politics, leveraging the different interpretations of a peace park to appeal to various groups at the same time—and unsettling what a peace park is and can be in the process. This all began when the activists were looking for a way to combine their different conservation and lobbying activities and, as they were fond of saying, started "thinking bigger."

"THINKING BIGGER"

The KESAN office was ensconced in a residential area down a maze of small side streets on the outskirts of Chiang Mai. The first time I visited the office I managed to get hopelessly lost on the way. I arrived over an hour late, dripping in sweat, my brain pickled from cycling around in circles in the midday sun. After cooling off a little in their air-conditioned meeting room, and after the activists had finished cracking jokes about my sense of direction, or lack thereof, I attempted to pitch a research collaboration with them. I began by describing their work in the Mutraw hills as a type of "insurgent conservation." Before I could finish my spiel, one of the leading activists, Ta Thoo, who sat behind a laptop adorned with stickers of KNU logos and Karen flags, interjected. He asserted that they are rather hostile to words such as *insurgent* and *rebel* due to the thorny connotations they have gathered over the decades of armed conflict in southeast Myanmar.[1]

James, a North American who described himself as a consultant to KESAN, his hair pulled back into long black ponytail, added that "I want to make it clear that KESAN is not working in parallel to the KNU. We work very much with the KNU. This work should be seen as part of the revolution, part of the struggle." He went on to elaborate how KESAN's efforts to protect the biodiversity of the Mutraw District of the Karen State came from within KNU's Karen Forestry Department KFD. Their conservation work in Mutraw sprang largely from the KFD's definition of a "protected landscape" (that they, in turn, appear to have adopted from the International Union for Conservation of Nature, or IUCN).[2] Ta Thoo continued that, in working from within the Forestry Department, the vast majority of their activities consisted of lobbying the KNU on land rights issues and how best to govern forest lands. Indeed, as a Thai researcher, Eh, who had worked closely with KESAN for some years, put it succinctly, "KESAN is more of a technical body [of the KNU] that deals with conservation issues." After putting this issue to bed, Ta Thoo went on to detail their current big conservation project in the Mutraw hills, the Salween Peace Park.

Looking up from his computer screen again after furiously typing, Ta Thoo explained to me how the first seeds of the peace park were sown in 2015 when they "started establishing wildlife sanctuaries and began to think bigger." They experimented with ways to combine all their smaller conservation and development projects in this area with their work protecting and promoting Indigenous *kaw* governance systems prevalent in southeast Myanmar in order to create a larger conservation zone. By working from within the KNU, they lobbied policymakers to compose and amend laws that would allow the Salween Peace Park to take root.

Ta Thoo went on to state that the Salween Peace Park was "one of the ways to work on the federal situation." However, he quickly added that it was "just an idea. A local solution that could not be applied in all places." He then concluded that the Salween Peace Park "is part of our movement to claim land and control this land as we are Karen."

* * *

Ta Thoo's talk of "thinking bigger" gestured toward the way KESAN was experimenting, stitching together its work lobbying the KNU and establishing smaller conservation zones in the Mutraw hills with the Indigenous *kaw* land possession practices (explored in chapters 2 and 3) in order to compose the Salween Peace Park. Glancing back at the map of this protected area presented in the introduction to this book, we see how these processes were taking shape. KESAN has spent decades laboring to create wildlife sanctuaries, to reaffirm (colonial-era) reserve forests, and to establish locally managed community forests. Through the Salween Peace Park, all these different patches of land were woven together with *kaw* or "customary territories" to create a peace park.

At its heart, the Salween Peace Park, much like each *kaw*, was itself a patchwork of different lands—that is it say, patches of heterogeneous yet related lands, bundled together to form a delineated space (see chapter 2; Tsing, Mathews, and Bubandt 2019). "Thinking bigger" for these activists entailed drawing these heterogeneous types of land together to form a contiguous space that would act as an Indigenous-run protected area, 6,747 km2 across. For scale, this makes the Salween Peace Park a little larger than the Everglades National Park in the United States and little under half the size of the Serengeti National Park in Tanzania. Akin to sister conservation projects in the south of the country (see chapter 4), this protected area in the Mutraw District of southeast Myanmar strived to push back against growing ceasefire territorialization.

By "thinking bigger" the activists behind the Salween Peace Park were also thinking across geographical and political scales. They were resisting threats of dispossession by "adapting"—that is to say, translating, mapping, and also rescaling—small-scale situated Indigenous practices, such as *kaw* lands, into a wider (trans)regional project. The peace park was weaving together conservation with a small *c*—which Terese Gagnon (2024; see also Nazarea 2005) describes as sensory and embodied practices of making good relations with landscapes—with Conservation with a capital *C*, of more formalized top-down efforts to create protected areas. In the process, the activists were building peace and autonomy by opening up a space for and prefiguring alternative modes of federalism that emerged from Indigenous land possession practices. The centrality of situated Indigenous land possession practices, and the way they were translated and rescaled into key aspects of the sprawling Salween Peace Park, becomes particularly salient in its official charter.

The introduction in the Salween Peace Park charter reads, "The Salween Peace Park is a grassroots people-centered alternative to the previous Myanmar government and foreign companies' plans for ecologically destructive and socially inequitable development in the Salween River basin." To this end, "the charter finds its inspiration in the core of the Indigenous Karen way of life, namely a worldview that sees land, forests, waters, and people, as inseparable. . . . The charter represents an adaption of the beliefs and values that the Indigenous Karen people have held for generations to a more structured system of governance and management" (Mutraw District et al. 2018, 4).

CLEARING A LEGAL SPACE FOR THE PEACE PARK

At the crack of dawn on Christmas Eve 2016, I joined the lion's share of the KESAN staff from their Chiang Mai office, along with several of their non-Karen consultants and interns, on the long car, boat, and tractor ride to Deh Bu Noh, the administrative capital of the KNU's Mutraw District in the Northern Karen State, to attend a public consultation meeting for the Salween Peace Park. It was there that I first met the three men whom I would later accompany as they attempted to protect their forest from overexploitation. Following the official opening of the public consultation meeting, the draft charter of the Salween Peace Park was read aloud, in full, to the crowd assembled in the large meeting hall at the edge of town. It was read to participants who had traveled far and wide from nearly all areas that fall inside the park's borders. This was so everyone in attendance, including those unable to read, could comment on and suggest amendments to the document before it was finalized. Following the consultation meeting, the charter was revised again (this was the second of three consultation meetings), and the final document was later presented at a series of smaller meetings followed by an election, held at the seat of each village tract within the Salween Peace Park area, throughout 2018. At each of these elections, representatives from each community that would become part of the peace park, 75.1 percent of the voting age population, voted in favor of endorsing the charter. On December 18 of the same year, the Salween Peace Park was officially established, becoming a legal entity in KNU law (albeit, this status was less clear in Myanmar state law; KESAN 2019). This landmark event was reached through a long, drawn-out process of clearing a space in the legal landscape where the Salween Peace Park could flourish.

KEY EVENTS RELATED TO THE SALWEEN PEACE PARK

2015	The KESAN activists begin "thinking bigger" about a protected area encompassing most of the Mutraw District New KNU land law launched, enshrining *kaw* lands
2016	First consultation meeting for the Salween Peace Park, followed by an international press release Second consultation meeting

2017	Beginning of test phase for *kaw* land titles Salween Peace Park becomes official KNU policy
2018	Third consultation meeting, followed by election Salween Peace Park is officially established
2022	Area expanded to include nine new village tracts in the Thaton/Doo Tha Htoo District

Chartering a Course to Conservation

Reading aloud this over-forty-page document, with continual breaks for questions and comments, was a laborious and time-consuming process. As I stood just outside the grand meeting hall where it was being presented, I noticed how many of the participants' patience quickly wore thin. People often slopped off to look for food, tobacco, betel, a place to snooze, or all of the above. But listening in, I heard how the charter opened with a bold "Preamble":

> We, the Indigenous Karen People of Mutraw,
> Recognizing our roots that transcend national boundaries;
> Respecting the natural world, which has sustained our people for generations;
> Honoring the memory of those who have struggled against all forms of injustice against the people and the Earth;
> In order to create and sustain a lasting peace in our lands, protect and maintain the environmental integrity of the Salween River basin, preserve our unique cultural heritage, and further the self-determination of our people;
> Do enact and establish:
> The Charter of the Salween Peace Park. (**Mutraw District et al. 2018, 6**)

Following the apparent nod to the preamble to the United States Constitution in evoking "we the people," the charter goes on to explicitly lay out that the "legitimacy of governance shall be determined collectively by the people of the Salween Peace Park" and "not disproportionately influenced or unilaterally determined by the KNU Mutraw District government or the Salween Peace Park Governing Committee" (Mutraw District et al. 2018, 12). Moreover, as Indigenous people, the residents of the Salween Peace

Park "have the right to manage and govern their own lands and the natural resources above and below the ground that are inalienably part of Indigenous territory," since "customary rights to ancestral domain take precedence over governance systems that have excluded the voices and perspectives of Indigenous Karen people" (11). The general thrust of the charter was that the Salween Peace Park should "devolve management responsibilities to decentralized committees that will be responsible for the day-to-day management of the collective and public affairs of the Salween Peace Park at the village level" (19).

Continuing to listen carefully, in the final chapter on land and land ownership, it became clear that terms used throughout, such as *decentralized committees*, *Indigenous territory*, and *ancestral domain*, were differing ways of referring to the practices and cosmologies tied to *kaw* lands, which I examine in part 1 of this book. In Article 107 (Section 5.1), the charter elaborates that "the land in the Salween Peace Park that are organized under the Indigenous *kaw* system shall be considered as land owned by the villages or communities that forms the *kaw*" (Mutraw District et al. 2018, 36). Consequently, while not stated explicitly, it was evident here that *kaw*, and the particular modes of ephemeral and nesting ownership and spectral sovereignty implicated in them, were not only "an integral part of Indigenous Karen culture" (37) but also integral to the workings of the Salween Peace Park as a whole. The "*kaw* customary lands" served as the backbone of the Salween Peace Park, enshrined as pockets of local autonomy. In effect, much like similar movements, the charter translated Indigenous practices and cosmologies, such as those tied to *kaw*, to forms that were more legible to both states and international conservation groups.

The charter rescaled Indigenous practices from small-scale situated politics (conservation with a small *c*) into (trans)national-scale environmental governance policy (Conservation with a big *C*). One practical example of this process of translation and rescaling comes in the section addressing access and use of—that is to say, relationships with—forests. Here, the charter dictates that "the integrity of sacred forest sites is inviolable, and the people of Salween Peace Park, regardless of faith or ancestral background, shall respect existing customary rules and regulations against access and use" (Mutraw District et al. 2018, 29).

By declaring the inviolability of such "sacred forest sites," the authors of the text intimated the patches of the landscape regularly referred to in the Mutraw hills as *ta thoo ta pgho* or simply *hsoo*, "potent" or "strong." As discussed in previous chapters, potent places such as the *loh* (glossed in the charter as "spirit dwelling sites"; see Mutraw District et al. 2018, 36) and Hpu

Noh Noh Deh, or "the path that drinks your blood," were wedded to day-to-day practices of treating the landscape as possessed—both occupied and owned by a plethora of spectral presences. Consequently, people refrained from clearing patches of forest in, and sometimes even attempted to avoid walking through, such potent places out of fear they might vex its spectral owner/s. Knowledge of these places was passed on not only via oral histories and *hta* (dramatic poems) but also through a robust set of *ta du ta htu*, or orally transmitted taboos. The charter translated and rescaled *ta du ta htu* into "customary rules and regulations" that it demands all inhabitants of the Salween Peace Park "shall respect" and that local rules and regulations should be determined "with respect to Indigenous Karen customs and traditions" (36).

Indeed, as the charter explicitly states from the start, it "finds its inspiration in" and builds on "an adaption" of Indigenous practices and cosmologies, which it attempts to marshal into "a more structured system of governance and management" (Mutraw District et al. 2018, 4). That is to say, akin to the burgeoning movements in Tanintharyi explored in chapter 4, the Salween Peace Park translated Indigenous practices and created counter-maps to push back against ceasefire territorialization and to repossess the landscape. This process of translation was, as I have shown, a deeply pragmatic affair, focused on making Indigenous land possession practices legible to national and transnational actors by making them "more structured." In doing so, these "adaptions" of Indigenous practices also rescaled them, from micro-level day-to-day politics to macro-level units of environmental governance, bolstering the legitimacy of the peace park.

KESAN was not simply scaling-up *kaw* to KNU state–level legal entities; it was constantly working multidirectionally and across scales. Delving deeper into the process of writing *kaw* into law, anthropologist Emily Hong (2017, 227) demonstrates how KESAN was upending common approaches that tend to oppose top-down legal wrangling to bottom-up resistance. In the 2015 update of KNU's land laws (that I address in the next section), for instance, KESAN built on micro-level *kaw* politics and simultaneously made explicit citations to macro-level laws—such as the United Nations Declaration on the Rights of Indigenous Peoples and the Voluntary Guidelines on the Responsible Governance of Tenure of Land, Fishers and Forests (from the Food and Agriculture Organization of the United Nations)—greatly strengthening the legal standing of *kaw* politics in the process (Hong 2017, 233).

The charter of the Salween Peace Park similarly relies heavily on multiscalar movements, making citations to other foundational documents. Along with the United States Constitution, intimated in the preamble, it constantly refers back to the United Nations Declaration on the Rights of Indigenous Peoples—especially to Article 3 on Indigenous peoples' "right to self-determination" (UN 2007). As the introduction proclaims, "the Charter *enshrines the right* of the indigenous Karen people to self-determination" (Mutraw District et al. 2018, 4; my emphasis). Paying attention to the strategic ways scale was deployed sheds light on the procedural ways in which scales were constantly made and remade and the manner in which the global and local were "mutually reproduced" (Hong 2017, 229; Milne 2022, 20; West 2006).

In the context of this book, I refer to this process of continual negotiation, of making and unmaking scales, as "messing with scale." In this framing I highlight the highly pragmatic and playful ways in which the activists deployed scale to suit the situation at hand, in a manner that tended to unsettle and subvert them. Through messing with scales, *kaw* were not simply scaled-up into legible, largely unchangeable, and scalable units of governance that could be rolled out in other areas of southeast Myanmar, as is often the case in big Conservation projects (Milne 2022, 14–15; Tsing 2012). A far more complex and messier picture was emerging. As Ta Thoo reminded me, the Salween Peace Park was "just an idea. A local solution that could not be applied in all places."

In accordance with the charter, much of the land that fell within the Salween Peace Park was grasped as owned and controlled first and foremost by the people of the given *kaw*. It was they who determined local rules and regulations of land tenure and use. By implication, Indigenous modes of ownership and sovereignty—ultimately resting in the hands of the *k'sah* and the other spectral presences discussed in part 1 of this book—were elicited. Thus, local rules and regulations, or *ta du ta htu*, were always "determined" by humans in relation to the appetites and gripes of their spectral sovereigns.[3] This militated against any notion of transforming *kaw* into scalable units of environmental governance that could be "rolled out" across southeast Myanmar.

The translation and rescaling of *kaw* carried out throughout the charter followed the activists' pragmatic politics: as a practical way to simultaneously bolster legitimacy through appealing to different scales while also unsettling and subverting these scales in the process. The activists were oriented not only toward countering the Myanmar state and affiliated investors but also to prefiguring new scales and new modes of politics that embodied a form of self-determination.

As many of the KESAN activists continued to stress to me, however, the charter and the Salween Peace Park itself did not materialize out of thin air. Both this legal document and the Indigenous-run protected area more generally cannot and should not be considered separately from the several decades of activism KESAN has put into supporting Pwakanyaw communities in both sustaining themselves and protecting their environments and in their continued advocacy for these communities, lobbying the KNU to build "good governance." The Salween Peace Park project emerged out of and was built upon a great deal of work in the background by KESAN activists clearing a space within the KNU legal landscape where this large-scale conservation project could take root. This legal gap was opened through lobbying the KNU aggressively both to shape land laws and to begin awarding collective land titles to *kaw* lands. Only then could the Salween Peace Park eventually blossom.

Lobbying, Land Laws, and Collective Tenure Titles

Spending time with these Chiang Mai–based activists, I learned that many of their efforts were invested in lobbying the KFD. Predominantly, this lobbying was conducted through the KNU's Central Land Committee, where several KESAN staff members had significant influence, and was foundational for the establishing of the Salween Peace Park. One of the first fruits of these combined labors came in the current land policy, officially approved by the KNU's highest legal body, the Executive Committee, in December 2015.

The current KNU land policy came about through many years of hard graft, petitioning local government members and working closely with external (transnational) activists and academics. One tangible outcome of this work was that KESAN staff were largely fluent not only in technical terminology but also academic terminology and current debates. Consequently, they were able to bring their combined engagement with other activists, academics, and non-government organizations such as the Transnational Institute to bear on the reworking of the land policy. This sustained contact left a deep impression on the final document. Traces of the activists' engagements with the wider world could be discerned in the ways ownership was dealt with explicitly in the newest iteration of the land policy, whereas previous versions skirted around the subject.

Take the first land policy from 1974. Here the KNU decreed, "the land must be in our hands." The 2005 update, however, proclaimed, "land to the native people." In the 1974 version, it was unclear who the possessive determiner "our" referred to: the policy's authors (i.e., KNU leaders) or the Indigenous people themselves? In the 2005 update, it remained opaque as to what specific rights were implied in stating that the land was "to" the Indigenous people: to use, to borrow, to buy? It was therefore striking that the newest iteration from 2015, a document strongly shaped by the influence of KESAN and its external activist-academic interlocutors, placed ownership firmly at the center.

The current land policy opens by proclaiming "people are owner [sic] of the land" (KNU 2015, 2). Delving deeper into this document, we find that its engagement with issues of ownership goes far beyond simple window dressing. In the following lines, this policy document states that since "land policies are never neutral" and as such "necessarily transform the status quo," it was essential to take a point of departure in *"socially-legitimate* customary occupation and use rights" (2). This point is repeated and reinforced throughout. The 2015 land policy then represents one of the first concerted efforts to translate and rescale on-the-ground land possession practices—that is to say, *kaw* politics and spectral sovereignty—into official KNU policy and law. In the current land policy, KESAN's twin priorities of environmental conservation and the protection of customary rights and practices are explicitly entwined for the first time. These labors to "think bigger" were finally bearing fruit. The deep imprint of KESAN's advocacy becomes clearer upon reading the KNU land policy document from 2015.

In Article 3.6 on "KNU Authorities-Managed Public Purpose Land," for example, there is a specific article on "Reserve Land" (Article 3.6.2) that effectively enshrines "Wildlife Protected Areas," "Reserved Forest," and "National Park Areas" into KNU law (KNU 2015, 34). This article dictates that these categories of land can only be established by free, prior, and informed consent (FPIC) together with the "customary authorities." Speaking with KESAN staff, they explained that the wording of this paragraph helped convince the KNU Executive Committee to accept the Salween Peace Park as official KNU policy in 2017. The peace park in effect fell into the category of "National Park," established through an explicit process of FPIC, together with the "customary authorities." Simultaneously, Article 3.3 refers directly to "'*Kaw*' Lands," effectively bringing Indigenous land possession practices into the KNU legal fold:

> Land, forests, fisheries, water and other related natural resources have social, cultural, spiritual, economic, environmental and political value to indigenous peoples and other communities with *Kaw* (customary tenure) systems. KNU Authorities must recognize, respect and always take into account these non-monetized values for peoples and village communities with *Kaw* tenure systems. (KNU 2015, 28)

Through the specific wording of this article, the KNU became legally obligated not only to recognize *kaw* land possession practices in the Mutraw hills but, in certain situations, to treat them as "socially-legitimate" modes of ownership and governance. The wording of the Salween Peace Park charter was therefore largely a restatement of existing KNU policy. What I find particularly compelling about this article on the KNU's land policy is that *kaw*, as they are conceived here—as modes of land possession and as political systems—were little known, let alone a part of day-to-day practices, beyond the Mutraw hills.[4] This fact suggests that this section of the land policy was penned with this particular stretch along the lower Salween River, or perhaps even the Salween Peace Park itself, in mind. Whether this was happenstance or the result of careful planning by KESAN is, perhaps, of lesser importance than the effect the new land policy had. This new legal framework helped pave the way for the Salween Peace Park, as a "National Park" composed of *kaw* that were treated as "socially-legitimate" modes of ownership and governance, to become KNU national policy.

While the 2015 land policy may have been one of the first of KESAN's attempts to "think bigger" to yield results, it was far from the last. Rather than resting on their laurels, these activists wasted no time in using the new land policy as a wedge, to slowly open up a gap in KNU policy and law for the Salween Peace Park to take root. The next step in thinking bigger came two years later in 2017.

The KNU's official website proclaims that their policy "is National Democracy. It fully recognises and encourages private ownership."[5] Accordingly, the KNU has long issued land titles to individual household plots and paddy fields, facilitating the transfer and, indeed, sale of land. In chapter 2, I illustrate one downstream implication of this policy where, as people in the Mutraw hills began establishing their own paddy fields and applying for titles to them, local land possession practices were slowly being stretched to the breaking point. In response to these transformations, together with other activists, KESAN worked behind the scenes to induce the KFD to issue collective land titles, in the form of community forest land titles. Community forest land titles recognize the collective tenure of a local community to a demarcated forested area. Community forests entail that the communities themselves are given a large degree of latitude in formulating day-to-day rules and regulations governing access and use of these areas and their enforcement. The rules and regulations laid down by a community that hold a collective title to their land are both semi-autonomous of, and have some legal backing from, local KNU and KFD authorities. While, as I demonstrate in chapter 5, the process of obtaining them was not always straightforward, this made community forest land titles highly attractive to many in the Mutraw hills. Off the back of the 2015 land policy and growing acceptance of community forest titles, KESAN pushed the KNU to extend collective land titles to *kaw* lands.

At the beginning of 2017, after years of lobbying, the KNU eventually acceded and began issuing *kaw* titles—with the proviso they start tentatively with a "test phase." This official decision allowed KESAN, together with the KFD and Karen Agriculture Department (KAD), to continue and intensify their work demarcating each *kaw* within the limits of the Salween Peace Park. The process of demarcations required careful and protracted collaboration with the inhabitants of each *kaw*. To achieve this, KESAN again worked across scales, building on the deep ties and trust they have forged with communities across the Mutraw hills over many years of extensive activist work and with KNU policy makers. Elders, activists, and experts were brought together with GPS technology to translate and map the indeterminate practices tied to *kaw* into discrete demarcated areas. Following the demarcation and mapping of each *kaw*, with the official go-ahead from the KNU, the next step (which happened after my fieldwork had ended) was for the residents to be awarded with titles to these (*kaw*) lands. This new form of tenure, much like community forests, entailed collective legal rights over the land but, beyond forested areas, also covered fallow fields, swidden patches, rivers, lakes, and mountains—indeed all territories within the *kaw*'s borders that were not individually held. Under a *kaw* land tenure title, the community themselves dictated the local rules and regulations, including the allocation of conservation areas such as community forests.

In one fell swoop, KESAN's protracted and intensive activism with local communities and their advocacy in the highest echelons of KNU governance finally culminated in a situation in which the various patches marked on the Salween Peace Park map (see map 1 in the introduction) went from purely illustrative to demonstrative of the de facto political organization of this area. These different categories of land—the reserve forests and wildlife sanctuaries, the community forests and *kaw* or "customary territories"—were gently shepherded into KNU policy in no small part through KESAN's diligent efforts.

This activism and advocacy, as I argue, emerged out of pragmatic politics of translation and constant messing with scales. KESAN simultaneously translated and messed with the scale of situated Indigenous practices, KNU policy, and global resolutions, bringing them to bear upon one another to garner legitimacy for the Salween Peace Park. These different forms of activism and advocacy were directed toward the same goal of wedging open a gap in the KNU's legal system and a physical space in the Mutraw hills to stage an encounter between different modes of politics, allowing the Salween Peace Park to take root and flourish.

In bringing together different scales—situated Indigenous land possession practices, KNU policy, and the transnational United Nations Declaration of the Rights of Indigenous People—these activists were subtly unsettling and subverting established notions of scales as self-contained, unable to form relationships with one another and arranged vertically in a neat and nested fashion (Ferguson and Gupta 2002; Tsing 2012). In doing so, they also upset notions of social movements as either top-down or bottom-up (Hong 2017). This becomes clear in the opening pages of the charter of the Salween Peace Park, where it is stated that "in the spirit of self-determination," the peace park aims to open up a space (or indeed "territory" as the charter declares) in which the Indigenous people themselves may "manage and govern their natural resources and lands" (Mutraw District et al. 2018, 3–4). These struggles to create a gap in KNU policy and a space for self-determination to flourish in the Mutraw hills became most evident on one of my last days in Chiang Mai.

On the same day that I met Saw Jonny for the last time at KESAN's main office, I learned that one of the final pieces of KESAN's ongoing struggle, to create "good governance" and clear a space in the legal landscape that would allow the Salween Peace Park to flourish, had fallen into place. Not long after Saw Jonny abruptly disappeared again, Doh K'Oh turned to me and rather casually informed me that, during the last meeting convened by the KNU's Executive Committee, the Salween Peace Park had been accepted into the KNU legal fold as official policy. As Ta Thoo had predicted in our first meeting almost a year earlier, by appealing to the KFD's policy of protected landscapes and the land policy (especially Article 3.6.2 on reserve land), this "crazy idea" (as Doh K'Oh referred to it) of an Indigenous-managed decentralized peace park had officially acceded to mainstream KNU policy, becoming part and parcel of their continued struggle for autonomy. Yet, as Ta Thoo continually stressed, the peace park itself was by no means the end goal of KESAN's combined labors. By naming this protected area a peace park, they were thinking very big indeed, gesturing toward a prefigurative politics that went far beyond both conservation and protective countermovements.

THAT WHICH WE CALL CONSERVATION: WHAT IS IN A NAME?

The ideas underpinning the Salween Peace Park sit uncomfortably alongside descriptions of peace parks in other places around the world. As mentioned above, peace parks are commonly spoken of as "transfrontier conservation areas" or "transborder protected areas." This left me to ponder: What exactly was KESAN implying by choosing to name this Indigenous-run protected area a peace park? Through my conversations with KESAN staff and their supporters I learned that the very indeterminacy and playfulness of the way they used the term *peace park* was central to the political efficacy of this protected area more generally. A conversation with the director of KESAN made this line of thinking clearer to me.

The first time I met the director was at KESAN's main office in Chiang Mai. Like many of his colleagues, he, too, sported a long ponytail, his reaching nearly all the way down his back, and he wore thin metal-framed glasses that kept slipping down his nose as he spoke, such that he was constantly pushing them up again with his index finger. Beaming as he introduced himself, he explained how they had not always envisioned the protected area along the lower Salween basin as a peace park. As Ta Thoo had mentioned earlier, when they first brainstormed how to stitch together their disparate conservation projects to their ongoing work protecting and promoting *kaw* lands to compose a wider protected area, they leaned heavily on the KNU's forest policy and the IUCN's terminology—that is, labeling it a *protected landscape*. However, they soon found such terminology too constricting for their means. The IUCN's category of "Protected Landscape" expressly aimed to "protect and sustain important landscapes/seascapes and the associated nature conservation and other values created by interactions with humans through traditional management practices."[6] In this definition, there is no provision for how these interactions would be protected and sustained in (former) war zones and heavily militarized areas, such as the Mutraw hills. The activists then began looking closer at the notion of a peace park. Thus, the origin story of the Salween Peace Park's conception was constantly reworked.

A few weeks after meeting the director, during the opening speech on the first day of the consultation meeting, I found that—not dissimilar to the highlanders' constant refashioning of colonial debris and of histories (see chapter 1)—he regularly reworked the tale of the peace park's formation to better fit the audience and situation at hand. In this particular version, he explained to the assembled crowd that KESAN first conceptualized this conservation area as a kind of wilderness (category Ib in IUCN's now defunct classification of protected areas) but, for obvious reasons, quickly found this characterization to be a poor fit. Eventually they settled on the notion of a peace park, translated into Pwakanyaw as Ta Mu Ta Hku K'Ruh (literally, pleasant-and-cool/peace garden). Much to his chagrin, the director added, Karen people often came up to him and said, "We hear that you are building a flower garden." To this he added, "I don't know where this rumor is coming from," followed by a hearty belly laugh. The last particle, *k'ruh*, usually denotes a patch of land beside a house where flowers and fruit trees are planted, or an allotment close by where fruits and vegetables for household consumption are grown—not unlike a flower garden.

When I inquired about this lexical slippage, the director conceded that it was a slightly unfortunate translation. They were unable to find a Pwakanyaw term that better encapsulated the aspirations and ideals of this project. However, as Walter Benjamin (2006, 250) argues, there is a value to "bad" translations in that they can lead to productive misunderstandings. Such lexical slippages were less errors than part and parcel of KESAN's pragmatic politics that aimed to cultivate indeterminacy as they messed with scales and evoked the "spirit of self-determination." This became most apparent when the director made public speeches about the Salween Peace Park.

As the public face of KESAN, with several decades of public speaking under his belt, the director had developed a well-rehearsed presentation of the Salween Peace Park, in both Pwakanyaw and English, which appealed to broad audiences. Each time I heard him speak about this conservation zone, he followed a similar routine, culminating in an articulation of the three core aspirations of this peace park. While in English he talked of these aspirations as "the three pillars" that the peace park rested upon, in Pwakanyaw he evoked a more poetic image. Holding up the first two fingers and thumb of his left hand so his fingertips formed a triangle, he talked to the crowd of these aspirations as the "hearthstones" that propped up this protected area. The three "hearthstones" were environmental integrity, cultural survival, and peace and self-determination.[7] The first two, to protect biodiversity and to protect Indigenous peoples' culture and livelihoods, were not entirely unexpected aspirations for a project led by a network of ecological and Indigenous activists. The final stone, however, intimated aspirations far beyond the remit of the other two.

The first two aspirations of the Salween Peace Park, taken on their own, gestured toward a protected area that resonated strongly with the IUCN's category of a "Protected Landscape," albeit a radical, bottom-up, Indigenous-run vision of this category. The third aspiration, however, by ingeniously bundling self-determination together with peace, radically refigured the whole project. While for the activists the third aspiration was what made this protected area in the Mutraw hills a peace park, this was in fact a highly unorthodox translation of the notion. By paying close attention to the discrepancy between how peace parks have been conceived previously and the aspirations of the Salween Peace Park, I hope to shed light on what the activists hoped to achieve with this radical experiment in conservation.

"Parks for Peace"

The CEO of the Peace Parks Foundation, Werner Myburgh, defined peace parks, or "transfrontier conservation areas," as a "way to 'link' those protected areas that are divided by an international boundary" (quoted in Büscher 2013, 27). The then–director general of the IUCN similarly stated that these "transboundary protected areas" should "involve a degree of cooperation across one or more boundaries, since plants and animals clearly do not recognize artificial boundaries" (Marton-LeFèvre 2007, xiii). Moreover, the South African environmental minister Pallo Jordan reiterated in his opening address to the IUCN meeting on Parks for Peace in 1997 that "the earth's environment is the common property of all humanity and creation, and what takes place in one country affects not only its neighbors, but many others well beyond its borders" (quoted in Marton-LeFèvre 2007, xiv). These various statements and the academic literature bring home how the guiding principle of the global peace park initiative is that peace between nations, ethnic groups, armies, and people can be forged through the practice of cooperating to conserve a protected area, straddling a boundary they share (Ali 2007; Büscher 2013).

Bringing this literature to bear on the Salween Peace Park project, however, we find that it straddled no borders. From its inception, the entirety of the Salween Peace Park rested within the borders of what the KNU claimed as its Mutraw District and the Karen National Liberation Army's 5th brigade (*thu kay yeh*), an area almost solely under KNU's jurisdiction. Up until 2022, when it was expanded to include nine new village tracts in the Thaton/Doo Tha Htoo District, the borders of this protected area aligned neatly with the KNU's political-economic boundaries while only partly corresponding to the ecological boundaries of the Salween River basin. The extent of cooperation involved in the Salween Peace Park was thus restricted to that between the different village tracts, townships, and political departments of the Mutraw division of the KNU, the KNLA, and the inhabitants of these highlands, human and otherwise.

When I took up this seeming incongruency with KESAN, between "standard" notions of peace parks as "transboundary protected areas" and the Salween Peace Park, James responded a little curtly that this was, of course, by no means new information to them. "But in any case," he added, what I was talking about were "international peace parks," while the project they were working on in the Mutraw District of Myanmar was a "national peace park." After quickly picking up that I was not entirely satisfied with this explanation, he changed tack. He softened his tone and explained that, in truth, "you have to do what works best." Getting to know these activists better, I encountered this highly pragmatic outlook time and time again.

The director, for example, often told of how he and some of the other activists had originally envisioned that the Salween Peace Park would straddle this great river, linking this conservation zone with the current Salawin National Park on the eastern bank in Thailand.[8] They hoped to then continue expanding the peace park outward, eventually covering the entire Salween basin, from its headwaters on the Tibetan Plateau to its mouth in the Gulf of Martaban. Given the political climate, however, a cross-border conservation zone was not yet feasible. In the meantime, the Thai government continued to forge ever closer links with their Myanmar counterparts following their "battlefields to marketplaces" strategy that began in the late 1980s (Brenner 2019, 40–46; Magee and Kelley 2009, 115), and special economic zones began cropping up all along their shared border (Aung 2023; Campbell 2018). As a result, the KESAN activists decided to begin small, first plowing ahead in Mutraw where they had the support of the KNU. With time, they planned to slowly expand this conservation zone into areas not held by the KNU when, or indeed if, the political climate shifted.

As the peace process continued to unravel, and as the ceasefire was increasingly punctuated by armed scuffles and land grabs, these activists held out little hope that the Myanmar state government would cooperate on this conservation project anytime soon. In response, they often attempted to "jump over," leap-frogging the Myanmar state "for now," seeking legitimacy for their project from the wider international community (cf. West 2006, 10). Almost as if to confirm this, the director ended our first conversation by apologizing that he had to dash off home and pack. He had to catch a flight in a few hours to Cancun in Mexico, where he was to attend the UN Biodiversity Conference (COP 13) in a panel on Biological Diversity and Conservation Monitoring.[9]

A great deal of the academic work on large-scale Conservation projects foregrounds the misunderstandings they tend to provoke, where the various actors involved grasp their aims in, at times, wildly different ways, leading to considerable conflict. In Paige West's (2006) classic monograph *Conservation Is Our Government Now*, for example, she focuses on a Conservation project in Papua New Guinea premised on the notion that biodiversity can be protected through the sustainable development of economic markets. Here, she demonstrates a fundamental disconnect whereby the NGO workers behind the protected area understood that they would get conservation from the local population in exchange for financial incentives and development, and the local population understood these exchanges as an opening for a relationship in which they would gain access to things they desperately needed, such as medicine and education. Much of West's ethnography centers on the violent conflicts this disconnect provoked and the seemingly Sisyphean task she was assigned of translating between these two groups (see also West 2005).

In the Salween Peace Park, however, the activists were actually leaning into and torquing certain misunderstandings. They found that the peace park translated differently for different actors in productive ways, allowing them to appeal to different audiences. For many Pwakanyaw speakers, Salween Peace Park as Ta Mu Ta Hku K'Ruh connoted a "flower/peace garden," evoking notions of a shared space. Furthermore, as I discuss below, a "peace garden" carries with it positive undertones of a plot of land for growing new ideas. As it so happened, these different connotations dovetailed with several of KESAN's central aims. For global Conservation organizations and other transnational groups, however, peace park implied a "transfrontier conservation area" that coincided with and reinforced their efforts to meet global development goals and targets on the protection of biodiversity and participation. While these various connotations did not mesh perfectly with the vision of the Salween Peace Park in its entirety, they did capture many important aspects of it and gestured toward a deferred future goal. It was precisely these misunderstandings of this "park for peace," including my own, that allowed KESAN to pitch the notion of the Salween Peace Park to different actors and evoke different connotations. Pragmatic translations in turn played into KESAN's ongoing messing with scale, in which they strategically deployed scale as they simultaneously upended it.

In the face of both resistance and silence from the Myanmar government, the activists once more messed with scale, leap-frogging directly from situated small-scale politics and practices, conservation with a small *c*, to the global scale of international Conservation organizations and bodies. This was done quite literally. While I had heard from Ta Thoo how KESAN was deeply engaged in a central government-led initiative in 2014 to revise state land laws (i.e., the VFV Law and Farmland Law), bar a few concessions (such as a partial recognition of customary lands), these laws continued to promote widespread land grabs and dispossession. Following these frustrated engagements with the central government, the director spoke of "jumping over" the national scale of the Myanmar state to negotiate with the UN directly at the global scale. This could be seen in the way the Salween Peace Park was hedged in global concerns for biodiversity loss and Indigenous effort to prevent it. By messing with scales, KESAN was, in process, effectively unsettling and remaking notions of how such "parks for peace" were conceived and practiced. The Salween Peace Park, therefore, outstripped notions of both "transfrontier conservation areas" and countermovements, prefiguring "a grassroots, people-centered alternative" (Mutraw District et al. 2018, 4).

PREFIGURING A KAWTHOOLEI IN MINIATURE AND "REAL FEDERAL SOLUTIONS"

What these activists were hoping to evoke by explicitly naming this conservation project a peace park becomes clearer still when the Salween Peace Park is considered alongside similar grassroots experiments in conservation, such as those addressed in chapter 4. When I discussed the Tenasserim River and Indigenous Peoples' Network's (TRIP NET) work on countermapping their landscapes with the director of KESAN, for instance, he was quick to point out that, while Saw Jonny is an old and good friend of KESAN, their two movements were of a fundamentally different kind. He took pains to point out that the Salween Peace Park played a pivotal role in KESAN's concerted efforts, in close accordance with the KNU, to generate "real federal solutions" to the ongoing peacebuilding efforts in southeast Myanmar. In the director's words, "We shall achieve this [federalism] through strong governance, not by sharing power. In this way [by sharing power] we do not have the decision-making power, allowing them [the Myanmar government/Tatmadaw] to build dams and other projects on our land. What we need is action, not debates." In laboring this point, he demonstrated that the aspirations of the Salween Peace Park went far beyond those of a peace park as they are conventionally conceived to a radically different way of understanding and practicing peace parks and conservation more generally.

The vision of this large-scale conservation project along the Salween basin was intimately entangled with, and inseparable from, the KNU's seven-decade-long struggle for greater autonomy. The ramifications of the ties between conservation and struggles for liberation crystallized for me during a long car ride with Doh K'Oh from the border back to Chiang Mai. The director had asked me to meet Doh K'Oh, one of KESAN's leading activists, who wore thick square glasses and had seemingly boundless reserves of energy, to discuss my upcoming fieldwork in the Mutraw hills. As it transpired, Doh K'Oh was (nominally at least) on "holiday" in a Thai border town, visiting his wife and children—yet still very much working. When I learned that he was there to be with his family, I tried to reschedule, only for him to insist, "It's fine, they are getting used to it by now." Thus, with his (understandably exasperated) family in tow, sitting at another table at a small café,

Doh K'Oh and I discussed suitable villages for my research. It was during this conversation that we agreed upon an area where "traditions are still strong" and that could still be reached during the height of the monsoon season. We continued our conversation on the ride back home to Chiang Mai the next day in his slick black pickup truck, but soon the topic turned to politics.

After a brief silence, Doh K'Oh turned to face me and said, "I don't know what federalism is." I was initially a little taken aback by this statement, especially given that it came from a person working so explicitly on federal solutions to armed conflict. Before I had time to comment, he pressed on, explaining in an increasingly animated fashion, how the Tatmadaw and transnational corporations were slowly "moving into areas and the war continues." Echoing a now familiar sentiment, he lamented that people were still steadily being displaced, even after armed conflict had largely abated. As he breathlessly exclaimed, "Refugees are beginning to return, but their customary lands are now palm oil or rubber plantations, and they have no way of securing their livelihoods."

After a short pause, Doh K'Oh asked rhetorically, "But what do they mean by a federal union?" The point he was alluding to, he swiftly interjected, was how can federalism work when the land slated to be "handed back," so to speak, was now occupied and effectively owned by corporations and the military? Here, he took what, as I mentioned previously, was often labeled the "hard-line" position. "They accuse us," he said—meaning the more militant sections of the KNU—"of being inflexible, yet they [the Tatmadaw] won't compromise on anything and keep demanding DDR [disarmament, demobilization, and reintegration]."[10] Now thoroughly riled up, he pressed on, referring to the Vacant Fallow and Virgin Land Law and Farmland Law: "And what is more, in their laws our fallow lands become unoccupied or waste land. Then they sell it. But it is not theirs to sell. It belongs to the Karen communities."

Building to a crescendo, he continued, "when they talk of federalism, like in the United States, they have no idea how they could actually achieve this, they just say 'it's coming, it's coming.'" This last part was accompanied by a sardonic laugh. By now rather impassioned, he added, "The way I see it, after sixty-seven, nearly sixty-eight years of war [now well over seventy years] where thousands if not tens of thousands have died, it is not okay to just give up." After a short break to catch his breath, he elaborated that, in some respects, he viewed the National Ceasefire Agreement (NCA) as a form of surrender. Yet unlike the hard-line general introduced in chapter 4, he quickly tempered this sentiment by adding, "It is not that I want fighting again. Nobody wants that to happen, but this 'national' [spitting out the word] ceasefire agreement lacks any real vision for a federal union." For him "there should be another way." He envisioned that federalism could only come about through self-governance, where the people themselves had a greater ability to decide their own destiny.

"This is why the Salween Peace Park came about," he concluded. The Salween Peace Park, for these activists, was a novel alternative approach to what most sides in the conflict agreed was the only way forward—to achieve a federal solution. Yet, as Doh K'Oh concluded, "People think we are crazy. Such a crazy idea, that it [the peace park] could be maintained by the Indigenous people; it has never been done before."

*   *   *

Over the course of this long car ride with Doh K'Oh, the lineaments of this "crazy idea" of a conservation zone, maintained by Indigenous people, gradually became more defined. In the conventional sense of a peace park, the Salween Peace Park is a pragmatic attempt to build a "transboundary protected area": a peace park in waiting. If, however, we take up Doh K'Oh and the other activists' invitation to follow where this "crazy idea" leads, we see that the Salween Peace Park is also a diminutive model, a sketch, of a radical experiment in building peace and federalism that simultaneously kept alive the KNU's protracted struggle for autonomy. In the process, the very notion of a peace park becomes unsettled and broadened far beyond a "transboundary protected area" to also embrace wider struggles for federalism and liberation.

This was exactly what Ta Thoo was pushing me to do on my first visit to KESAN's main office. As I have shown, he spoke of the Salween Peace Park as "just an idea, a local solution that could not be applied in all places," on the one hand, and as "one of the ways to work on the federal situation" such that both KNU and Indigenous sovereignty could be retained and enhanced, on the other. In his words, the Salween Peace Park was "part of our movement to claim land and control this land, as we are Karen." He emphasized that this project should be led by the people themselves, "as part of their rights as Indigenous people." The peace park was then part and parcel with the KESAN's ongoing attempts to prefigure modes of alter-politics: radically different ways of building federalism and autonomy.

The architects of the Salween Peace Park were deeply invested in what Hong describes as a "prefigurative politics that embodies political autonomy" as they attempted to "build federalism from the 'ground up'" (2017,

233). This prefigurative orientation distanced the Salween Peace Park from the (counter)movements I describe in chapter 4. Rather than simply turning the Myanmar state's attempts to make these lands legible and investible on their head by reversing the valences, the Salween Peace Park was an experiment in "a grassroots people-centered alternative" (Mutraw District et al. 2018, 4) to this dialectic.

KESAN was prefiguring an alternative way in which federalism might be practically achieved in one specific landscape, at one particular juncture, where "the struggle and the goal, the real and the ideal become one in the present" (Maeckelbergh 2009, 67): one "local solution," as Ta Thoo insisted. These efforts were not simply prefiguring. By giving form to the indeterminable, they were also "a figuration of the future . . . materializing the otherwise in the here and now," as Stine Krøijer (2010, 149) puts it. The groundwork of clearing a space within the KNU legal system allowed these activists to open up a gap in these highlands. In this interstitial space, alternative modes of (re)possessing landscapes were encouraged to come into contact and become intertwined, prefiguring a federal union and evoking "the spirit of self-determination" by building on actually existing practices of everyday autonomy.

Returning to the director's quip that he still encountered villagers who referred to the Salween Peace Park as a flower garden, since the Pwakanyaw translation of *peace park* can be literally rendered as "peace garden," these villagers may have not been so far off the mark after all. In a sense, the Salween Peace Park, as KESAN conceived it, was not unlike a *k'ruh*, a garden patch. It was a space for cultivating new ideas of how peace could practically be achieved.

In the Salween Peace Park, Indigenous land possession practices such as those described in part 1 of this book—patchworks of different categories of land, held together by shared practices and cosmologies of ephemeral and nesting ownership, and the sovereignty of the spectral realm—were cultivated, and subtly translated and rescaled, then grafted onto wider notions of federalism and autonomy. The Salween Peace Park was then itself a patchwork in the sense that it was composed not of various "units" of lands, scaled up to form a protected area, but of heterogeneous "patches" (Tsing, Deger et al. 2024; Tsing, Mathews, and Bubandt 2019) roughly stitched together to form a possessed landscape.

Along similar lines, when speaking to an academic with many years of experience as an adviser to the nationwide peace process, I was initially taken aback when they confided in me that, while positive toward the Salween Peace Park, they worried it may simply become "a diminutive Kawthoolei"—a miniature version of the KNU's protracted and stymied struggle for autonomy. With this statement, they appeared to echo a common sentiment that certain (hard-line) factions of the KNU were myopic when it came to the peace process. However, spending time with the KESAN activists, I learned that describing this protected area in the Mutraw hills as a diminutive Kawthoolei, rather than being a cutting critique, quite succinctly summed up the vision behind it.

Depicting the Salween Peace Park as a miniature version of the ongoing struggle for federalism and greater autonomy evokes similar imagery to that of a peace garden. Both as a diminutive model and as a garden patch, the Salween Peace Park emerged as a space where different modes of politics could come into contact: a space for cultivating new ideas and practices of how both peace and autonomy might be attained, offering an alternative vision. Ta Thoo made a similar point when he stressed that this conservation project up in the Mutraw hills was simply "one way to work on the federal situation . . . a local solution," not the only way. Far from being myopic, simply rehashing hackneyed notions of ethno-nationalism rooted in "Blut und Boden," or blood and soil (which the academic seemed to intimate with "diminutive Kawthoolei"), the Salween Peace Park may be grasped as one specific and local way—highly pragmatic, practical, but also playful—to unsettle and rethink stymied notions, not only of conservation and federalism but also of peacebuilding and autonomy. The third aspiration of the Salween Peace Park, to attain "peace and self-determination," pushed this protected area beyond a "protected landscape" to embrace a "park for peace." Following this aspiration, the peace park aimed to act as a model or a garden for cultivating alternative ways of engendering federalism and peace through conservation.

Through the third aspiration of the Salween Peace Park, the call for self-determination was smuggled in with an unequivocally laudable call for peace. Consequently, the commitment to build peace in the highlands along the Salween River was inextricably tied to the KNU's revolutionary commitment to achieve greater autonomy for the Indigenous peoples of these uplands. The commitment to conservation and peace was married to the commitment to the liberation of the inhabitants of the Mutraw hills. To better grasp the wider vision of this protected area, I describe the Salween Peace Park as a form of liberation conservation. To unravel the differing implications of the notion of liberation conservation, I return to the car ride back to Chiang Mai with Doh K'Oh.

CONSERVATION AS SELF-DETERMINATION

Back in the pickup truck, Doh K'Oh had begun to wind down after venting his frustration toward the current peace process. It was already getting dark, and the deep forests of one of Thailand's national parks slipped past the windowpanes as we sat quietly in the cab of the truck. Breaking this silence, I eventually asked him how he first came to work with KESAN. He smiled sweetly, but wearily, and began telling the story of how KESAN was formed.

KESAN has its origins in the Mae Ra Moe refugee camp in Thailand in 1997 as a small-scale environmental protection organization, the Karen Nature Conservation Group. This organization was formed by a group of friends, including Doh K'Oh, who wanted to help clean up the vast amount of rubbish piling up in the refugee camp they all lived in. In the camp they first met the *goh la wah* (white foreigner) whom they still fondly refer to as simply *Hpu* (grandfather). Hpu, who still works with them as a consultant, was volunteering at the refugee camp at the time, teaching young refugees about environmental issues and environmental movements from all over the world. Around this time Hpu helped form the first, though short-lived, multiethnic environmental alliance for people from Myanmar. This encounter with Hpu and environmentalism more generally helped spur this group of friends to start "thinking bigger," beyond the confines of the camp, or "temporary shelter area" as they were officially designated.

By 2001, these young refugees had raised sufficient funds to found the Karen Environmental and Social Action Network, or KESAN. The first major environmental report they produced under this new moniker was on illegal logging in 2004. These were wild times, Doh K'Oh added. At one point, to gather information for the report, he was embedded with a troop of KNLA soldiers to document illegal logging camps. Two heavily armed soldiers were detailed to protect him, but Doh K'Oh himself had only a camera to point at the loggers and Tatmadaw troops securing the area. The memory of these times caused him to pause for a moment and chuckle to himself before he affirmed that he would never do this sort of work again. Back then he was young and brave, but he has a wife and children to think of now. He still has the report and the pictures from this time at home somewhere, as a keepsake. Continuing to chat, he went on to stretch even further back in his history.

As the trees and forests turned to 7-Elevens and city streets through the windowpanes of the truck, Doh K'Oh told me how his family was, in fact, from the Mutraw hills. His parents were from a village cluster with its own *kaw*, perhaps one and half day's hike north of Ta K'Thwee Duh. But he himself was not born there. At the time his mother was pregnant with him, the Tatmadaw had begun intensifying their counterinsurgency program, continually making incursions deeper into these highland areas. When armed conflict made its way to their front door, his parents and four older siblings were forced to flee, first hiding in the jungle. During this time, two of his uncles attempted to return to their granaries to fetch rice and were captured by Tatmadaw soldiers. Both men were then summarily executed. This event left an indelible mark on Doh K'Oh. He restated this tale several times, stressing, "they [his uncles] were not soldiers, only farmers, but they were murdered along with many others."[11] Following these incidents, his parents, like countless others, eventually fled the area entirely, coming to rest in what he termed a "revolutionary area," just behind the former KNU headquarters in Manerplaw (literally, field of victory).

A former KNU general, whom I met while he was visiting the Karen diaspora in the United States, described Manerplaw as the "second capital of Burma" during the 1970s and 1980s. For a time, it acted as the focal point for the revolution against the reigning junta, after 1988 also hosting most of the exiled National League for Democracy.[12] Subsequently, both of Doh K'Oh's parents became what he called "revolutionaries." Indeed, nearly all of the founding members of KESAN had similar trajectories, with deep roots in the "revolutionary area" around Manerplaw and kin well positioned within the KNU/KNLA. One of the other leading activists in KESAN, for example, was the grandchild of a former KNU chairman and a cousin of the former vice-chairman.

Doh K'Oh was the only one of his siblings who did not follow directly in his parents' footsteps by joining the KNU/KNLA. He walked his own path, attending school in the nearby refugee camp where his parents later came to join him. While he regularly shuttled between the camp and Manerplaw, it was in the refugee camp, with other children of "revolutionaries," that the idea of what was to become KESAN first took form. Like many of KESAN's founding members, he was officially registered as a refugee by the United Nations High Commissioner for Refugees (UNHCR) in 2005 and qualified for their resettlement program to a third country. His parents had, in fact, already taken up this offer and resettled to the heart of the Karen diaspora in the United States, in St. Paul, Minnesota. When I asked him why he did not accompany his parents to the United States, he stated plainly, "I have chosen to stay as I want to fight for my people, and it is too hard to do that from so far away."

As the landscape over Doh K'Oh's shoulder faded back into the deep greens of forests, he explained that the current wave of ecological and

Indigenous movements in southeast Myanmar can be understood in terms of generations. The young women and men who first took up arms against the Myanmar government in 1949, such as the then-chairman of the KNU, Mutu Say Poe, were the "first generation" of revolutionaries. As they grew older, the second generation took up the mantel. This new wave was most commonly the children of the first generation, such as the hard-line general I met in Chiang Mai and Baw Kyaw Heh, the de facto leader of the Mutraw District. These men (only one woman was able to reach the highest ranks of the KNU at this time, herself a granddaughter of a former chairman) became the new vanguard of the revolution. I never got around to asking him, but I assume that Doh K'Oh's parents were counted among this second generation of revolutionaries. Today, as these leaders, too, grew old and weary, Doh K'Oh and his KESAN compatriots saw themselves as the "coming generation," the third wave of revolutionaries. He pointed out that, despite multiple waves of revolutionaries, the highest echelons of the KNU were still stacked with those from the first generation, such as both the then-chairman and then-vice-chairman. What was more, he lamented, these leaders were getting older and more stuck in their ways; they were steadily becoming less receptive to new ideas. As a result, it was up to his "coming generation" to push for more power and newer ways to carry on this old and tired struggle for greater autonomy.

For Doh K'Oh, this coming generation should not be seen as rebels. "We are not rebellious," he insisted, "however, like our parents before us, we *are* revolutionaries." While the generations before them made revolution by bearing arms and pointing them at the Tatmadaw to effect change and gain autonomy, his generation was trying a new tack. Rather than bearing M16s and mortars, they now carry around digital cameras and GPS devices. These new technologies were pointed not only at Tatmadaw troops but increasingly also at themselves, forging a new path through Indigenous practices with the same goal of effecting change and attaining autonomy, albeit via a different route.

* * *

What bound these different generations together was their shared revolutionary zeal to continue the struggle for self-determination. As James urged the first time I spoke to him, we must grasp the KESAN's experiments in conservation as "part of the revolution, as part of the struggle, not separate from it." A visiting villager elder from the neighboring district of Taw Oo (Taungoo) of Kawthoolei in the north succinctly captured this sentiment when he told the crowd at the second consultation meeting of the Salween Peace Park at the end of 2016, "When you cut down a teak tree, an ironwood tree does not grow in its place. A new teak grows from the same stump. It is the same with the new generation; they grow out of the old." For these activists the struggle to conserve biodiversity and to build peace was tightly bound up with, and inseparable from, wider struggles for liberation.

Recalling Michel Foucault's inversion of Carl von Clausewitz's famous adage, we might say that through the Salween Peace Park, conservation and environmental politics were the continuation of revolutionary war by other means.[13] KESAN's activism and advocacy were part of the third wave of the KNU's struggle for liberation to attain the "Karen-land" of Kawthoolei. However, through the process of clearing a legal space and opening up a gap in these highlands where different modes of politics could come into contact and become entwined, the Salween Peace Park continually overflowed and unsettled the protracted KNU struggle for the state of Kawthoolei. This made possible radically alternate modes of self-determination, politics, and being enmeshed with the world.

KESAN's protracted labors to establish this Indigenous-run protected area could not be disentangled from their continued revolutionary commitments to attain greater autonomy for the Pwakanyaw/Karen people. Taking seriously Doh K'Oh's insistence that "like our parents before us, we are revolutionaries," the pragmatic politics underpinning the Salween Peace Park was this "coming" generation's renewed attempts to continue the long arc of KNU's struggle to establish and legitimize their own (revolutionary) state, only by other means. In a sense, this Indigenous-run protected area was indeed a diminutive Kawthoolei, answering San C. Po's (1928) revolutionary call at the turn of the last century for an autonomous territory to act as their "home country," the establishing of a "Karen-land" that has guided the KNU struggle for liberation since its inception. At the same time, it was radically refiguring this struggle, gesturing toward more convivial and relational modes of autonomy.

Delving deeper into the Indigenous practices and cosmologies that the Salween Peace Park translated and rescaled into environmental policy, I found that the pockets of autonomy generated by spectral sovereignty (discussed in chapter 3) and local experiments in conservation (such as those described in chapters 4 and 5) were always nesting in, and indeed dependent upon, asymmetric relations to spectral persons, who were the true owners of the landscape. People in these highlands were continually engaged in the labor of "making friends," building relations of conviviality with the spectral sovereigns and the landscapes they possessed. Through these relations, the villagers could make claims on powerful others, be they KNU leaders or the Ta Htee Ta Daw K'sah, the sovereign of all specters.

Like the mushroom growing on a termite mound, as the senior KNU official in Tanintharyi put it, or a dandelion pushing its way through the cracks in the pavement, in the minuscule gaps between things, life finds a way. But life is always interdependent on other forms of life. The Salween Peace Park, and the other radical experiments in conservation that this book explores, illustrate a novel mode of revolutionary politics: a modality of autonomy that was deeply convivial and relational. I want to close this book by revisiting the tagline of the Salween Peace Park: "all living things sharing peace." In studying Indigenous practices and cosmologies and how they were translated and rescaled, I argue we can better understand both how people related to the more-than-human world and how radical alternatives to conservation and armed conflict were emerging in southeast Myanmar.

Epilogue

Pugmarks in the Sand

IN mid-September 2017, I made my way to the Karen Environmental and Social Action Network's main office one last time. I was there to say my goodbyes and give a short debriefing on my findings before heading home. On the basement floor, I found Doh K'Oh and the others hunched over their computers. After some small talk, catching up on one another's lives, I began detailing the eight months I had spent in the Mutraw hills by describing one of the experiences that had stuck with me the most. I explained how I was struck by the way people in these highlands often treated their landscapes as not simply alive, but possessed by spectral persons such as *kaw k'sah*, or "owners of the earth," and how they constantly negotiated and "made friends" with landscapes and the specters who possessed them, with tigers often acting as moral guardians to the *kaw k'sah*.

I began hearing tales about tigers even before I stepped foot in the village. When people in the regional center of Deh Bu Noh, where I first visited to clear my paperwork at the local KNU office, heard I would be staying along the Bu Thoe ridge that towers above this tiny town, the first thing they told me was "Watch out for tigers!" I anticipated that these comments would lead to stories of bloodthirsty beasts preying on livestock and human flesh, or even of tigers as metaphors for marauding Myanmar Army soldiers with whom Karen soldiers still occasionally clashed. Instead, they proceeded to speak of how tigers usually appear whenever somebody makes a *k'ma*, punctuating this claim with squeals of laughter. While (as I have shown) *k'ma* literally means "a mistake"—that is to say, a breach of taboo—what they were referring to was *k'ma poe mu poe hkwa*, or "a girl and boy mistake," implying a breach of the taboo against premarital sex. In this instance, they were less concerned about the endangered big cat, or saying something

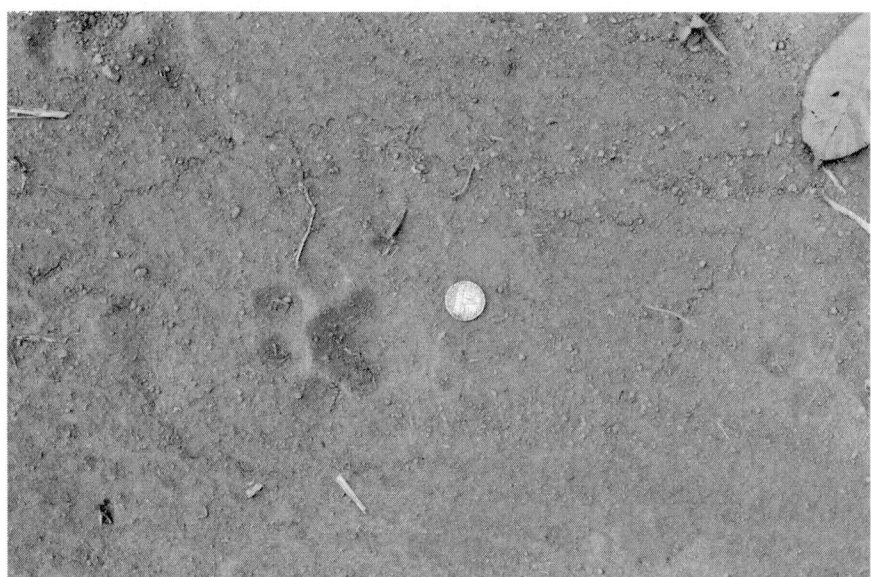
FIGURE 9. Tiger pugmarks in the sand along the "car road."

about over seventy years of armed conflict, than with playfully ribbing me about traveling with a young unmarried female field assistant, Naw Paw.

Arriving in the village, I found that the human residents still shared this ridge with at least three *baw thoe*—that is, tigers. During my second week, I was shown fresh pugmarks of a female and her cub along the dusty road that cuts along the top of this ridge (see figure 9).[1] To the west of the road was the rocky forest of Way Pgha, where tigers often rested as they prowled around these uplands. Tiger sightings along this ridge regularly provoked less fear for the safety of children and livestock than contemplation and discussion as to why a tiger had appeared in this specific place at this specific time. Each appearance was shrouded in speculation and doubt. While it was first reasoned that these tigers appeared on the road beside the village in relation to my arrival, the leading consensus was that it was actually related to the three Thai monks who (as described in chapter 5) attempted to build a small pagoda on the highest peak in this area, Ta Bu Kyoh, just before I arrived. As one elder, Hpu Gay, who lived in the house opposite my own, explained, this was most likely the work of the *kaw k'sah*. He told me how the *kaw k'sah* would often send one of her tigers, her "livestock," to prowl the edges of the village when people made *k'ma*, only relenting when the *k'ma* had been addressed.

The tiger was the first warning, heralding the great misfortune the *kaw k'sah* would soon pile upon on the people. Shortly afterward the land would start becoming *koh*, "hot" and feverish, affecting the crops, livestock, and humans in the area. The arrival of a tiger was thus followed by a flurry of negotiations, attempting to propitiate, placate, and plead with the *kaw k'sah* to "cool" down relations again and return peace and conviviality to the area.

It was decidedly uncertain as to whether these moral tigers, who made their presence known after breaches of taboo, were the same animals that conservationists are deeply concerned about (as in *Pantera tigris corbetti*, or Indochinese tigers). In an attempt to clear this up, I asked a group of elders whether the tigers that villagers accidentally caught in their *htu*, or "deathfall traps," in their fields and those caught in conservationists' camera traps were the *kaw k'sah*, her emissaries, or simply run-of-the-mill tigers. After a small pause to think, they usually equivocated, not committing to a definite answer one way or another.

In the following months, I learned that, on at least one occasion, tigers were not heard, nor their traces seen, following a case of premarital sex (such as that of Naw Maw Htaw, whom we meet in chapter 3). When, sometime later, several of the soldiers at a nearby Karen National Liberation Army checkpoint reported that they caught a fleeting glimpse of a large male tiger, the villagers brushed off any significance of its appearance at this particular place and time. Indeed, as other elders attested, when they were young, tigers regularly entered the village and took their livestock. Sometimes tigers were the *kaw k'sah*'s emissary, sometimes her physical manifestation, but more often than not, a tiger was just a tiger. While in some cases the appearance of a tiger had profound political effects, such as rerouting roads and preventing the construction of religious monuments, in other cases they were simply mentioned in passing, as one might mention seeing a villager from the neighboring area. These differing perspectives were far from settled and constantly shifting.

When I finished telling this tale to Doh K'Oh, he blurted out incredulously, "But you don't really believe it, right?" This question gave me pause to ponder: Do people in the Mutraw hills have to believe in these practices for them to have deep-reaching effects on their lives and politics?

* * *

This conversation with Doh K'Oh at the end of my fieldwork brings us full circle, back to where this book began, in questions on how to grasp such "worldly" practices (Tsing 2005): practices in which the line between inert and animate, the spectral and the biotic, and between the profound and the banal was indeterminate and constantly redrawn in relation to the situation at hand. In exploring these vexed questions, established notions of ownership and sovereignty become unsettled and subverted.

To address these questions and attempt to gather up the different threads I weave throughout this book, I return to the tagline of the Salween Peace Park: "All living things sharing peace." I begin by exploring "all living things," delving deeper into how I approached working with people who practice Thoo Hkoh/ Moh La Pa Lah (animist/ancestral ways). Through this exploration I show how such approaches might help us better understand the shifting relations between people, politics, environments, and other unseen more-than-humans. I then move on to the second half of the tagline: "sharing peace." Here I tentatively sketch out how experiments in conservation and autonomy in the Mutraw hills might inform radical alternatives to top-down protected areas and armed conflict in Myanmar and beyond.

"ALL LIVING THINGS"

Over the course of my fieldwork in the Mutraw hills, and particularly when I attempted to sum it up to Doh K'Oh, I found that the line between specters, mountains, and tigers was less than clear, constantly being redrawn. As I argue in the introduction, in some instances a mountain was the seat of the *kaw k'sah* and a tiger its worldly emissary, but in others a mountain was just a rock formation and a tiger was just a big cat. How a set of pugmarks in the sand was understood shifted from case to case.

Returning to the discussions I open this book with, much of the work on people broadly categorized under the rubric of *animist* has circled around the question of what is, or should be, considered alive. As I have shown, the two most common approaches to broaching this issue have been, in broad brushstrokes, (1) to parcel out these practices and cosmologies as "belief systems" or "worldviews" that are metaphorical representations of real events (Evans-Pritchard 1976; Hornborg 2017a, 2017b; Leach 1954; Spiro [1967] 1996) or (2) to take these practices and cosmologies seriously, hypostatized as part and parcel of people's everyday reality as radically (read, ontologically) different worlds (de la Cadena 2015; Holbraad and Pedersen 2017; Latour 2005).

My modest intervention into these highly vexed debates has been to take a different tack. Taking a lead from my interlocutors, my focus has been less on what *is* and what actually exists and more on what *works*—that is, on what has an effect on people's everyday lives. I found that people were less enamored (at least far less than most anthropologists) with questions pertaining to whether unseen more-than-humans really existed than they were attentive to the effects they had on people's day-to-day lives, their traces, and how they could respond to and negotiate with these beings. In doing so, I have taken my interlocutors' own practices and cosmological sensibilities, along with their uncertainties and doubts, seriously.

I describe this methodological orientation as a move toward a playful "more-than-human political ecology" that gives equal attention to both people's deep entanglements with ecologies and to the political underpinnings of these entanglements. In focusing on the interface of these imperatives, I found that people's relations with ecologies were continually made and unmade, leading to a great deal of indeterminacy and doubt. As Rita Astuti (2017) points out, the people we work with seem to contradict themselves and change their minds on a regular basis. To address the muddle that can result from such contradictions, in this book I have taken a similar approach to that of Astuti in striving to "take people seriously"—constantly emphasizing the ways people's relations with the world are riddled with indeterminacy and doubt and shot through with a distinct playfulness in the sense of both levity and of experimentation.

To better grapple with these issues, I have drawn on, and tweaked slightly, Violet Cho's (2023) understanding of belief (*tana*) as inseparable from and animated by practice/action (*tama*). She found that the Christian communities she studied were infused with a strong sense of pragmatism, drawn together not simply through their shared belief in God but also through shared action—such as prayer and caring for and protecting one another. Such actions were necessary to face down the "calamitous effects of colonialism and post-colonial states," as she puts it so vividly (46). *Tana* entails not only belief but also trust and confidence and derives its power from *tama*, or the capacity to act on and have an effect on the world. Thus, people only believed (*tana*) in the animacy of any given thing after discerning its actions (*tama*) on their lives and bodies and only trusted/had confidence (*tana*) in any given mode of sovereignty after discerning its capacity to have an effect (*tama*) on local politics.

In tacking toward a more-than-human political ecology, I attempted to better grasp shifting entanglements between spectral persons and politics by holding open questions as to what exists and what is alive and what is not (cf. Dooren et al. 2016). Indeed, as philosopher Simon Critchley notes, "if we are doing politics, we cannot and should not pin our hopes on any ontology . . . politics is the disruption of the ontological domain" (2007, 105). In this manner, especially in the context of chronic conflict, not only is the line defining what is alive constantly redrawn, but so is the line between different forms of life: for example, spectral and biotic. As I have shown, war spills beyond everyday life into the cosmos itself, perpetually making and unmaking them both (cf. Ruiz-Serna 2023, 3). Accordingly, I play with the manifold connotations of the term *spectral* in this book: in the sense of ineffable, indeterminate, and labile and to denote something/someone whose presence is often sensed but never quite seen—understood to be just off the visual spectrum.

The multifaceted connotations of specters become clearer in how the suffix *-khah* in Pwakanyaw can denote both spectral persons, such as *ta mu khah*, and other hard-to-see things, such as insects. The term *bu khah*, for example, usually refers to the tiny green/yellow insects that feed on rice seedlings, but it is also used to refer to bacterial infections of rice. As such, insects, bacteria, viruses, and other microorganisms were regularly grasped similarly as spectral, in the sense of being just off the visual spectrum (cf. Herrera 2018), and thus could only be discerned through the traces they left and the effects they had on human lives, bodies, and crops. Returning to the vignette above, I found that tigers were often treated in a similar fashion.

While the older villagers often told tales of having tangled with tigers in their youth, many of the younger generation's only glimpses of tigers were of those caught in traps and long dead. For the vast majority of the people residing in these highlands, the presence of tigers, like that of specters, could never be discerned directly but rather through the traces they left: pugmarks imprinted on the dusty road, scat left along a small jungle path, or the sound of their roar heard distantly. As Amitav Ghosh notes, there remains an "irreducible element of mystery" and "uncanniness" (2016, 30) surrounding tigers. In everyday life people did not always distinguish between tigers and specters since, in most instances, both could only be discerned in the traces they left and the effects they had on their lives. To an extent, the Myanmar state itself had a similar spectral quality, often only discerned in its effects, its traces: in the whirling propellers of drones heard overhead or felt surging through rumors of Tatmadaw spies moving among them.

Consequently, drawing on this method might help better grasp the shifting entanglements not only between politics and specters but also more widely between people, states, and other things that are difficult to perceive, such as tigers, insects, bacteria, and viruses. This move implies drawing on a more pragmatic approach (Cho 2023; Lambek 1996). Rather than spilling endless amounts of ink on whether such entities actually exist, attention is trained on sensing and experimenting with the traces and imprints they leave and the effects that they have on people's everyday lives and politics (Tsing, Swanson et al. 2017). In this sense, a more-than-human political ecology takes seriously both people's doubts and what is significant to them, "what is at stake" and what "really matters," in Arthur Kleinman's (1997, 327, 315) phrasing.

Throughout, I have argued that, attending to the continually shifting line between the inert and the animate, and between spectral and biotic life, affords us the ability to perceive alternative modes of ownership and sovereignty: modes of politics that might generatively unsettle the current political impasse of intractable armed conflict in southeast Myanmar and perhaps beyond. By translating and rescaling Indigenous practices and cosmologies, the radical experiments in conservation and autonomy I examine in this book offered a radical alternative to the "unproductive and endless oppositions" (Hage 2015, 62) of armed conflict in the highlands along the Salween River by attempting to transform these former battle zones into spaces for "all living things sharing peace."

"SHARING PEACE"

Delving deeper into Indigenous practices and cosmologies, I have shown how these highlands might be best grasped as actually existing spaces of autonomy—an autonomy rooted in deep interdependencies. Human sovereignty and local politics in these highlands were largely concerned with asymmetrical negotiation with the spectral owners of the earth and in maneuvering oneself into what James Ferguson terms as more "desirable forms" (2013, 237) of dependence. Thus, a mode of politics emerged that was predicated on making and maintaining "good relations" (TallBear 2019; see also Wildcat 2013) with the spectral realm and other humans, through feasting and drinking together: of "making friends," as people often put it. These highlands were a contact zone, not only of violence and asymmetrical relations of power but also of relations of conviviality and care. I end this book by offering a tentative sketch of how these findings relate to wider debates and ongoing efforts to protect biodiversity and mitigate conflict in and also far beyond Myanmar.

In exploring how largely asymmetrical relations between people and the relative autonomy of these highlands were dependent on and nesting in encompassing hierarchical relations to the spectral realm, these findings speak to a growing interest in understanding sovereignty globally as "a process of contingent negotiation" (Martin 2014, 343; see also Kirksey 2012; Rutherford 2012). I follow Andrew Ong's argument that the kind of sovereignty and autonomy generated by Indigenous practices and in situ experiments with conservation can be best understood as *relational*: "enacted through engaging with the 'outside' by creating intermittent, oscillating political relations" (2023, 8). Spectral sovereignty and the ways it was drawn on, translated, and rescaled to create pockets of Indigenous autonomy highlighted how it was always relational, entangled and interdependent, defined by encounter and interaction (Ong, *Stalemate*, 2023, 12; see also W. Brown 2010). These practices, and the ways they were translated and rescaled, were then prefigurative, figuring the future in the here and now (cf. Krøijer 2010; Maeckelbergh 2009).

The various experiments in conservation and autonomy that I examine in this book were not *"just* an idea," as the activist Ta Thoo so modestly claimed; they were more than simply a plan or a possibility. They were actively figuring a radically alternative way of protecting biodiversity and striving for greater autonomy in landscapes upended by war. By 2020, the practices underpinning the Salween Peace Park that wove together the KNU's state politics and spectral sovereignty were starting to travel and take root in other areas of Myanmar. They were also starting to gain recognition and acclaim far beyond the borders of this nation-state.

In southern Myanmar, where, as I describe in chapter 4, an ensemble of activists and farmers were pushing back against threats of "green territoriality" (Woods 2019), several different movements began linking up into the so-called Tanawthari Landscape of Life. Taking its cue from the Salween Peace Park, this large-scale conservation project was similarly sewing together seven Indigenous territories to form an "Indigenous Conserved Landscape, a symbol of the symbiotic relationship between nature and humans, and a proposal for future peace, environmental protection, food sovereignty, and self-determination" (CAT 2020, 10). Indeed, as the director of KESAN, who was part of the alliance of activists behind this project, summed it up, "Conservation of small areas will not work. Indigenous peoples conserve their territories through a landscape approach by seeing the interconnections through the landscape—we have seen this through the example of the Salween Peace Park. Now it is time for governments, international organisations, businesses and the UN to learn from indigenous people" (ICCAS 2023). This seemed to indeed be the case, and right up until the coup of February 2021, global organizations were starting to take notice.

On September 29, 2020, the Salween Peace Park received the Equator Prize from the United Nations Development Programme in recognition of their "outstanding community efforts to reduce poverty through the conservation and sustainable use of biodiversity . . . laying the foundation for a global movement of local successes that are collectively making a contribution to achieving the Sustainable Development Goals (SDGs)" (Equator Initiative 2020). Two months on, in November 2020, the director of KESAN was awarded the Goldman Environmental Prize, spoken of as the Green Nobel, for his work on the Salween Peace Park.

In this light, the Salween Peace Park might be grasped in the context of growing globe-spanning movements that Bram Büscher and Robert Fletcher (2020) describe as the conservation revolution. For these authors, "a revolution in conservation is brewing" that is moving beyond "people versus park" disputes to embrace radical alternative approaches (1). The Indigenous-run protected area along the Salween River resonated strongly with the radical alternative Büscher and Fletcher put forward of "convivial conservation," which rejects both nature-people dichotomies and capitalist economic systems that demand continual growth. Beyond modes of conservation that attempt to turn the environment into "nature capital" and "environmental services," convivial conservation points to the need to find better ways "to 'con vivire,' live with (the rest of) nature" (9–10). Yet, while these authors discuss these "radical alternatives" in order to forward a "scientifically grounded, *political* platform and paradigm" (12), the Salween Peace Park was a concrete and situated example of an actually existing radical alternative to both conservation and peacebuilding. As such, following the establishment of this peace park offers us a window on how revolution in conservation might be achieved in practice in Myanmar and, indeed, far beyond. All this building momentum and hope, however, was interrupted just two short months after the Salween Peace Park was awarded these prizes.

Apocalypse, Again!

At the crack of dawn on February 1, 2021, armored vehicles trundled into the state capital of Nay Pyi Daw, heralding the latest military coup and the return to protracted armed conflict. Many seasoned researchers and commentators, myself included, were shocked by this turn of events, fearing all the gains that had been made in the transitional decade (2011–21) would come to nought. But glancing back I realized that my interlocutors had been warning me about this moment, time and time again. The current coup was, after all, far from the first time they had experienced such an apocalyptic event. In fact, in that same conversation with Doh K'Oh, I shared another experience from my time in the Mutraw hills that had left a deep impression on me, of how people regularly prophesized that all-out war would return in 2020.

During my second to last week in Ta K'Thwee Duh, I went to visit one of the village elders I had grown particularly close to, Hpu Waw. He greeted me, telling me morosely, "This may be the last time we get to chat. I have to take a trip out of the village soon, and fear you will not be around when I get back." Then he brightened up, adding, "But then again, maybe next time I see you will be in Yu Wah Duh." As it transpired, he remained deeply distrustful as to my real intentions, even after all these months. He assumed that, upon leaving the village, I would join the Chinese prospectors who were planning to survey neighboring Yu Wah Duh Kaw for minerals (mentioned in chapter 4). Quickly noticing my growing agitation toward this line of conversation (one we had followed many times before), he pivoted to telling me how he thought that conflicts over resources and land would be the spark that ignites the next cycle of armed conflict in Myanmar.

Like many of the highlanders I had spoken to in the last few months, he held the view that the year 2020 would mark the return of war to the Mutraw hills. He told me that "it was already foreseen by the [now long dead] oracle Wee Hta Baw Mu." In these prophetic visions, the first thing Wee Hta Baw Mu predicted was that, in the lead-up of the return of apocalyptic war "along Bu Thoe ridge, the only footprints to be seen will be the pugmarks of tigers and leopards." This prophesy Hpu Waw claimed "has already been fulfilled as people now ride motorbikes and wear flip-flops. Human footprints are rarely seen along the path at the top of this mountain now." This also intimated that people would begin to forget Thoo Hkoh ways and begin breaking many *ta du ta htu* (taboos), vexing the specters and provoking them to send their tigers. The second prophecy was that "the pigs will come and dig up the ground." He elaborated that this, too, has been fulfilled since "the pigs in this prophecy are the people and machinery that came to dig up the soil to create the road and to excavate the ground searching for valuable minerals." With all these things coming to pass, the final prediction of apocalyptic war returning was imminent, he explained.

While 2020 also figured in his telling of this prophecy, when I asked why exactly it would happen in that year, he backtracked a little, insisting that "we can, of course, never know such things with any real certainty. It might still not happen." Again, this tale was shot through with doubt. And yet he remained convinced that the war was looming. When talking of what would happen when this war finally arrives, he narrated a series of events that appeared to be purloined directly from the stories of the Rapture in the last book of the Bible (remembering that Hpu Waw strongly identified as Thoo Hkoh). As he told it, when this war comes, the great demiurge Y'wa will "come and separate the rice seed from the husk," again adapting the tale by drawing on metaphors rooted in people's everyday life. "Y'wa will bring his winnowing tray to winnow away the bad people from the good," he explained, swapping out biblical images of separating the sheep from the lambs with local notions of the rice seed and husk.

Hpu Waw concluded this tale by explaining that Wee Hta Baw Mu's final prediction was that there would be three outbreaks of war and the third instance would be the most intense, taking on apocalyptic proportions. Prior to 2012, there were already two outbreaks of conflict, so if the ceasefire did not hold, the next would be the third and final war, when Y'wa would start winnowing. He added, however, that none of this was a foregone conclusion. It could still be averted. Others told of how this catastrophic third wave of war would usher in a period of unprecedented peace. They pointed to how Pwakanyaw of these highlands had lived through multiple apocalypses and were still there. War was like a revenant that kept returning but that could still be negotiated with, to continue to eke out an existence. Speaking to the activists from KESAN following the coup, I found that KESAN saw the situation similarly—as apocalypse, again!

In the teeth of the violent conflict that has roiled nearly every corner of Myanmar, as almost all international collaboration has dried up, these radical and pragmatic experiments in conservation and autonomy are ongoing. In 2022, the Salween Peace Park expanded from 5,485 km^2 to 6,747 km^2. Moreover, KESAN continues to organize a general assembly each year, inviting people from all the villages incorporated into this protected area to vote for a new leader and plot and plan a new future in these treacherous times. At the 5th General Assembly from December 18–20, 2023, one of the governing committee members commented, "The Burma military attacks us with airstrikes. Of course, our people live in fear every day. Nevertheless, to successfully implement our many tasks, and to achieve the three goals of our Salween Peace Park, we will not back down. We have to work harder so that the whole world will recognise our park" (KESAN 2024).

The Indigenous people of these highlands, like Indigenous peoples around the world, were no strangers to catastrophe. They had already lived through the "calamitous effects of colonialism and post-colonial states," as Cho (2023, 46) puts it. In this light, the various experiments in conservation and sovereignty that I explore in this book might be seen as their way of preparing for the next apocalypse and paving the way for what comes after it. By word and by deed these radical Indigenous thinkers were living proof that "another world is possible." Only time will tell what that world might look like.

NOTES

INTRODUCTION

1. On the one hand, in referring to landscapes along the Mutraw highlands as "contested," I am simply pointing to the manner in which various armed actors made competing claims upon them. Chiefly, the Myanmar state/Tatmadaw and the KNU/KNLA. On the other hand, by evoking the term *contested landscapes*, I elude to the way in which, as Barbara Bender notes, "the study landscape is much more than an academic exercise—it *is* about the complexity of people's lives, historical contingency, contestation, motion and change" ([2001] 2020, 2). Accordingly, beyond territorial claims, landscapes are also the site of contesting cosmological claims, such as those over the "visible and invisible, the animate and the inanimate" (Yeh and Coggins 2014, 204).
2. Karen Environmental and Social Action Research (KESAN), press release, May 26, 2016, https://kesan.asia/press-released-battlefields-to-refuge-the-salween-peace-park-in-burmas-karen-state/.
3. During the period in which I conducted the bulk of my fieldwork (2016–17), the Salween Peace Park covered 5,485 km^2, but was expanded to 6,747 km^2 in 2021. I use the most recent figure to foreground the fact that this work is still ongoing, despite the current conflict. I return to this point in the epilogue to this book.
4. This said, the border between the biotic and the spectral was often far from clear-cut. The suffix *-khah* denotes both hungry specters, such as *ta mu khah*, as well as other hard-to-see things, such as insects like *htee khah*, a kind of water-dwelling insect. Something similar existed in the English language in Elizabethan times, when, for Shakespeare at least, "bug" was once also a synonym for ghosts (MacNeal 2017, 9ff.). I return to this point in the epilogue to this book.

5. These policies tied in to the colonial model of a "plural society," in which different groups lived side by side but separate, only meeting in the marketplace (Furnivall 1948, 304), sharing a striking resemblance to later models of liberal peace (Paris 2004).
6. Indicative of the continued symbolic importance of Thee Mu Hta, it was the first Tatmadaw base to be retaken by the KNLA when full-blown war returned to this area in March 2021 (Myanmar Now 2021).
7. As a consequence, this tree was often referred to as *Mu Khah Hklur*, or the Mu Khah Banyan.
8. While I later heard other tales that spoke of Y'wa's mother, people consistently insist that this mother figure was neither Mu Khah nor her daughter.
9. As I demonstrate in chapter 1, however, this story became more layered and considerably more complex as I delved deeper. I found that other stories tell of how the original inhabitants of the highlands came to a landscape that was already possessed, not only by various spectral presences but also by a semi-mythical group called the K'wa.

1. POSSESSED LANDSCAPES

1. This kind of colonial nostalgia is common across highland areas of what was once British India (Karlsson 2017).
2. The suffix *-kaw* following the name of a village denotes the lands surrounding and belonging to this settlement. I return to the term *kaw*, and deal with it in much greater detail, in chapters 2 and 3.
3. As I show in chapter 3, this phenomenon stretches far beyond Southeast Asia.
4. This is a common feature among swidden-cultivating peoples from the Amazonas (Butt Colson 1973; Viegas 2016) to South and Southeast Asia (Karlsson 2011; Li 2014a). I return to this point in chapter 2.
5. As we see here, in day-to-day terms people often spoke of a tree, a rock, a mountain, a pond, or a swath of land as having a *k'la* (a spirit), a *nah htee* (tutelary spirit/*nat*), or some other spectral presence who was spoken of as its *k'sah*, its owner. It is this emic practice that I gloss as possession/possessed to capture the entwined senses of both haunting and owning.

2. ALTERNATING OWNERSHIP

1. Occasionally it is also used as a prefix. Northern Thailand is known as Kaw Kyaw Teh.
2. In the north of the Salween Peace Park, there was a *kaw* called Kaw They Ghoo that consisted of several village clusters. This "federal *kaw*," as they

called it, came about due to one man, Saw Thay Ghoo, exchanging several golden drums for the right to these lands/*kaw*, which he then named after himself. Yet this, from what I can ascertain, was the exception that proves the rule (Paul, personal communication, March 13, 2017; for more details, see Paul 2018).

3. Her husband—the man with a rude word embossed on his baseball cap, introduced in the opening vignette of this book—was unfortunately also one of the most accomplished rice wine consumers (together with his friend Hpa Kha Pa), such that Naw Daw rarely profited from this enterprise.

3. SPECTRAL SOVEREIGNTY

1. One elder did relay to me his concerns that the cargo the road brought with it, such as T-shirts, instant noodles, and digital technologies, threatened to corrupt the youth and lead them to abandon traditional practices and eventually the village. These comments were, however, largely scoffed at by his fellow villagers.
2. During my research in the refugee camps in Thailand in 2013, I learned this was not always the case in all areas of southeast Myanmar. One woman from a village downstream of the Salween, near Hpa-An City, told me how her mother was the village headman when she was a child. This area was under dual KNU/Tatmadaw control at the time, and the Tatmadaw soldiers would regularly beat the headman when he could not meet their (often unreasonable) demands. Reasoning that the soldiers might go easier on a woman, the villagers voted in her mother.
3. I was never able to glean a clear answer as to why this title could only be inherited patrilineally, to the oldest or youngest son of the current holder, while all other forms of inheritance were traced bilaterally. In part this may be due to how, as I show above, only men could inherit the rites associated with making and maintaining relations with the spectral owners. However, the *htee hpoe kaw k'sah* himself, and elders I consulted, were adamant that this title could not "skip a generation" and be inherited by the eldest son of the current holder's daughter. It could only be passed from father to son, regularly leading the *htee hpoe kaw k'sah* generation to "be lost."

4. COUNTERMOVEMENTS

1. These accusations largely stemmed from the contentious KNU election held in 2012, right before the initial ceasefire was signed. They were further fueled by a flurry of unsubstantiated claims that the KNU chairman

received 2 million USD in bribes from the Euro-Burma Office (Naing 2016).
2. As it so happened, the headmaster was the only person who actually obeyed these orders. Everyone else, not unreasonably, surmised that given their almost total absence from day-to-day life, these commanders would never be able to enforce such an order. The villagers continued to invite me to their fields as they wished, with no fear of being reprimanded.
3. Fascinatingly, people used the phrase *ta thoo ta pgho* to describe not only potent/powerful places but also, as in situations such as this, areas where potential "valuable things" might be hidden, such as gold. This led to many productive misunderstandings.
4. I would like to extend an extra thanks to Nick Cheesman for assistance translating this sign from Burmese to English.
5. The conference sessions were named after the first Panglong Conference held in February 1947. At this conference various ethnic minority leaders met and agreed to join the Union of Burma, effectively paving the way for independence the following year.
6. I return to this point in the following section.
7. This argument bears a striking resemblance to the one made by James Ferguson in his book *The Anti-Politics Machine* (1994), which was similarly inspired by Michel Foucault's "governmentality lectures" (2003). Ferguson posits that, much like the "peace trap" described above, political realities are commonly translated into "technical" issues to be solved by development professionals, all the while strengthening the state's presence in the area (see also Li 2007).
8. This animosity toward swidden cultivation echoes findings across the border, as well as those further afield (Forsyth and Walker 2008; Karlsson 2011; Peluso and Vandergeest 2011).
9. In Ta K'Thwee Duh village, the umbilical cords of neonates were placed inside a bamboo tube and affixed to one particular vibrant tree that grew at the top of the village. Akin to an umbilical cord forest, this one tree served the purpose of keeping the children's *k'la* strong and vibrant (like the tree), protecting them from malevolent spectral presences.
10. The notion of translations has accumulated a great deal of theoretical baggage since Benjamin. It has become central to science and technology studies and actor-network theory (Callon 1984; Star and Griesemer 1989) and more recently to studies affiliated with the so-called ontological turn (de la Cadena 2015; Viveiros de Castro 2004b).

5. ALTER-POLITICS

1. In Buddhism this practice is known as *Upodatha*. During certain phases of the moon, not only monks but also laypeople observe the five pre-

cepts, including abstaining from killing living beings and from becoming intoxicated.
2. As I demonstrate in chapter 4, this was the monk embroiled both in the incident in Thee Mu Hta and in the DKBA's split from the KNU in 1997.
3. Slightly confusingly, a natural clearing along the top of the Bu Thoe ridge, some fifteen minutes' walk from Ta K'Thwee Duh, was said to be flat because it was at this spot in which the Ta Htee Ta Daw K'sah wrestled with Y'wa. Similarly, a mountain in the neighboring district was then said to be Y'wa's bust that petrified after he was killed.
4. While meaning literally "nature," *nay suh* connotes all the contents of the earth that were not made by man, such as the land, the sea, the air, the animals, the fish, and the plants.

6. LIBERATION CONSERVATION

1. So-called non-state armed groups (NSAGs) such as the KNU were regularly referred to by the Tatmadaw as "insurgents" and "rebels" and their revolutions as "insurgencies." This categorization was often treated as synonymous with "terrorist" and was long used as a justification for the Tatmadaw's brutal "four cuts" counterinsurgency. Indeed, as Martin Smith (1999, 259) notes, the Tatmadaw long referred to the armed opposition groups as "bandits" and "extremists" and thus did not accord them with political status. More recently, the Arakan Rohingya Salvation Army (ARSA) and Arakan Army (AA) were variously labeled as "extremist terrorists" and "insurgents" by the Tatmadaw in order to justify a pattern of targeting civilians that a UN fact-finding mission described as amounting to "genocidal intent" (OHCHR 2020).
2. These categories of protected areas used by the IUCN are now obsolete but can still be found archived here: https://www.eea.europa.eu/themes/biodiversity/protected-areas/facts-and-figures/IUCN-management-categories.
3. This point elicits a whole host of questions around the "rights of nature" and debates as to whether spectral or "non-secular" beings can and should be written into law. For a comprehensive review of the central debates around more-than-human law and justice, please consult Sophie Chao, Karin Bolender, and Eben Kirksey's *The Promise of Multispecies Justice* (2022).
4. I found a broad consensus among the activists, Indigenous people, and academics alike in regard to this point.
5. See https://knuhq.org/en/about/background, archived from the original on January 19, 2025, https://web.archive.org/web/20241217172418/https://knuhq.org/en/about/background.
6. This source is now defunct, but see https://web.archive.org/web

/20180711023854/https://www.iucn.org/theme/protected-areas/about/protected-areas-categories/category-v-protected-landscapeseascape.
7. These three principles were first laid out in a briefer, the revised version of which can be downloaded here: https://kesan.asia/wp-content/uploads/2017/12/Salween-Peace-Park-briefer-Eng-Oct-2019-revised.pdf.
8. In KNLA company, he regularly claimed that the second in command of the KNLA and de facto leader of the Mutraw District, Baw Kyaw Heh, first came up with the idea after visiting the Salawin National Park on the Thai side of the river. In this telling, Baw Kyaw Heh then tasked KESAN with realizing his vision.
9. For more information about this conference, see https://whc.unesco.org/fr/actualites/1601.
10. Similarly, the Tatmadaw placed the blame for a flare-up of conflict in 2020 on the western edges of the Salween Peace Park squarely on the KNU, who they said was unable to "look at the bigger picture," all while the Tatmadaw continued to conduct an unauthorized widening of a military road between two of their army camps in KNU country, in clear violation of the NCA agreement (Weng 2020).
11. Accounts such as Doh K'Oh's, of mass displacements and treatment of all civilians in "black zones" as possible combatants, have been meticulously documented over the years by the Karen Human Rights Group (see KHRG 2000, 2010).
12. In a fascinating twist of fate, following the coup in 2021, history repeated itself. As peaceful protests turned increasingly bloody, urban youth, activists, and the exile government once more returned to the border, receiving shelter and training from established armed groups such as the KNLA.
13. Foucault inverted Clausewitz's famous adage that war is the continuation of politics by other means to argue that politics is the continuation of war by other means.

EPILOGUE

1. As people were fond of explaining, just like humans, tigers prefer to take the dusty road rather than traipse through the often overgrown forest paths.

REFERENCES

Agamben, Giorgio. 1998. *Homo Sacer: Sovereign Power and Bare Life*. Translated by Daniel Heller-Roazen. Stanford University Press.

Ali, Saleem H., ed. 2007. *Peace Parks: Conservation and Conflict Resolution*. MIT Press.

Allen, T. F. H., and Thomas B. Starr. 1982. *Hierarchy: Perspectives for Ecological Complexity*. University of Chicago Press.

Allerton, Catherine. 2009. "Introduction: Spiritual Landscapes of Southeast Asia." *Anthropological Forum* 19 (3): 235–51. https://doi.org/10.1080/00664670903278387.

Allerton, Catherine. 2013. *Potent Landscapes: Place and Mobility in Eastern Indonesia*. University of Hawai'i Press.

Anderson, Benedict R. O'G. 1990. "The Idea of Power in Javanese Culture." In *Language and Power: Exploring Political Cultures in Indonesia*. Cornell University Press.

Apter, Andrew. 2017. "Ethnographic X-Files and Holbraad's Double-Bind: Reflections on an Ontological Turn of Events." *HAU: Journal of Ethnographic Theory* 7 (1): 287–302. https://doi.org/10.14318/hau7.1.021.

Aragon, Lorraine V. 2003. "Expanding Spiritual Territories: Owners of the Land, Missionization, and Migration in Central Sulawesi." In *Founders' Cults in Southeast Asia: Ancestors, Polity, and Identity*, edited by Nicola Tannenbaum and Cornelia Ann Kammerer. Yale University Press.

Arensen, Lisa. 2022. "Living with Landmines: Inhabiting a War-Altered Landscape." *Journal of Material Culture* 27 (2): 91–106. https://doi.org/10.1177/1359183521997506.

Århem, Kaj. 2016. "Southeast Asian Animism in Context." In *Animism in Southeast Asia*, edited by Kaj Århem and Guido Sprenger. Routledge.

Astuti, Rita. 2017. "Taking People Seriously." *HAU: Journal of Ethnographic Theory* 7 (1): 105–22. https://doi.org/10.14318/hau7.1.012.

Aung, Geoffrey. 2018. "Postcolonial Capitalism and the Politics of Dispossession: Political Trajectories in Southern Myanmar." *European Journal of East Asian Studies* 17 (2): 193–227. https://doi.org/10.1163/15700615-01702006.

Aung, Geoffrey. 2023. "The Frontier in Heterogeneous Time: Finance, Temporality, and an Economic Zone on Hold." *Journal of Cultural Economy* 16 (3): 377–91. https://doi.org/10.1080/17530350.2022.2098517.

Barbesgaard, Mads. 2019. "Landscapes of Dispossession: The Production of Space in Northern Tanintharyi, Myanmar." PhD thesis, Lund University.

Barclay, Harold. 1998. *People Without Government: An Anthropology of Anarchy*. 2nd rev. ed. Kahn & Averill.

Bender, Barbara. (2001) 2020. Introduction to *Contested Landscapes: Movement, Exile and Place*, edited by Barbara Bender and Margot Winer. Routledge.

Benjamin, Walter. 2004. *Walter Benjamin: Selected Writings, 1: 1913–1926*. Edited by Marcus Bullock and Michael W. Jennings. Harvard University Press.

Benjamin, Walter. 2006. *Walter Benjamin: Selected Writings, 3: 1935–1938*. Edited by Howard Eiland and Michael W. Jennings. Harvard University Press.

Bennett, Jane. 2010. *Vibrant Matter: A Political Ecology of Things*. Duke University Press.

Bernstein, Henry. 2014. "Food Sovereignty via the 'Peasant Way': A Sceptical View." *Journal of Peasant Studies* 41 (6): 1031–63. https://doi.org/10.1080/03066150.2013.852082.

Bessire, Lucas, and David Bond. 2014. "Ontological Anthropology and the Deferral of Critique." *American Ethnologist* 41 (3): 440–56. https://doi.org/10.1111/amet.12083.

Bielo, James S. 2015. *Anthropology of Religion: The Basics*. Routledge.

BirdLife International. 2018. *Buceros bicornis*. The IUCN Red List of Threatened Species. https://doi.org/10.2305/IUCN.UK.2018-2.RLTS.T22682453A131870948.en.

Bishara, Amahl. 2017. "Sovereignty and Popular Sovereignty for Palestinians and Beyond." *Cultural Anthropology* 32 (3): 349–58. https://doi.org/10.14506/ca32.3.04.

Bonilla, Yarimar. 2017. "Unsettling Sovereignty." *Cultural Anthropology* 32 (3): 330–39. https://doi.org/10.14506/ca32.3.02.

Borneman, John. 2002. "Reconciliation After Ethnic Cleansing: Listening, Retribution, Affiliation." *Public Culture* 14 (2): 281–304. https://doi.org/10.1215/08992363-14-2-281.

Bourguignon, Erika. 1976. *Possession*. Chandler & Sharp Publishers.

Boutry, Maxime, Celine Allaverdian, Marie Mellac et al. 2017. *Land Tenure in Rural Lowland Myanmar: From Historical Perspectives to Contemporary Realities in the Dry Zone and the Delta*. GRET. https://gret.org/en/publication/land-tenure-in-rural-lowland-myanmar-from-historical-perspectives-to-contemporary-realities-in-the-dry-zone-and-the-delta/.

Brac de la Perrière, Bénédicte. 2015. "Possession and Rebirth in Burma (Myanmar)." *Contemporary Buddhism: An Interdisciplinary Journal* 16 (1): 61–74. https://doi.org/10.1080/14639947.2015.1013000.

Brenner, David. 2019. *Rebel Politics: A Political Sociology of Armed Struggle in Myanmar's Borderlands*. Cornell University Press.

Bright, Saw John. 2019. "Rites, Rights, and Water Justice in Karen State: A Case Study of Community-Based Water Governance and the Hatgyi Dam." In *Knowing the Salween River: Resource Politics of a Contested Transboundary River*, edited by Carl Middleton and Vanessa Lamb. Springer International Publishing.

Brightman, Marc, Carlos Fausto, and Vanessa Grotti. 2016. "Introduction: Altering Ownership in Amazonia." In *Ownership and Nurture: Studies in Native Amazonian Property Relations*, edited by Marc Brightman, Carlos Fausto, and Vanessa Grotti. Berghahn Books.

Brockington, Dan. 2002. *Fortress Conservation: The Preservation of the Mkomazi Game Reserve, Tanzania*. Indiana University Press.

Brown, Michael A. 2004. "Heritage as Property." In *Property in Question: Value Transformation in the Global Economy*, edited by Caroline Humphrey and Katherine Verdery. Berg Publishers.

Brown, Wendy. 2010. *Walled States, Waning Sovereignty*. Zone Books.

Buadaeng, Kwanchewan. 2003. *Buddhism, Christianity and the Ancestors: Religion and Pragmatism in a Skaw Karen Community of North Thailand*. Social Research Institute, Chiang Mai University.

Bubandt, Nils. 2014. *The Empty Seashell: Witchcraft and Doubt on an Indonesian Island*. Cornell University Press.

Bubandt, Nils. 2017. "Haunted Geologies: Spirits, Stones, and the Necropolitics of the Anthropocene." In *Arts of Living on a Damaged Planet*, edited by Anna Lowenhaupt Tsing, Heather Swanson, Elaine Gan, and Nils Bubandt. University of Minnesota Press.

Bubandt, Nils, Astrid Oberborbeck Andersen, and Rachel Cypher, eds. 2023. *Rubber Boots Methods for the Anthropocene: Doing Fieldwork in Multispecies Worlds*. University of Minnesota Press.

Burma Gazetteer. 1910. *Salween District: Volume A*. Government Printing, Burma.

Büscher, Bram. 2013. *Transforming the Frontier: Peace Parks and the Politics of Neoliberal Conservation in Southern Africa*. Duke University Press.

Büscher, Bram, and Robert Fletcher. 2020. *The Conservation Revolution: Radical Ideas for Saving Nature Beyond the Anthropocene.* Verso.

Butt Colson, Audrey. 1973. "Inter-Tribal Trade in the Guiana Highlands." *Antropológica* 34.

Cadena, Marisol de la. 2010. "Indigenous Cosmopolitics in the Andes: Conceptual Reflections Beyond 'Politics.'" *Cultural Anthropology* 25 (2): 334–70. https://doi.org/10.1111/j.1548-1360.2010.01061.x.

Cadena, Marisol de la. 2015. *Earth Beings: Ecologies of Practice Across Andean Worlds.* Duke University Press.

Callon, Michel. 1984. "Some Elements of a Sociology of Translation: Domestication of the Scallops and the Fishermen of St Brieuc Bay." *Sociological Review* 32 (1_suppl): 196–233. https://doi.org/10.1111/j.1467-954X.1984.tb00113.x.

Campbell, Stephen. 2018. *Border Capitalism, Disrupted: Precarity and Struggle in a Southeast Asian Industrial Zone.* Cornell University Press.

CAT (Conservation Alliance of Tanawthari). 2020. *Tanawthari Landscape of Life: A Grassroots Alternative to Top-Down Conservation in Tanintharyi Region.* https://www.iccaconsortium.org/wp-content/uploads/2020/05/Tanawthari-Landscape-of-Life-A-grassroots-alternative-to-top-down-conservation-in-Tanintharyi-Region.pdf.

Chambers, Justine. 2024. *Pursuing Morality: Buddhism and Everyday Ethics in Southeastern Myanmar.* National University of Singapore Press.

Chao, Sophie. 2022. *In the Shadow of the Palms: More-Than-Human Becomings in West Papua.* Duke University Press.

Chao, Sophie, Karin Bolender, and Eben Kirksey, eds. 2022. *The Promise of Multispecies Justice.* Duke University Press.

Cheesman, Nick. 2002. "Seeing 'Karen' in the Union of Myanmar." *Asian Ethnicity* 3 (2): 199–220. https://doi.org/10.1080/14631360220132736.

Cho, Violet. 2014. "The Academic Life of Savages." *Journal of Burma Studies* 18 (1): 23–31. https://doi.org/10.1353/jbs.2014.0003.

Cho, Violet. 2023. "Constructing Taohpwoh: Journeying Through Pwakanyaw Christian Model Communities and Its Indigenous Social Paradigm." PhD thesis, Australian National University. https://openresearch-repository.anu.edu.au/handle/1885/287423.

Christie, Clive. 2000. "The Karens: Loyalism and Self-Determination." In *Turbulent Times and Enduring People: Mountain Minorities in the South-East Asian Massif,* edited by Jean Michaud. Curzon. Routledge

Chua, Liana, Joanna Cook, Nicholas Long, and Lee Wilson. 2012. "Introduction: Power and Orientation in Southeast Asia." In *Southeast Asian Perspec-*

tives on Power, edited by Liana Chua, Joanna Cook, Nicholas Long, and Lee Wilson. Routledge.

Clastres, Pierre. 1987. *Society Against the State: Essays in Political Anthropology*. Translated by Robert Hurley and Abe Stein. Zone Books.

Clifford, James. 1997. *Routes: Travel and Translation in the Late Twentieth Century*. Harvard University Press.

Clifford, James. 2003. *On the Edges of Anthropology: Interviews*. Prickly Paradigm Press.

Cole, Tomas. 2020. "'Power-Hurt': The Pains of Kindness Among Disabled Karen Refugees in Thailand." *Ethnos* 85 (2): 224–40. https://doi.org/10.1080/00141844.2018.1542411.

Comaroff, Joshua, and Ong Ker-Shing. 2016. "Paramilitary Gardening." *Why Singapore Blog*. https://whysingaporeblog.files.wordpress.com/2016/09/paramilitary-gardening.pdf.

Critchley, Simon. 2007. *Infinitely Demanding: Ethics of Commitment, Politics of Resistance*. Verso.

Crosson, J. Brent. 2019. "What Possessed You? Spirits, Property, and Political Sovereignty at the Limits of 'Possession.'" *Ethnos* 84 (4): 546–56. https://doi.org/10.1080/00141844.2017.1401704.

Derrida, Jacques. 1994. *Specters of Marx: The State of the Debt, the Work of Mourning and the New International*. Translated by Peggy Kamuf. Routledge.

Descola, Philippe. 2013. *Beyond Nature and Culture*. Translated by Janet Lloyd. University of Chicago Press.

Desjarlais, Robert R. 1992. *Body and Emotion: The Aesthetics of Illness and Healing in the Nepal Himalayas*. University of Pennsylvania Press.

Despret, Vinciane, and Michel Meuret. 2016. "Cosmoecological Sheep and the Arts of Living on a Damaged Planet." *Environmental Humanities* 8 (1): 24–36. https://doi.org/10.1215/22011919-3527704.

Dooren, Thom van, Eben Kirksey, and Ursula Münster. 2016. "Multispecies Studies: Cultivating Arts of Attentiveness." *Environmental Humanities* 8 (1): 1–23. https://doi.org/10.1215/22011919-3527695.

Empson, Rebecca, and Lauren Bonilla. 2019. "Introduction: Temporary Possession." *Fieldsights*, March 29. https://culanth.org/fieldsights/introduction-temporary-possession.

Endicott, Kirk. 2011. "Cooperative Autonomy: Social Solidarity Among the Batek of Malaysia." In *Anarchic Solidarity: Autonomy, Equality, and Fellowship in Southeast Asia*, edited by Thomas Gibson and Kenneth Sillander. Yale University Press.

Errington, Shelly. 1990. "Recasting Sex, Gender and Power: A Theoretical and Regional Overview." In *Power and Difference: Gender in Island Southeast Asia*, edited by Jane Monnig Atkinson and Shelly Errington. Stanford University Press.

Errington, Shelly. 2012. "The Subject of Power in Southeast Asia." In *Southeast Asian Perspectives on Power*, edited by Liana Chua, Joanna Cook, Nicholas Long, and Lee Wilson. Routledge.

Escobar, Arturo. 1999. "After Nature: Steps to an Antiessentialist Political Ecology." *Current Anthropology* 40 (1): 1–16. https://doi.org/10.1086/515799.

Equator Initiative. 2020. "What's the Equator Prize?" United Nations Development Programme. https://www.equatorinitiative.org/equator-prize/.

Evans-Pritchard, E. E. 1976. *Witchcraft, Oracles, and Magic Among the Azande*. Clarendon.

Faier, Lieba. 2009. *Intimate Encounters: Filipina Women and the Remaking of Rural Japan*. University of California Press.

Fairhead, James, Melissa Leach, and Ian Scoones. 2012. "Green Grabbing: A New Appropriation of Nature?" *Journal of Peasant Studies* 39 (2): 237–61. https://doi.org/10.1080/03066150.2012.671770.

Favret-Saada, Jeanne. 1980. *Deadly Words: Witchcraft in the Bocage*. Cambridge University Press.

Ferguson, James. 1994. *The Anti-Politics Machine: "Development," Depoliticization, and Bureaucratic Power in Lesotho*. University of Minnesota Press.

Ferguson, James. 2013. "Declarations of Dependence: Labour, Personhood, and Welfare in Southern Africa." *Journal of the Royal Anthropological Institute* 19 (2): 223–42. https://doi.org/10.1111/1467-9655.12023.

Ferguson, James, and Akhil Gupta. 2002. "Spatializing States: Toward an Ethnography of Neoliberal Governmentality." *American Ethnologist* 29 (4): 981–1002.

Ferguson, Jane M. 2014. "The Scramble for the Waste Lands: Tracking Colonial Legacies, Counterinsurgency and International Investment Through the Lens of Land Laws in Burma/Myanmar." *Singapore Journal of Tropical Geography* 35 (3): 295–311. https://doi.org/10.1111/sjtg.12078.

Forsyth, Tim, and Andrew Walker. 2008. *Forest Guardians, Forest Destroyers: The Politics of Environmental Knowledge in Northern Thailand*. University of Washington Press.

Forth, Gregory L. 1998. *Beneath the Volcano: Religion, Cosmology and Spirit Classification Among the Nage of Eastern Indonesia*. Brill.

Foucault, Michel. 2003. *"Society Must Be Defended": Lectures at the Collège de France, 1975–1976*. Edited by Mauro Bertani and Alessandro Fontana. Translated by David Macey. Picador.

Fujimura, Hitomi. 2020. "The Emergence of *Dawkalu* in the Karen Ethnic Claim in the 1880s and the Beginning of Contestations for 'Native Races.'" In *Living with Myanmar*, edited by Justine Chambers, Charlotte Galloway, and Jonathan Liljeblad. ISEAS-Yusof Ishak Institute.

Furnivall, J. S. 1948. *Colonial Policy and Practice: A Comparative Study of Burma and Netherlands India*. Cambridge University Press.

Furnivall, J. S. 1960. *The Governance of Modern Burma*. 2nd ed. Institute of Pacific Relations.

Gagnon, Terese V., ed. 2024. *Embodying Biodiversity: Sensory Conservation as Refuge and Sovereignty*. University of Arizona Press.

Galtung, Johan. 1967. "Theories of Peace: A Synthetic Approach to Peace Thinking." International Peace Research Institute. https://www.transcend.org/files/Galtung_Book_unpub_Theories_of_Peace_-_A_Synthetic_Approach_to_Peace_Thinking_1967.pdf.

Gan, Elaine, Anna Tsing, Heather Swanson, and Nils Bubandt. 2017. "Introduction: Haunted Landscapes of the Anthropocene." In *Arts of Living on a Damaged Planet*, edited by Anna Lowenhaupt Tsing, Heather Swanson, Elaine Gan, and Nils Bubandt. University of Minnesota Press.

Ghosh, Amitav. 2016. *The Great Derangement: Climate Change and the Unthinkable*. University of Chicago Press.

Gibson, Thomas, and Kenneth Sillander. 2011. *Anarchic Solidarity: Autonomy, Equality, and Fellowship in Southeast Asia*. Yale University Press.

Gilroy, Paul. 2004. *After Empire: Melancholia or Convivial Culture?* Routledge.

Good, Byron J. 1993. "Medical Anthropology and the Problem of Belief." In *Medicine, Rationality, and Experience: An Anthropological Perspective*. Lewis Henry Morgan Lectures. Cambridge University Press.

Goodrich, John, Hariyo T. Wibisono, Dale Miquelle et al. 2015. *Panthera tigris*. The IUCN Red List of Threatened Species. https://doi.org/10.2305/IUCN.UK.2015-2.RLTS.T15955A50659951.en.

Govindrajan, Radhika. 2018. *Animal Intimacies: Interspecies Relatedness in India's Central Himalayas*. University of Chicago Press.

Govindrajan, Radhika. 2022. "Spectral Justice." In *The Promise of Multispecies Justice*, edited by Sophie Chao, Karin Bolender, and Eben Kirksey. Duke University Press.

Graeber, David. 2012. *Debt: The First 5,000 Years*. Melville House.

Graeber, David. 2015. "Radical Alterity Is Just Another Way of Saying 'Reality': A Reply to Eduardo Viveiros de Castro." *HAU: Journal of Ethnographic Theory* 5 (2): 1–41. https://doi.org/10.14318/hau5.2.003.

Gravers, Mikael. 1999. *Nationalism as Political Paranoia in Burma: An Essay on the Historical Practice of Power*. Curzon.

Gravers, Mikael. 2007. "Conversion and Identity: Religion and the Formation of Karen Ethnic Identity in Burma." In *Exploring Ethnic Diversity in Burma*, edited by Mikael Gravers. NIAS Press.

Guillou, Anne Yvonne. 2017. "Potent Places and Animism in Southeast Asia." *Asia Pacific Journal of Anthropology* 18 (5): 389–99. https://doi.org/10.1080/14442213.2017.1401324.

Hage, Ghassan. 2015. *Alter-Politics: Critical Anthropology and the Radical Imagination*. Melbourne University Press.

Hansen, Thomas Blom. 2006. "Performers of Sovereignty: On the Privatization of Security in Urban South Africa." *Critique of Anthropology* 26 (3): 279–95. https://doi.org/10.1177/0308275X06066583.

Hansen, Thomas Blom, and Finn Stepputat. 2006. "Sovereignty Revisited." *Annual Review of Anthropology* 35 (1): 295–315. https://doi.org/10.1146/annurev.anthro.35.081705.123317.

Haraway, Donna J. 2007. *When Species Meet*. University of Minnesota Press.

Harrisson, Annika Pohl. 2021. "Fish Caught in Clear Water: Encompassed State-Making in South-East Myanmar." *Territory, Politics, Governance* 9 (4): 533–52. https://doi.org/10.1080/21622671.2020.1743200.

Harrisson, Annika Pohl, and Helene Maria Kyed. 2019. "Ceasefire State-Making and Justice Provision by Ethnic Armed Groups in Southeast Myanmar." *Sojourn: Journal of Social Issues in Southeast Asia* 34 (2): 290–326. https://doi.org/10.1355/sj34-2c.

Hartman, Saidiya. 2019. *Wayward Lives, Beautiful Experiments: Intimate Histories of Social Upheaval*. W. W. Norton.

Harvey, David. 2003. "Accumulation by Dispossession." In *The New Imperialism*. Oxford University Press.

Harvey, David. 2004. "The 'New' Imperialism: Accumulation by Dispossession." *Socialist Register* 40:63–87.

Harvey, Penny, and Hannah Knox. 2015. *Roads: An Anthropology of Infrastructure and Expertise*. Cornell University Press.

Hauʻofa, Epeli. 2008. *We Are the Ocean: Selected Works*. University of Hawaiʻi Press.

Hayami, Yōko. 1993. "To Be Karen and to Be Cool: Community, Morality and Identity Among Sgaw Karen in Northern Thailand." *Cahiers des sciences humaines* 29 (4): 747–62.

Hayami, Yōko. 2004. *Between Hills and Plains: Power and Practice in Socio-Religious Dynamics Among Karen*. Trans Pacific Press.

Herrera, César E. Giraldo. 2018. *Microbes and Other Shamanic Beings*. Palgrave Macmillan.

Hetherington, Kregg. 2011. *Guerrilla Auditors: The Politics of Transparency in Neoliberal Paraguay.* Duke University Press.

Hobbes, Thomas. 1651. *Leviathan: Or the Matter, Forme, & Power of a Common-Wealth Ecclesiasticall and Civill.* London.

Holbraad, Martin, and Morten Axel Pedersen. 2017. *The Ontological Turn: An Anthropological Exposition.* Cambridge University Press.

Holbraad, Martin, Morten Axel Pedersen, and Eduardo Viveiros de Castro. 2014. "The Politics of Ontology: Anthropological Positions." *Fieldsights*, January 13. https://culanth.org/fieldsights/the-politics-of-ontology-anthropological-positions.

Holt, John Clifford. 2009. *Spirits of the Place: Buddhism and Lao Religious Culture.* University of Hawai'i Press.

Hong, Emily. 2017. "Scaling Struggles over Land and Law: Autonomy, Investment, and Interlegality in Myanmar's Borderlands." *Geoforum* 82 (June): 225–36. https://doi.org/10.1016/j.geoforum.2017.01.017.

Hornborg, Alf. 2017a. "Convictions, Beliefs, and the Suspension of Disbelief: On the Insidious Logic of Neoliberalism." *HAU: Journal of Ethnographic Theory* 7 (1): 553–58. https://doi.org/10.14318/hau7.1.042.

Hornborg, Alf. 2017b. "Dithering While the Planet Burns: Anthropologists' Approaches to the Anthropocene." *Reviews in Anthropology* 46 (2–3): 61–77. https://doi.org/10.1080/00938157.2017.1343023.

Horstmann, Alexander. 2011a. "Ethical Dilemmas and Identifications of Faith-Based Humanitarian Organizations in the Karen Refugee Crisis." *Journal of Refugee Studies* 24 (3): 513–32. https://doi.org/10.1093/jrs/fer031.

Horstmann, Alexander. 2011b. "Sacred Networks and Struggles Among the Karen Baptists Across the Thailand-Burma Border." *Moussons*, no. 17:85–104. https://doi.org/10.4000/moussons.551.

Howell, Signe. 2002. "Nesting, Eclipsing and Hierarchy. Processes of Gendered Values Among Lio." *Social Anthropology* 10 (2): 159–72. https://doi.org/10.1111/j.1469-8676.2002.tb00052.x.

Htoo, Sheila. n.d. "The Salween Peace Park: An Alternative Vision of Building Genuine 'Peace' from Grassroot Indigenous-Led Conservation Movement in Karen State of Southeast Myanmar/Burma." PhD thesis, York University.

Huard, Stéphen. 2019. "Beyond the Village Headman: Transformations of the Local Polity in Central Myanmar (1750s–2010s)." PhD thesis, School of International Development, University of East Anglia.

Huard, Stéphen. 2020. "Nobody Owns the Land: How Inheritance Shapes Land Relations in the Central Plain of Myanmar." *Journal of Burma Studies* 24 (1): 79–117. https://doi.org/10.1353/jbs.2020.0004.

ICCAs. 2023. "Tanawthari Landscape of Life: A Community-Led Alternative to Top-Down Conservation." ICCA Consortium, last updated June 13, 2023. https://www.iccaconsortium.org/index.php/2020/05/22/tanawthari-landscape-of-life-a-community-led-alternative-to-top-down-conservation/.

Illich, Ivan. (1973) 1975. *Tools for Conviviality*. Fontana/Collins.

Ingold, Tim. 2000. *The Perception of the Environment: Essays on Livelihood, Dwelling and Skill*. Routledge.

Ingold, Tim. 2006. "Rethinking the Animate, Re-animating Thought." *Ethnos* 71 (1): 9–20. https://doi.org/10.1080/00141840600603111.

Ingold, Tim. 2011. *Being Alive: Essays on Movement, Knowledge and Description*. Routledge.

Isaacs, Jenny R., and Ariel Otruba. 2019. "Guest Introduction: More-than-Human Contact Zones." *Environment and Planning E: Nature and Space* 2 (4): 697–711. https://doi.org/10.1177/2514848619855369.

Jackson, Michael. 1996. "Introduction: Phenomenology, Radical Empiricism, and Anthropological Critique." In *Things as They Are: New Directions in Phenomenological Anthropology*, edited by Michael Jackson. Indiana University Press.

James, William. 1907. *Pragmatism: A New Name for Some Old Ways of Thinking*. Longmans, Green.

Jolliffe, Kim. 2016. *Ceasefires, Governance, and Development: The Karen National Union in Times of Change*. Asia Foundation.

Kammerer, Cornelia Ann, and Nicola Tannenbaum. 2003. Introduction to *Founders' Cults in Southeast Asia: Ancestors, Polity, and Identity*, edited by Nicola Tannenbaum and Cornelia Ann Kammerer. Yale University Press.

Karen Rivers Watch. 2016. "Press Release by KRW on Recent Fighting in Karen State." Press release, September 29. https://kesan.asia/press-release-by-krw-on-recent-fighting-in-karen-state/.

Karlsson, Bengt G. 2011. *Unruly Hills: A Political Ecology of India's Northeast*. Berghahn Books.

Karlsson, Bengt G. 2017. "Shillong: Tribal Urbanity in the Northeast Indian Borderland." *IIAS: The Newsletter* 77:32–33.

Karlsson, Bengt G. 2018. "After Political Ecology." *Anthropology Today* 34 (2): 22–24. https://doi.org/10.1111/1467-8322.12422.

Kasfir, Nelson. 2015. "Rebel Governance—Constructing a Field of Inquiry: Definitions, Scope, Patterns, Order, Causes." In *Rebel Governance in Civil War*, edited by Ana Arjona, Nelson Kasfir, and Zachariah Mampilly. Cambridge University Press.

Kauffmann, H. E. 1971. "Stone Memorials of the Lawā (Northwest Thailand)." *Journal of the Siam Society* 59 (1): 129–51.

Kauffmann, H. E. 1977. "Some Social and Religious Institutions of the Lawā (Northwestern Thailand). Part II." *Journal of the Siam Society Bangkok* 65 (1): 181–226.

Keeler, Ward. 2017. *The Traffic in Hierarchy: Masculinity and Its Others in Buddhist Burma.* University of Hawai'i Press.

KESAN (Karen Environmental and Social Action Network). 2019. "Celebrating the Salween Peace Park Proclamation." Karen Environmental and Social Action Network, January 9. http://kesan.asia/celebrating-the-salween-peace-park-proclamation/.

KESAN (Karen Environmental and Social Action Network). 2024. "The 5th General Assembly of the Salween Peace Park." Karen Environmental and Social Action Network, February 13. https://kesan.asia/the-5th-general-assembly-of-the-salween-peace-park/.

Keyes, Charles F. (1977) 1995. *The Golden Peninsula: Culture and Adaptation in Mainland Southeast Asia.* University of Hawai'i Press.

Keyes, Charles F. 2003. "Afterword: The Politics of 'Karen-ness' in Thailand." In *Living at the Edge of Thai Society: The Karen in the Highlands of Northern Thailand,* edited by Claudio O. Delang. RoutledgeCurzon.

Khayyat, Munira. 2022. *A Landscape of War: Ecologies of Resistance and Survival in South Lebanon.* University of California Press.

KHRG (Karen Human Rights Group). 2000. *Suffering in Silence: The Human Rights Nightmare of the Karen People of Burma.* Edited by Claudio O. Delang. Universal Publishers.

KHRG (Karen Human Rights Group). 2009. *Patterns of Abuse: Photographs of Rural Life in a Militarized Karen State.* Karen Human Rights Group.

KHRG (Karen Human Rights Group). 2012. *Uncertain Ground: Landmines in Eastern Burma.* http://web.archive.org/web/20121020032542/http://www.khrg.org/khrg2012/khrg1201.pdf.

KHRG (Karen Human Rights Group). 2019. "Statement: 12 March 2019, Day One." https://khrg.org/sites/khrg.org/files/report-docs/statement_vfv_day_one.pdf.

Kim, Eleana J. 2016. "Toward an Anthropology of Landmines: Rogue Infrastructure and Military Waste in the Korean DMZ." *Cultural Anthropology* 31 (2): 162–87. https://doi.org/10.14506/ca31.2.02.

Kim, Eleana J. 2022. *Making Peace with Nature: Ecological Encounters Along the Korean DMZ.* Duke University Press.

Kimmerer, Robin Wall. (2013) 2020. *Braiding Sweetgrass: Indigenous Wisdom, Scientific Knowledge, and the Teachings of Plants.* Penguin Books.

Kirksey, Eben. 2012. *Freedom in Entangled Worlds: West Papua and the Architecture of Global Power.* Duke University Press.

Klein, Naomi. 2008. *The Shock Doctrine: The Rise of Disaster Capitalism*. Picador.

Kleinman, Arthur. 1997. "'Everything That Really Matters': Social Suffering, Subjectivity, and the Remaking of Human Experience in a Disordering World." *Harvard Theological Review* 90 (3): 315–36. https://doi.org/10.1017/S0017816000006374.

KNU (Karen National Union). 2015. *Land Policy*. December. https://www.tni.org/files/article-downloads/knu_land_policy_eng.pdf.

Krøijer, Stine. 2010. "Figurations of the Future: On the Form and Temporality of Protests Among Left Radical Activists in Europe." *Social Analysis: The International Journal of Anthropology* 54 (3): 139–52. https://doi.org/10.3167/sa.2010.540309.

Kwon, Heonik. 2008. *Ghosts of War in Vietnam*. Cambridge University Press.

Kyed, Helene Maria, ed. 2020. *Everyday Justice in Myanmar: Informal Resolutions and State Evasion in a Time of Contested Transition*. NIAS Press.

Kyed, Helene Maria, and Mikael Gravers. 2014. "The Future of Armed Actors: Sustainable Peace in Myanmar." Danish Institute for International Studies policy brief, September, 2014.

Lambek, Michael. 1981. *Human Spirits: A Cultural Account of Trance in Mayotte*. Cambridge University Press.

Lambek, Michael. 1996. "Afterword: Spirits and Their Histories." In *Spirits in Culture, History, and Mind*, edited by Jeannette Marie Mageo and Alan Howard. Routledge.

Landmine and Cluster Munition Monitor. 2013. "Myanmar/Burma: Casualties and Victim Assistance." Last updated October 30, 2013. http://archives.the-monitor.org/index.php/cp/display/region_profiles/theme/2869.

Latour, Bruno. 1993. *We Have Never Been Modern*. Translated by Catherine Porter. Harvard University Press.

Latour, Bruno. 2002. *War of the Worlds: What About Peace?* Translated by Charlotte Bigg. Edited by John Tresch. Prickly Paradigm Press.

Latour, Bruno. 2004. "Whose Cosmos, Which Cosmopolitics? Comments on the Peace Terms of Ulrich Beck." *Common Knowledge* 10 (3): 450–62. https://doi.org/10.1215/0961754X-10-3-450.

Latour, Bruno. 2005. *Reassembling the Social: An Introduction to Actor-Network-Theory*. Oxford University Press.

Leach, E. R. 1954. *Political Systems of Highland Burma: A Study of Kachin Social Structure*. Harvard University Press.

Lehman, F. K. 2003. "The Relevance of the Founders' Cult for Understanding the Political Systems of the Peoples of Northern Southeast Asia and Its Chinese Borderlands." In *Founders' Cults in Southeast Asia: Ancestors, Polity, and Identity*, edited by Nicola Tannenbaum and Cornelia Ann Kammerer. Yale University Press.

Li, Tania Murray. 2007. *The Will to Improve: Governmentality, Development, and the Practice of Politics*. Duke University Press.

Li, Tania Murray. 2010. "Indigeneity, Capitalism, and the Management of Dispossession." *Current Anthropology* 51 (3): 385–414. https://doi.org/10.1086/651942.

Li, Tania Murray. 2014a. *Land's End: Capitalist Relations on an Indigenous Frontier*. Duke University Press.

Li, Tania Murray. 2014b. "What Is Land? Assembling a Resource for Global Investment." *Transactions of the Institute of British Geographers* 39 (4): 589–602. https://doi.org/10.1111/tran.12065.

Lintner, Bertil. 2015. *Burmas historia*. Svenska Historiska Media Förlag AB.

Locke, John. (1689) 2003. *Two Treatises of Government and a Letter Concerning Toleration*. Edited by Ian Shapiro. Yale University Press.

Löfving, Staffan. 2007. "Liberal Emplacement: Violence, Home, and the Transforming Space of Popular Protest in Central America." *Focaal* 2007 (49): 45–61. https://doi.org/10.3167/foc.2007.490105.

Loong, Shona. 2025. "More-Than-Rebel Territory: War, Resistance, and Relations in the Salween Peace Park." *Annals of the American Association of Geographers*, published online, April 2. https://doi.org/10.1080/24694452.2025.2478262.

Lund, Christian. 2018. "Predatory Peace: Dispossession at Aceh's Oil Palm Frontier." *Journal of Peasant Studies* 45 (2): 431–52. https://doi.org/10.1080/03066150.2017.1351434.

Lwin, Nan. 2019. "Daw Aung San Suu Kyi Pitches Investors on Rakhine State." *The Irrawaddy*, February 22. https://www.irrawaddy.com/business/daw-aung-san-suu-kyi-pitches-investors-rakhine-state.html.

Mac Ginty, Roger. 2008. "Indigenous Peace-Making Versus the Liberal Peace." *Cooperation and Conflict* 43 (2): 139–63. https://doi.org/10.1177/0010836708089080.

MacNeal, David. 2017. *Bugged: The Insects Who Rule the World and the People Obsessed with Them*. St. Martin's Press.

Maeckelbergh, Marianne. 2009. *The Will of the Many: How the Alterglobalisation Movement Is Changing the Face of Democracy*. Pluto Press.

Magee, Darrin, and Shawn Kelley. 2009. "Damming the Salween River." In *Contested Waterscapes in the Mekong Region: Hydropower, Livelihoods and Governance*, edited by François Molle, Tira Foran, and Mira Käkönen. Routledge.

Makki, Fouad. 2014. "Development by Dispossession: *Terra Nullius* and the Social-Ecology of New Enclosures in Ethiopia." *Rural Sociology* 79 (1): 79–103. https://doi.org/10.1111/ruso.12033.

Mampilly, Zachariah Cherian. 2011. *Rebel Rulers: Insurgent Governance and Civilian Life During War*. Cornell University Press.

Marshall, Harry Ignatius. 1922. *The Karen People of Burma: A Study in Anthropology and Ethnology*. Ohio State University.

Martin, Keir. 2014. "Sovereignty and Freedom in West Papua and Beyond." *Oceania* 84 (3): 342–48. https://doi.org/10.1002/ocea.5064.

Marton-LeFèvre, Julia. 2007. Foreword to *Peace Parks: Conservation and Conflict Resolution*, edited by Saleem H. Ali. MIT Press.

Marx, Karl, and Friedrich Engels. (1848) 2008. *The Communist Manifesto*. Pluto Press.

Masco, Joseph, and Deborah A. Thomas. 2023. "Introduction: Feeling Unhinged." In *Sovereignty Unhinged: An Illustrated Primer for the Study of Present Intensities, Disavowals, and Temporal Derangements*, edited by Deborah A. Thomas and Joseph Masco, 1–23. Duke University Press.

Mauss, Marcel. (1925) 2002. *The Gift: The Form and Reason for Exchange in Archaic Societies*. Translated by W. D. Halls. Routledge.

McConnachie, Kirsten. 2014. *Governing Refugees: Justice, Order and Legal Pluralism*. Routledge.

Mehtta, Megnaa. 2022. "Nonhuman Governance: Care and Violence in South Asian Animism." *Comparative Studies of South Asia, Africa and the Middle East* 42 (3): 584–602. https://doi.org/10.1215/1089201X-10148247.

Middleton, Beth Rose. 2015. "*Jahát Jatítotòdom*: Toward an Indigenous Political Ecology." In *The International Handbook of Political Ecology*, edited by Raymond L. Bryant. Edward Elgar Publishing.

Middleton, Carl, Alec Scott, and Vanessa Lamb. 2019. "Hydropower Politics and Conflict on the Salween River." In *Knowing the Salween River: Resource Politics of a Contested Transboundary River*, edited by Carl Middleton and Vanessa Lamb. Springer International Publishing.

Milne, Sarah. 2022. *Corporate Nature: An Insider's Ethnography of Global Conservation*. University of Arizona Press.

Moo, Hsa, and Brennan O'Connor. 2018. "Villagers Flee as Specter of War Returns to Northern Karen State." *The Irrawaddy*, March 30. https://www.irrawaddy.com/opinion/guest-column/villagers-flee-specter-war-returns-northern-karen-state.html.

Morris, Brian. 2014. *Anthropology, Ecology, and Anarchism: A Brian Morris Reader*. PM Press.

Myanmar Now. 2021. "KNU Seizes Control of Tatmadaw Base in Kayin State." *Myanmar Now*, March 27. https://myanmar-now.org/en/news/knu-seizes-control-of-tatmadaw-base-in-kayin-state/.

Mutraw District, Salween Peace Park Steering Committee, and Karen National Union. 2018. *Charter of the Salween Peace Park*. December 2018. https://kesan.asia/wp-content/uploads/2018/12/SPP-Charter-Eng.pdf.

Naing, Saw Yan. 2016. "Upcoming Karen Congress Elections Uncertain." *The Irrawaddy*, November 3. https://www.irrawaddy.com/news/burma/upcoming-karen-congress-elections-uncertain.html.

Nathan, Tobie. 2004. "The Phasmid and the Twig." *Common Knowledge* 10 (3): 518–31. https://doi.org/10.1215/0961754X-10-3-518.

Nazarea, Virginia D. 2005. *Heirloom Seeds and Their Keepers: Marginality and Memory in the Conservation of Biological Diversity*. University of Arizona Press.

Neumann, Roderick P. 2005. *Making Political Ecology*. Hodder Arnold.

Nyein, Nyein. 2020. "Thousands of Villagers in Myanmar's Karen State Protest Army Killings of Civilians." *The Irrawaddy*, June 28. https://www.irrawaddy.com/news/burma/thousands-villagers-myanmars-karen-state-protest-army-killings-civilians.html.

OHCHR (Office of the United Nations High Commissioner for Human Rights). 2020. "Detailed Findings of the Independent International Fact-Finding Mission on Myanmar." United Nations Human Rights Council. https://www.ohchr.org/Documents/HRBodies/HRCouncil/FFM-Myanmar/20190916/A_HRC_42_CRP.5.pdf.

Ong, Aihwa. 2006. *Neoliberalism as Exception: Mutations in Citizenship and Sovereignty*. Duke University Press.

Ong, Andrew. 2023. *Stalemate: Autonomy and Insurgency on the China-Myanmar Border*. Cornell University Press.

Pannell, Sandra. 2007. "Of Gods and Monsters: Indigenous Sea Cosmologies, Promiscuous Geographies and the Depths of Local Sovereignty." In *A World of Water: Rain, Rivers and Seas in Southeast Asian Histories*, edited by Peter Boomgaard. KITLV Press.

Paris, Roland. 2004. *At War's End: Building Peace After Civil Conflict*. Cambridge University Press.

Paul, Andrew. 2018. "'With the Salween Peace Park, We Can Survive as a Nation': Karen Environmental Relations and the Politics of an Indigenous Conservation Project." Master's thesis, York University, Toronto.

Pedersen, Morten Axel. 2011. *Not Quite Shamans: Spirit Worlds and Political Lives in Northern Mongolia*. Cornell University Press.

Peluso, Nancy Lee. 1995. "Whose Woods Are These? Counter-Mapping Forest Territories in Kalimantan, Indonesia." *Antipode* 27 (4): 383–406. https://doi.org/10.1111/j.1467-8330.1995.tb00286.x.

Peluso, Nancy Lee, and Peter Vandergeest. 2011. "Taking the Jungle out of the Forest: Counter-Insurgency and the Making of National Natures." In *Global Political Ecology*, edited by Richard Peet, Paul Robbins, and Michael J. Watts. Routledge.

Peluso, Nancy Lee, and Michael Watts. 2001. *Violent Environments*. Cornell University Press.

Polanyi, Karl. (1944) 2001. *The Great Transformation: The Political and Economic Origins of Our Time*. 2nd ed. Beacon Press.

Povinelli, Elizabeth A. 2011. "Routes/Worlds." *e-flux*, no. 27. https://www.e-flux.com/journal/27/67991/routes-worlds/.

Povinelli, Elizabeth A. 2012. "The Will to Be Otherwise/The Effort of Endurance." *South Atlantic Quarterly* 111 (3): 453–75. https://doi.org/10.1215/00382876-1596236.

Pratt, Mary Louise. 1991. "Arts of the Contact Zone." *Profession*, 33–40.

Pratt, Mary Louise. 2008. *Imperial Eyes: Travel Writing and Transculturation*. 2nd ed. Routledge.

Radcliffe-Brown, A. R. 1952. *Structure and Function in Primitive Society: Essays and Addresses*. Free Press.

Rajah, Ananda. 1990. "Ethnicity, Nationalism, and the Nation-State: The Karen in Burma and Thailand." In *Ethnic Groups Across National Boundaries in Mainland Southeast Asia*, edited by Gehan Wijeyewardene. Institute of Southeast Asian Studies.

Renard, Ronald D. 2003. "Studying Peoples Often Called Karen." In *Living at the Edge of Thai Society: The Karen in the Highlands of Northern Thailand*, edited by Claudio O. Delang. RoutledgeCurzon.

Rhoads, Elizabeth L., and Courtney T. Wittekind. 2018. "Rethinking Land and Property in a 'Transitioning' Myanmar: Representations of Isolation, Neglect, and Natural Decline." *Journal of Burma Studies* 22 (2): 171–213. https://doi.org/10.1353/jbs.2018.0011.

Richmond, Oliver P., and Roger Mac Ginty. 2015. "Where Now for the Critique of the Liberal Peace?" *Cooperation and Conflict* 50 (2): 171–89. https://doi.org/10.1177/0010836714545691.

RKIPN (Rays of Kamoethway Indigenous People Nature). 2016. "We Will Manage Our Own Natural Resources: Karen Indigenous People in Kamoethway Demonstrate the Importance of Local Solutions and Community-Driven Conservation." https://www.burmapartnership.net/wp-content/uploads/2016/03/Book_We-Will-Manage-Our-Own-Natural-Resources-English.pdf.

Robbins, Paul. 2012. *Political Ecology: A Critical Introduction*. 2nd ed. Wiley-Blackwell.

Ruiz-Serna, Daniel. 2023. *When Forests Run Amok: War and Its Afterlives in Indigenous and Afro-Colombian Territories*. Duke University Press.

Rutherford, Danilyn. 2012. *Laughing at Leviathan: Sovereignty and Audience in West Papua*. University of Chicago Press.

Sadan, Mandy. 2013. *Being and Becoming Kachin: Histories Beyond the State in the Borderworlds of Burma*. Oxford University Press.

Sahlins, Marshall. 2014. "On the Ontological Scheme of *Beyond Nature and Culture*." *HAU: Journal of Ethnographic Theory* 4 (1): 281–90. https://doi.org/10.14318/hau4.1.013.

Sahlins, Marshall. 2017. "The Original Political Society." *HAU: Journal of Ethnographic Theory* 7 (2): 91–128. https://doi.org/10.14318/hau7.2.014.

San C. Po. 1928. *Burma and the Karens*. Elliot Stock.

Schwenkel, Christina. 2017. "Haunted Infrastructure: Religious Ruins and Urban Obstruction in Vietnam." *City & Society* 29 (3): 413–34. https://doi.org/10.1111/ciso.12142.

Scotson, Lorraine, Gabriella Fredriksson, D. Augeri, Cheryl Cheah, Dusit Ngoprasert, and Wai-Ming Wong. 2017. *Helarctos malayanus*. The IUCN Red List of Threatened Species. https://doi.org/10.2305/IUCN.UK.2017-3.RLTS.T9760A45033547.en.

Scott, James C. 1998. *Seeing Like a State: How Certain Schemes to Improve the Human Condition Have Failed*. Yale University Press.

Scott, James C. 2009. *The Art of Not Being Governed: An Anarchist History of Upland Southeast Asia*. Yale University Press.

Shah, Alpa. 2013. "The Intimacy of Insurgency: Beyond Coercion, Greed or Grievance in Maoist India." *Economy and Society* 42 (3): 480–506. https://doi.org/10.1080/03085147.2013.783662.

Sikor, Thomas, and Christian Lund, eds. 2010. *The Politics of Possession: Property, Authority, and Access to Natural Resources*. John Wiley & Sons.

Simpson, Audra. 2014. *Mohawk Interruptus: Political Life Across the Borders of Settler States*. Duke University Press.

Skidmore, Monique. 2004. *Karaoke Fascism: Burma and the Politics of Fear*. University of Pennsylvania Press.

Smith, Martin. 1999. *Burma: Insurgency and the Politics of Ethnicity*, updated ed. Zed Books.

South, Ashley. 2008. *Ethnic Politics in Burma: States of Conflict*. Routledge.

South, Ashley. 2018. "'Hybrid Governance' and the Politics of Legitimacy in the Myanmar Peace Process." *Journal of Contemporary Asia* 48 (1): 50–66. https://doi.org/10.1080/00472336.2017.1387280.

South, Ashley, and Maria Katsabanis. 2007. *Displacement and Dispossession: Forced Migration and Land Rights in Burma*. Centre on Housing Rights and Evictions (COHRE).

Spiro, Melford E. (1967) 1996. *Burmese Supernaturalism: A Study in the Explanation and Reduction of Suffering*. Routledge.

Springate-Baginski, Oliver. 2018. *Decriminalise Agro-Forestry: A Primer on Shifting Cultivation in Myanmar*. The Transnational Institute. https://www.tni.org/files/publication-downloads/tni_p_shifting_cultivation_220518_online.pdf.

Springer, Simon. 2013. "Violent Accumulation: A Postanarchist Critique of Property, Dispossession, and the State of Exception in Neoliberalizing Cambodia." *Annals of the Association of American Geographers* 103 (3): 608–26. https://doi.org/10.1080/00045608.2011.628259.

Star, Susan Leigh, and James R. Griesemer. 1989. "Institutional Ecology, 'Translations' and Boundary Objects: Amateurs and Professionals in Berkeley's Museum of Vertebrate Zoology, 1907–39." *Social Studies of Science* 19 (3): 387–420.

Stengers, Isabelle. (1997) 2010. *Cosmopolitics I*. Translated by Robert Bononno. University of Minnesota Press.

Stengers, Isabelle. 2011. "Comparison as a Matter of Concern." *Common Knowledge* 17 (1): 48–63. https://doi.org/10.1215/0961754X-2010-035.

Stoler, Ann Laura. 2008. "Imperial Debris: Reflections on Ruins and Ruination." *Cultural Anthropology* 23 (2): 191–219. https://doi.org/10.1111/j.1548-1360.2008.00007.x.

Stoler, Ann Laura, ed. 2013. *Imperial Debris: On Ruins and Ruination*. Duke University Press.

Swancutt, Katherine. 2019. "Animism." In *The Open Encyclopedia of Anthropology*, edited by Felix Stein. https://doi.org/10.29164/19anim.

TallBear, Kim. 2019. "Caretaking Relations, Not American Dreaming." *Kalfou* 6 (1). https://doi.org/10.15367/kf.v6i1.228.

Tambiah, S. J. 1976. *World Conqueror and World Renouncer: A Study of Buddhism and Polity in Thailand Against a Historical Background*. Cambridge University Press.

Tan, See Seng. 2019. *The Responsibility to Provide in Southeast Asia: Towards an Ethical Explanation*. Bristol University Press.

Tannenbaum, Nicola. 2000. "Protest, Tree Ordination, and the Changing Context of Political Ritual." *Ethnology* 39 (2): 109–27. https://doi.org/10.2307/3773838.

Tarkapaw Youth Group. 2015. *"We Used to Fear Bullets, Now We Fear Bulldozers": Dirty Coal Mining by Military Cronies & Thai Companies, Ban*

Chaung, Dawei District, Myanmar. https://www.burmalibrary.org/docs21/TRIPN-2015-10-We_Used_to_Fear_Bullets-Now_We_Fear_Bulldozers-en-red.pdf.

Taylor, Robert H. 2009. *The State in Myanmar*. NUS Press.

Thomas, Deborah A., and Joseph Masco, eds. 2023. *Sovereignty Unhinged: An Illustrated Primer for the Study of Present Intensities, Disavowals, and Temporal Derangements*. Duke University Press.

Thwe, Pascal Khoo. 2003. *From the Land of Green Ghosts: A Burmese Odyssey*. Harper Perennial.

Todd, Zoe. 2016. "An Indigenous Feminist's Take on the Ontological Turn: 'Ontology' Is Just Another Word for Colonialism." *Journal of Historical Sociology* 29 (1): 4–22. https://doi.org/10.1111/johs.12124.

Trakansuphakon, Prasert. 2006. *Pga K'nyau Knowledge on Rotational Farming in Northern Thailand*. IKAP-Network.

Tsing, Anna Lowenhaupt. 2005. *Friction: An Ethnography of Global Connection*. Princeton University Press.

Tsing, Anna Lowenhaupt. 2012. "On Nonscalability: The Living World Is Not Amenable to Precision-Nested Scales." *Common Knowledge* 18 (3): 505–24. https://doi.org/10.1215/0961754X-1630424.

Tsing, Anna Lowenhaupt, Jennifer Deger, Alder Keleman Saxena, and Feifei Zhou. 2024. *Field Guide to the Patchy Anthropocene: The New Nature*. Stanford University Press.

Tsing, Anna Lowenhaupt, Andrew S. Mathews, and Nils Bubandt. 2019. "Patchy Anthropocene: Landscape Structure, Multispecies History, and the Retooling of Anthropology: An Introduction to Supplement 20." *Current Anthropology* 60 (S20): S186–97. https://doi.org/10.1086/703391.

Tsing, Anna Lowenhaupt, Heather Swanson, Elaine Gan, and Nils Bubandt, eds. 2017. *Arts of Living on a Damaged Planet*. University of Minnesota Press.

Tuck, Eve, and K. Wayne Yang. 2012. "Decolonization Is Not a Metaphor." *Decolonization: Indigeneity, Education & Society* 1 (1): 1–40.

Tylor, Edward B. 1920. *Primitive Culture*, vol. 1. John Murray.

UN (United Nations). 2007. *United Nations Declaration on the Rights of Indigenous Peoples*. https://www.un.org/development/desa/indigenouspeoples/wp-content/uploads/sites/19/2018/11/UNDRIP_E_web.pdf.

Viegas, Susana de Matos. 2016. "Temporalities of Ownership: Land Possession and Its Transformations Among the Tupinambá (Bahia, Brazil)." In *Ownership and Nurture: Studies in Native Amazonian Property Relations*, edited by Marc Brightman, Carlos Fausto, and Vanessa Grotti. Berghahn Books.

Vigh, Henrik. 2006. *Navigating Terrains of War: Youth and Soldiering in Guinea-Bissau*. Berghahn Books.

Vigh, Henrik. 2008. "Crisis and Chronicity: Anthropological Perspectives on Continuous Conflict and Decline." *Ethnos* 73 (1): 5–24. https://doi.org/10.1080/00141840801927509.

Vigh, Henrik, and David Brehm Sausdal. 2014. "From Essence Back to Existence: Anthropology Beyond the Ontological Turn." *Anthropological Theory* 14 (1): 49–73. https://doi.org/10.1177/1463499614524401.

Viveiros de Castro, Eduardo. 2004a. "Exchanging Perspectives: The Transformation of Objects into Subjects in Amerindian Ontologies." *Common Knowledge* 10 (3): 463–84. https://doi.org/10.1215/0961754X-10-3-463.

Viveiros de Castro, Eduardo. 2004b. "Perspectival Anthropology and the Method of Controlled Equivocation." *Tipití: Journal of the Society for the Anthropology of Lowland South America* 2 (1): 3–22.

Viveiros de Castro, Eduardo. 2014. *Cannibal Metaphysics: For a Post-structural Anthropology*. Edited and translated by Peter Skafish. University of Minnesota Press.

Volk, Tyler. 1995. *Metapatterns: Across Space, Time, and Mind*. Columbia University Press.

Wade, J. 1896. *A Dictionary of the Sgau Karen Language*. American Baptist Mission Press.

Walton, Matthew J. 2008. "Ethnicity, Conflict, and History in Burma: The Myths of Panglong." *Asian Survey* 48 (6): 889–910. https://doi.org/10.1525/as.2008.48.6.889.

Watson, Iain. 2014. "Rethinking Peace Parks in Korea." *Peace Review* 26 (1): 102–11. https://doi.org/10.1080/10402659.2013.846685.

Weng, Lawi. 2020. "KNU Rejects Myanmar General's Appeal to 'See the Big Picture.'" *The Irrawaddy*, February 25. https://www.irrawaddy.com/news/burma/knu-rejects-myanmar-generals-appeal-see-big-picture.html.

West, Paige. 2005. "Translation, Value, and Space: Theorizing an Ethnographic and Engaged Environmental Anthropology." *American Anthropologist* 107 (4): 632–42. https://doi.org/10.1525/aa.2005.107.4.632.

West, Paige. 2006. *Conservation Is Our Government Now: The Politics of Ecology in Papua New Guinea*. Duke University Press.

Wildcat, Daniel R. 2013. "Introduction: Climate Change and Indigenous Peoples of the USA." *Climatic Change* 120 (3): 509–15. https://doi.org/10.1007/s10584-013-0849-6.

Willerslev, Rane. 2007. *Soul Hunters: Hunting, Animism, and Personhood Among the Siberian Yukaghirs*. University of California Press.

Wilson, Helen F. 2019. "Contact Zones: Multispecies Scholarship Through Imperial Eyes." *Environment and Planning E: Nature and Space* 2 (4): 712–31. https://doi.org/10.1177/2514848619862191.

Winichakul, Thongchai. 1994. *Siam Mapped: A History of the Geo-Body of a Nation*. University of Hawai'i Press.

Woods, Kevin. 2011. "Ceasefire Capitalism: Military–Private Partnerships, Resource Concessions and Military–State Building in the Burma–China Borderlands." *Journal of Peasant Studies* 38 (4): 747–70. https://doi.org/10.1080/03066150.2011.607699.

Woods, Kevin. 2019. "Green Territoriality: Conservation as State Territorialization in a Resource Frontier." *Human Ecology* 47 (2): 217–32. https://doi.org/10.1007/s10745-019-0063-x.

Yeh, Emily T., and Chris Coggins, eds. 2014. *Mapping Shangrila: Contested Landscapes in the Sino-Tibetan Borderlands*. University of Washington Press.

Yeoh, Brenda S. A., and Katie Willis. 2005. "Singaporean and British Transmigrants in China and the Cultural Politics of 'Contact Zones.'" *Journal of Ethnic and Migration Studies* 31 (2): 269–85. https://doi.org/10.1080/1369183042000339927.

Zani, Leah. 2019. *Bomb Children: Life in the Former Battlefields of Laos*. Duke University Press.

INDEX

Page numbers in *italic* refer to illustrations.

activism, 5, 8, 111–17, 142, 151, 154, 169; ecological, 17, 95, 109; Indigenous, 17, 95
agriculture, 55, 61, 67, 105, 106, 110; war zones and, 100. *See also* cultivation
agroforestry, 39, 105
Allen, Tim, 59
alter-politics, 89, 117, 118, 125–28, *127*, 163
Amerindians, 45
anarchy, 83, 84; term, 11, 69
ancestors, x, xi, 19, 46, 66, 78–79, 137; death of, 43; making peace with, ix; respect for, 1, 119
Anderson, Benedict, 23
animism. *See* Thoo Hkoh
anthropology, 7, 116; political, 22, 23
anti-politics, 126, 127
Anti-Politics Machine, The (Ferguson), 186n7
Arakan Army (AA), 187n1
Arakan Rohingya Salvation Army (ARSA), 187n1
Astutui, Rita, 175
Aung San, 15
Aung San Suu Kyi, 15, 102

autonomy, 89, 95, 177; experiments in, 11–13, 142, 178; Indigenous, 12, 113, 178; pockets of, 169; spaces of, 139–41; struggle for, 163
aw loh (snatch/consume a person's soul), 38, 44, 48, 49, 51, 116

Bah Hpaw (syncretic form of Buddhism), 20, 120, 121, 122, 132; described, 119
Ban Chaung coal mine, 105
Baw Kyaw Heh, 168, 188n8
belief, xi, 23, 25, 245, 174, 175; cultural, 88; notion of, 21, 22; supernatural, 22, 41
Bender, Barbara, 183n1
Benjamin, Walter, 116, 157, 186n10
BIA (Burma Independence Army), 14, 15
biodiversity, 160, 169, 177, 178–79
Biodiversity Conference (COP 13), UN, 159
biomedicine, 49
biotic life, 176, 177
black zones, 15, 16, 108, 109
Bleh Mah Loh River, 37, 62, 63

Bonilla, Yarimar, 88
Boutry, Maxime, 77
British Empire, 13, 31
British Royal Air Force, 31
brown zones, 108
Bryant, Raymond, xin2
Bu Thoe ridge, 7, 11, 15, 52, 68, 69; KNU state and, 84; Myanmar state and, 84; roadbuilding on, 70, 139; tea shops on, 71
Bubandt, Nils, 10, 26, 66
Buddhism, 20, 94, 96, 97, 119–20, 124, 128, 131–33. *See also* Bah Hpaw
Burma, Union of, 15, 186n5
Burma Independence Army (BIA), 14, 15
Büscher, Bram, 140, 179

capitalism, ix, 98. *See also* ceasefire capitalism
car road (*kah kleh*), 52, 54, 55, 57, 68, *172*; construction of, 56, 70, 71, 85, 121, 126
ceasefire capitalism, 11, 104, 106, 107, 109
ceasefire territorialization, 11, 104–7, 107–10, 113, 118; attempts at, 114; creeping, 115, 123–24; forms of, 133
Central Land Committee, KNU, 151
Cheesman, Nick, 186n4
Chiang Mai, 7, 97, 110, 143, 155, 156; activism in, 151; KNU in, 93
Cho, Violet, 14, 25, 175, 181
Clausewitz, Carl von, 169, 188n13
Clifford, James, 9
collaboration, 104, 112, 125, 143, 154, 181
colonialism, 31, 36, 73, 103, 107, 126, 181
commons, 55, 56, 57; as patchworks, 65–68
Communist Manifesto, The (Marx), 33

conflict, x, 9, 10, 16, 101, 105, 109; armed, 177; cool, 120; mitigating, 177; peaceful, 97, 98; radical alternatives to, 170
conservation, x, 3, 9, 16, 145, 177; chartering course for, 147–51; experiments with, 117, 142, 178; fortress, 112; Indigenous, 12, 118–19, 139; initiatives, ix, xi, 112, 113; liberation, 12, 141, 143, 165; peace through, 165; radical alternatives to, 170; revolution in, 143, 179; as self-determination, 165–70; sovereignty and, 4; transfrontier, 155–61; zones, 5, 12, 142, 144, 159, 163
Conservation Is Our Government Now (West), 159
conservation projects, x, 3, 113, 143, 150, 159. *See also* liberation: conservation
consultation meetings, 3, 137, 146, 169
contact zones, 21, 89, 125, 139, 177; more-than-human, 11, 50, 126; violent, 9–10
conviviality, 8, 11, 173, 177, 179; spaces of, 139–41
cosmology, 8, 10, 41, 89, 95, 96, 126, 164, 170, 174, 175; Indigenous, 20, 70, 177–81; politics and, 21–24; Thoo Hkoh, 17, 21, 116, 117, 119, 133
cosmopolitics, 23, 126, 136, 140
counterinsurgency, 11–12, 15, 24, 102, 108–9, 167; cool/peaceful forms of, 94, 95–99; creeping, 123–24; "four cuts," 108, 187n1; military, 106; peaceful, 97; soft, 113, 123; state-sponsored, 104
counter-mapping, 12, 113–17
countermovements, 8, 95, 109, 116, 155, 161, 164
Critchley, Simon, 140, 175

cultivation, 59, 64, 75, 129; landscapes for, 42; pattern of, 57; rice, 55, 58, 61, 62, 107. *See also* agriculture
culture, 4, 10, 88, 157; generification of, 116
customary rights, protecting, 152
customary territories, 12, 36, 53, 154

de la Cadena, Marisol, 22–23, 24, 51
deadfall traps, 36–38, 173
Declaration on the Rights of Indigenous People, UN, 150, 155
Deh Bu Noh, 71, 72, 146, 171; consultation meeting in, 3, 137
demilitarized zone (DMZ), 99, 136
Democratic Karen Buddhist Army (DKBA), 97, 124, 133, 187n2
democratization, xi, 101
Department of Transportation and Communication, 72
dependency, 10, 73, 139–40, 177
Derrida, Jacques, 33, 34
Despret, Vinciane, 51
development, 16, 97, 103, 112, 179; economic/capitalist, 109; sustainable, 159
dispossession, 24, 93, 97, 109, 111–13; accumulation by, 98; creeping, 104; economic encroachment and, 98, 99; fears of, 107, 123–24; mass, 17; processes of, 8, 98, 104; risks of, 103; technologies of, 95; threats of, 5, 8, 12, 98, 111, 115; violence and, 11, 16
DKBA (Democratic Karen Buddhist Army), 97, 124, 133, 187n2
DMZ (demilitarized zone), 99, 136

Earth Beings, 23, 24
ecologies, 3, 9, 26, 136, 175
economic activity, 13, 102, 110–13, 118

economic encroachment. *See under* dispossession
EGATi, 102
entanglements, 4–5, 22, 99; more-than-human, 24; politics and, 176–77; shifting, 175, 176; specters and, 176–77
environment: degradation of, 131; protecting, 4, 113, 139, 151, 166, 178; spectral hands and, 136–39
environmentalism, x, 110, 157, 166
ethnography, 11, 47, 112
Euro-Burma Office, 186n1
Everglades National Park, 145
Executive Committee, KNU, 111, 151, 152, 155
extractivism, 8, 102, 105, 112

Farmland Law, 106, 160, 162
federalism, 145, 161–65; peace building and, 163; self-governance and, 163
Ferguson, James, 177, 186n7
Fletcher, Robert, 140, 179
Food and Agricultural Organization, 149
food crisis, 105
Forest Department, 113, 114, 128–29
forest sites, sacred, 148
forestry, agro-, 39, 105
forests, ix–x, 58; community, 2, 153; cultural, 116; Indigenous people/ancestors and, xi; overexploitation of, 129–30; possessing, 1–2; protected, 1, 128–29, 134, 144
Foucault, Michel, 169, 186n7, 188n13
"four cuts" campaign, 15, 16, 102, 108–9, 187n1
free, prior, and informed consent (FPIC), 152
friends, making, 128–33, 133–36, 177. See also *ray daw*

frontier zones, 13, 15, 105

Gagnon, Terese, 145
galactic polities, 9, 73, 107
Galtung, Johan, 101
geo-body, 107, 115
Ghosh, Amitav, 176
ghosts, 8, 30, 34, 38, 44, 183n4; green, 43; term, 42
goh la wah (white foreigner), 19, 165
Goldman Environmental Prize, 179
governance, 3, 146; environmental, 150; indirect, 13; political, 74; rebel, 72; sovereignty and, 88
Govindrajan, Radhika, 86
Graeber, David, 84
Gravers, Mikael, 13

Hage, Ghassan, 12, 126, 127
Hallowell, Alfred Irving, 24, 47
Haraway, Donna, 21
Hartman, Saidiya, 8
Harvey, Penny, 73
Hatgyi hydroelectric dam, 70, 102–3
Hau'ofa, Epeli, 18, 36
Hayami, Yoko, 19–20
headman, 75, 80; consulting, 82; role of, 76, 77, 78
hee hkoh htee, 53, 78, 79, 80, 122, 125
hee loh (borrowed), 11, 29, 42, 54–55, 57, 60
helmets, 21, *33*
histories: contact, 9, 13–20, 30; human/more-than-human, 9; Indigenous, 13, 17–20; oral, 19, 20, 36, 42, 44; war, 13–20
hkoh hkee (backward/inverted), 46, 131
hku, 43, 53, 54, 58, 60; tenure of, 59; term, 56

Hpu Noh Deh (a spectral person), 38, 39, 40, 41, 43, 48, 57, 65, 148
Hpu Noh Deh Kleh ("the path that drinks your blood"), 38–43, *40*, 61
Hpu Noh Noh Deh (specter), 65
Hpu Wah, 98
Hpu Waw, 31, 32, 51, 79, 180, 181
hsoo (strong/potent), 29, 37, 38, 39, 65, 66, 148
Htoo, Sheila, 100, 101
Huard, Stéphen, 60, 77
human becoming, 14
hunting, 32, 67, 129; banning, 130, 132

Indigenous peoples, 3, 8, 12, 17, 147–48; animism and, 45; colonialism and, 178, 181; concepts of, 23, 116; peace making by, ix
Indigenous practices, 8, 24, 55, 88, 168, 170
Ingold, Tim, 24, 26, 42, 47
insurgency, 15, 24, 108, 143, 187n1
internally displaced people (IDP), 100
International Monetary Fund (IMF), 101
international non-governmental organizations (INGOs), 16
International Union for Conservation of Nature (IUCN), 144, 187n2; Parks for Peace and, 158; protected landscapes and, 156; Red List of, 129
Irrawaddy Delta, 15
IUCN. *See* International Union for Conservation of Nature

Jackson, Michael, 26

Kachin Independence Army (KIA), 103, 104
Kachin Independence Organisation, 71
Kachin State, 108

KAD (Kawthoolei Agricultural Department), 63–64, 154
kah kleh. *See* car road
Kamoethway (Tanintharyi District), 112, 113, 115, 116
Karen. *See* Pwakanyaw
Karen Department of Health and Welfare, 73
Karen Education and Culture Department, 73
Karen Environmental and Social Action Network (KESAN), 152, 155, 157, 159, 160; activism of, xiii, 5, 12, 137, 150, 154, 169; federalism and, 164; founding of, 166; influence of, 149, 151; KFD and, 153; KNU and, 144, 149, 153; peace park and, 143, 151, 156; thinking bigger and, 144, 145; visiting, 115, 143, 171
Karen Forestry Department (KFD), 130, 137, 144, 151; forest titles and, 131; KAD and, 154; KESAN and, 153; protective landscapes and, 155
Karen Human Rights Group (KHRG), 100, 105, 188n11
Karen National Association (KNA), 14
Karen National Liberation Army (KNLA), 173, 188n12; formation of, 15; KNU and, 76, 77, 158, 167; presence of, 16; Tatmadaw and, 96, 184n6
Karen National Union (KNU), 53, 75; activity of, 110–13; agriculture and, 63–64; autonomy and, 140, 163; clashes with, 100; contact zones and, 125; counterinsurgency and, 123; counterstate and, 126; as de facto state, 11, 69; "distance-demolishing" technologies and, 72; DKBA and, 133, 187n2; election and, 185–86n1;

establishment of, 14–15, 73; field ownership and, 64; forest titles and, 131; governance of, 72, 151; judiciary system of, 80–81; *kaw* and, 152, 154; KESAN and, 144, 149, 153; KIA and, 103; KNLA and, 76, 77, 158, 167; KWO and, 81; land titles and, 131; landmines and, 34; leadership of, 93, 124; legal system of, 154, 164; liberation and, 169; NCA and, 93; policy of, 128, 152, 153, 154, 155, 156; politics of, 123, 126, 127, 131, 165, 178; road-building and, 7, 52, 71, 78, 122–23, 139; Salween Peace Park and, 4; self-determination and, 5, 119, 143; sovereignty of, 74, 88, 125, 128, 133; spectral realm and, 127; Tanintharyi and, 110–13; Tatmadaw and, 35, 70, 112; tax collection and, 76
Karen Nature Conservation Group, 166
Karen Revolution, 15–17, 118
Karen State, 13, 82, 95, 144
Karen Women's Organisation (KWO), 81, 119
Karen-land, 126, 169
Karen-ness, notion of, 14
kaw, 36, 38, 53, 54, 55; described, 66; federal, 184–85n2; mapping, 154; owners of, 78, 81, 82; as patchworks, 65–68, 145; promoting, 156; regimes of ownership and, 56–62; titles to, 153, 154
kaw k'sah (owners/lords), 55, 78, 86–87, 120–22, 134; contact zones and, 125; intervention of, 54, 85, 123, 128; rule of, 140; sovereignty of, 88, 126; tigers and, 24, 25; *tirakuna* and, 23; wrath of, 53, 82, 95
Kawthoolei, 14, 16, 71, 72, 126, 127, 168, 169; prefiguring, 161–65

Kawthoolei Agricultural Department (KAD), 63–64, 154
KESAN. *See* Karen Environmental and Social Action Network
KFD. *See* Karen Forestry Department
Khao Kwan (foundation in Thailand), 110, 113
Khayyat, Minura, 9, 35
KHRG (Karen Human Rights Group), 100, 105, 188n11
KIA (Kachin Independence Army), 103, 104
Kim, Eleana, 35, 102, 136
kinship, 44, 60, 66
k'la (spirit/shade), 38–39, 46, 47, 50, 51, 116, 131, 132; of rice, 48
Kleinman, Arthur, 177
k'ma (mistake), 84, 86, 121, 125, 171, 172
KNLA. *See* Karen National Liberation Army
Knox, Hannah, 73
KNU. *See* Karen National Union
"KNU Authorities-Managed Public Purpose Land," 152
Krøijer, Stine, 164
k'sah, 29, 40, 42, 43–44, 47; ownership by, 11, 57, 60, 61, 65, 66, 78, 85; praying to, 18; presence of, 48
K'wa (ethnic group), 29, 37, 42, 184n9
KWO (Karen Women's Organisation), 81, 119
Kwon, Heonik, 34, 51

labor: corvée, 76; forced, 108; physical, 60; ritual, 60
Lambek, Michael, 25
land laws, 104–10, 151–55. *See also* Vacant, Fallow and Virgin Land Management Law
land rushes, 104–10

land titles, 64, 131. *See also* tenure: titles
landmines, 34–36, 108
landscapes, 5, 7, 9, 10, 29, 30; contested, 3, 8, 183n1; cultural, 11, 42; described, 66; haunting, 11; landmines in, 34–36; legal, 146; natural, 11, 42, 43; negotiated, 51; political, 26; possessing, 106–7, 119, 135, 139, 141, 164; protected, 144, 155, 156, 157; social relations with, 46; spectral sovereigns and, 136; spiritual, 42; territorialization of, 131
Latour, Bruno, 126
Leach, Edmund, 22
Lehman, F. K., 87
Ler Mu Plaw, 70
liberalization, 99; political/economic, 101
liberation, 163, 169; conservation, 12, 141, 143, 165
loh (dwelling place of the dead), 1, 2, 3, 8, 131, 132, 137, 138; protecting, 61, 139
Loo Seh Buh. *See* Mu Kaw Lee
lu ta (offering of food), 11, 51, 79, 95, 119
Lund, Christian, 103, 104

Mae Ra Moe (refugee camp), 165, 166
making friends, 128–33, 133–36, 177. *See also ray daw*
Manerplaw, 97, 124, 167
mapping, 95, 106, 107, 108, 114–15, 154; as political act, 115; processes of, 113
Marx, Karl, 98
Mathews, Andrew, 66
Mauss, Marcel, 89
Mehtta, Megnaa, 88–89
Meuret, Michel, 51, 66
militarization, 95, 97, 100
Milne, Sarah, 112

mining, xi, 105; gold, 111, 123, 186n3
Ministry of Environmental Conservation and Forestry Management, 112
missionaries, 13, 14, 16, 17, 19, 20, 80
Moh La Pa Lah. *See* Thoo Koh
monks, 119, 121, 122, 123, 128, 139, 172; community forest and, 2; rituals and, 132; trees and, 131–33
morality, 24, 60, 81, 83
Mu Kaw Lee (the great trickster/Lucifer), 37
Mu Khah, 17, 18, 184n8
Mutraw District, 3, 13, 24, 67, 71; monsoon in, 1; political landscape of, 7; Salween Peace Park and, 5
Mutraw hills, 7, 8, 10, 12, 13; autonomy in, 174; ceasefire territorialization in, 133; conflict in, 108, 109; conservation in, 118, 174; dispossession in, 99; encounters in, 119; entanglements in, 99, 100; green ghosts in, 43; justice in, 86; landscapes along, 85, 183n1; militarization of, 95; ownership in, 96; protecting, 156; self-determination in, 155; tenure in, 105; VFV Law and, 107; war in, 180
Mutu Say Poe, 168
Myaing Gyi Ngu, 96
Myanmar Army. *See* Tatmadaw
Myanmar Posts and Telecommunications, 71
Myburgh, Werner, 157

nah htee (specter possessing a certain body of water), 43, 49, 50, 51, 184n5
National Ceasefire Agreement (NCA), 93, 101, 162, 188n10
National League for Democracy, 167
Native Americans, ideas/values of, x
natural resources, 22, 98
Naw Eh Oo, 18, 20
Nay Pyi Daw, 179
NCA. *See* National Ceasefire Agreement
Ne Win, 15
nesting, 55, 58–59, 62, 65, 67; hierarchy of, 136; ownership and, 106, 148, 164; sovereignty and, 88–89
New Mon State Party, 71
non-governmental organizations (NGOs), 7, 16, 73, 159
non-state armed groups (NSAGs), 71, 72, 104, 187n1
Northern Karen State, 13, 146
NSAGs. *See* non-state armed groups

obligations, ecology of, 51, 66
Ong, Andrew, 100–101, 177–78
overhunting, 128, 129–30
ownership, 126, 174; ephemeral, 54, 55, 58–59, 61, 62, 65, 67, 164; hegemonic concepts of, 85; human, 62, 65, 65–66; Indigenous, 89, 106, 142; individual, 8, 57; layers of, 55, 59; modes of, 30, 42, 54, 55, 57, 59, 64; nested, 57–61, 164; private, 61, 153; regimes of, 8, 56–62; sovereignty and, 8, 68; spectral, 11, 42, 47, 55, 60, 61, 62, 66, 79, 80, 88, 96, 106; usufruct, 58, 60–61, 65, 78

paddy fields, 61–62, 63, 64
pagodas, 34, 94, 95–99, 102, 121, 122, 130, 172; building, 96, 123, 125, 126, 133
Panglong Conference, 186n5
Panglong peace conference, 21st Century, 101
Parks for Peace, 158

Paul, Andrew, 44
peace, 18, 157, 164, 173; conference sessions, 101; conservation and, 165; cosmopolitical, 140; negative, 99–104; positive, 101; predatory, 99–104; sharing, 174, 177–81
peace garden, 160, 165
Peace Pagoda, 97
peace parks, x, 143, 157, 158, 179; term, 156, 164. *See also* Salween Peace Park
Peace Parks Foundation, 158
peace traps, 97, 102, 186n7
peacebuilding, ix, x, xi, 3, 4, 101, 163, 179
Peluso, Nancy, 115, 116
PETRONAS (oil and gas company), 112
pgha htoo lee hpoe ("Indigenous"), 66–67
pgha meh ay play thweh (elders), 83
phantoms, collective, 34
Po, San C., 169
Polanyi, Karl, 109, 111
political ecology, more-than-human, 20–26, 175
politics, x, 13, 26, 41, 42, 85, 88, 94, 118, 159, 178, 179; alternate mode of, 70, 89; cosmologies and, 21–24; entanglements and, 176–77; *kaw*, 74–84, 152; local, 69, 175; modes of, 127, 128, 138–39, 140; national/transnational, 12; pagoda, 119–23; pragmatic, 150; revolutionary, 4, 123–28, 170; roadbuilding and, 69; social worlds and, 24
possessed (term), 9, 30, 40, 46
possessed objects, 34
possession, 54, 89, 95, 106–7, 141; Indigenous, 12, 95, 106, 114, 115, 145, 155; of land, 113, 153, 164; landscapes of, 7–9; politics of, 21, 24, 42; by spirit, 40

power: imbalances of, 9–10; political, 53, 81
practices, 10, 21, 41, 96, 174, 175; Indigenous, 5–6, 70, 116, 149, 177; protecting, 152
Pratt, Mary Louise, 9, 13, 125, 126
property: individual, 60; private, 62, 64; rights to, 115
protected areas, transboundary, 158
pugmarks, 121, 172, *172*, 174, 176, 180
Pwakanyaw, 13–14, 19, 31, 43, 49; Christian, 21, 25; communities, 14, 81, 162; diaspora of, 167; Salween Peace Park and, 148; self-determination and, 150; traditions, 113

Rakhine, 102
ray daw (making friends), 10, 129, 135. *See also* making friends
realms: human, 13, 40, 50; more-than-human, 13, 126; spectral, 11, 30, 40, 41, 48, 50, 51, 74, 80, 86, 89, 127, 177
Red List, ICUN, 129
refugees, 4, 16, 162, 166, 167, 185n2
relationships, 54, 107, 125, 128, 148, 155, 160; formal, 22; gendered, 80; hierarchical, 65; open-ended, 140; political, 178; repairing, 82, 85, 86; symbiotic, 178
revolution, 9; histories of, 13–20
rice, 48, 63, 135; bacterial infections of, 176; cultivation of, 55, 58, 61, 62, 107
rice wine, 75, 134, 185n3
rituals, 48, 49, 50, 53, 60, 62, 120, 132, 133
roadbuilding, 56, 67, 85, 121, 126; KNU and, 52, 78, 122–23, 139; politics/sovereignty and, 69; tales of, 70
Rohingya crisis, 102
Ruiz-Serna, Daniel, 41

Sahlins, Marshall, 89
Salawin National Park, 159, 188n8
Salween District, 13, 70, 96
Salween Peace Park, x, 3, 7, 8, 51, 70, 76, 139; autonomy for, 67; charter of, 147, 148, 149, 150, 153, 155; conservation and, 5, 141, 142, 155–61, 178, 179; consultation meeting for, 137, 146, 169; cooperation over, 143; countermovements and, 164; development of, x–xi, 4, 12, 144, 151, 153, 155, 156, 157, 160, 181; environmental policy and, 169; as a "flower garden" (Ta Mu Ta Hku K'Ruh), 156–57, 160, 164; Hatgyi dam and, 102–3; Indigenous people and, 17, 147–48; key events related to, 146–47; land possession and, 164; legal space for, 146–55; liberation conservation and, 12; map of, 5, 154; ownership/sovereignty and, 89; peace and, 165; politics and, 5, 165; preservation and, 5, 178; prizes for, 178, 179; self-determination and, 143, 165; thinking bigger and, 144, 145; as transboundary protected area, 163
Salween Peace Park Governing Committee, 147
Salween River, 7, 9, 10, 11, 15; armed conflict along, 177; development along, 145; fighting along, 35; KNU and, 165; militarization along, 100, 102; political predicaments along, 13, 14; possessed highlands along, 29; protected area along, 156; traffic along, 71
scale: experiments in, 11–13; messing with, 150
Scott, James C., 106
SDGs (Sustainable Development Goals, 112, 179

Second Anglo-Burmese War, 13
self-determination, 4, 5, 71, 119, 142, 155, 164, 178; conservation as, 165–70; local, 140; right to, 150; spirit of, 157; struggle for, 143
Serengeti National Park, 145
shrines, 122; household, 120, *121*
Sikor, Thomas, 104
Simpson, Audra, 58, 88
Sinohydro, 102
Skidmore, Monique, 99
Smith, Martin, 16, 108
social relations, 10, 43, 44, 46, 60, 83
sovereignty, 10–11, 74, 106, 124–26, 128; conservation and, 4; food, 178; fractured/mutated forms of, 88; generating, 178; governance and, 88; hegemonic notions of, 70, 85, 88; Indigenous, 3, 4, 88, 89, 142, 163; modes of, 125, 140; ownership and, 8, 68; spectral, 11, 12, 69, 89, 97, 118, 127, 128, 134, 135–36, 139, 152, 178; state, 8, 70–74, 88, 104; understanding, 177; unsettling, 87–89
spaces: interstitial, 139–42; legal, 146–55; non-state, 9, 69
special economic zones, 159
specters, 46, 48, 50, 51, 87, 174; ecologies and, 136; entanglements and, 176–77; human affairs and, 139; place-based, 42; possessive, 41; tigers and, 176
spectral (term), 8, 10, 69, 84, 176, 177
spectral persons/presences, 10–11, 30, 38, 40, 42, 46, 65, 66, 69, 87
spirits, 38, 40, 44, 46, 49, 50; of the dead, 89; making peace with, ix; term, 42
State Law and Order Reconciliation Council (SLORC), 99

State Peace and Development Council, 99
Stengers, Isabelle, 23, 126, 128
Stoler, Ann, 33
Suphanburi, 110
Sustainable Development Goals (SDGs), 112, 179
swidden farming, 14, 42, 58, 104–5, 106, 116, 186n8
swidden patches, 35, 59, 63; clearing, 54; construction and, 53; cultivating, 54, 56, 57, 74; maintaining, 43; ownership of, 61, 65, 66, 78, 79
symbiotic events, 12, 125–28

Ta Bu Kyoh (mountain), 53, 54, 74, 85, 86, 87, 120, 121, 126, 172; capturing, 124; pagoda at, 122, 123, 133
ta du ta htu. See taboos
ta du ta pluh, 44, 45
ta du ta yah hku (cool/peaceful conflict), 94, 95, 96, 102, 118, 120, 123, 124, 133
Ta Htee Ta Daw K'sah (the sovereign of all specters), 133, 134, 135, 138, 170; offerings to, 136; sovereignty of, 137, 139, 140
Ta K'Thwee Duh, 7, 8, 15, 17, 29; Buddhists in, 119; ceasefire capitalism and, 105; environmental concerns in, 131; fieldwork in, 47; monks in, 128; overhunting and, 128, 130
Ta K'Thwee Duh Kaw, 36, 56, 62, 63, 65, 67, 74, 124; boundaries of, 75; pagoda in, 96
ta lu ("the spirit house"), 49, 50
ta mu khah (spectral people), 38, 39–40, 42, 43, 44, 45, 48, 55, 176
ta mu ta hku (peace), 96, 160

ta taw ta loh (that which is true), 46, 134
ta taw ta loh kaw (the realm of that which is true), 46, 131, 134
ta thoo ta pgho (potency), 18, 37, 65, 66, 89, 148, 186n3
taboos (*ta du ta htu*), 60, 62, 87; observing, 11, 43, 67; transmitting, 149; violating, 44, 58, 121, 171, 173, 180
tama (action), 50; *tana* ("belief") and, 21, 25, 175
Tambiah, Stanley, 73
Tanawthari Landscape of Life, 178
Tanintharyi (region), 14, 105, 109, 116, 149, 170; activism in, 114; conservation initiatives in, 113; countermapping in, 117; countermovements in, 111–12; economic activity in, 110–13; as frontier, 110; gold mining in, 123; green territoriality in, 110–13; KNU activity in, 110–13
Tanintharyi Nature Reserve Project (TNRP), 112, 115
Tannenbaum, Nicola, 133
Tarkapaw Youth Group, 105
Tatmadaw, 5, 111, 133, 162, 168, 176; bargaining with, 104; "black zone"/"fire free zone" and, 7; clashes with, 100; countering, 131; counterinsurgency by, 11–12, 15, 94, 108–9, 187n1; KNU and, 9, 112, 188n10; land concessions and, 104; landmines and, 34; Manerplaw and, 124; militarization by, 97, 100; Mutraw highlands and, 108; rapprochement with, 93; resistance to, 126, 127; roadbuilding and, 70; territorialization of, 97; Thee Mu Hta and, 107
Tatmadaw army, 95, 100
Tatmadaw soldiers, 71, 96, 166, 167, 168

Taw Oo (Taungoo), 168
technology, 107; digital, 185n1; "distance-demolishing," 72; legal, 104; legislative, 106
Tenasserim River and Indigenous Peoples' Network (TRIP NET), 110, 161
tenure, 58–59, 59–60, 150; collective, 153; customary, 105, 152; Indigenous, 59, 61; titles, 151–55
territoriality, 95, 106, 131; green, 110–13, 178; military, 104, 109; state, 109; technology of, 107, 115. *See also* ceasefire territorialization
territories, customary, 12, 36, 53, 154
Thanbyah, T., 14
Thaton (Doo Tha Htoo) District, 13, 158
Thee Mu Hta (military base), 103, 109, 184n6; cautionary tale of, 97, 98, 123, 124, 133; Tatmadaw and, 15–16, 96–97, 107
thinking bigger, 143–45
Thoo Hkoh ("animism"), 133, 173, 174, 175, 180; definition of, 17, 21–22; practices, 116, 117, 119; rites of, 49; *tana* and, 25; violence and, 24
Thoo K'Bee Duh, 85–86
tigers, 4, 24, 25, 82, 87, 129, 171; political effects of, 173; presence of, 176; pugmarks of, 121, 172, *172*, 174, 176, 180; sightings of, 172; specters and, 176
TNRP (Tanintharyi Nature Reserve Project), 112, 115
Total (oil and gas company), 112
Toungoo (Ta-Oo) Division, 13
transboundary protected areas, 143, 163
translation, 10, 113–17; experiments in, 11–13; pragmatic, 160
Transnational Institute, 151

trees: Buddhist monks and, 131–33; transformative, 61–62
TRIP NET (Tenasserim River and Indigenous Peoples' Network), 110, 161
Tsing, Anna Lowenhaupt, 66
21st Century Panglong peace conference, 101

U Thuzana, 97, 120, 124
Umbilical Cord Forest, 116, 186n9
UNHCR (United Nations High Commissioner for Refugees), 4, 167
Union of Burma, 15, 186n5
United Nationalities Federal Council (UNFC), 103–4
United Nations, 101, 112, 149
United Nations Biodiversity Conference (COP 13), 159
United Nations Declaration on the Rights of Indigenous People, 150, 155
United Nations Development Programme (UNDP), 178
United Nations High Commissioner for Refugees (UNHCR), 4, 167
usufruct, 42, 58, 61, 60, 62, 65, 66, 75, 78

Vacant, Fallow and Virgin Land Management Law (VFV Law, 2012), 105, 106, 107, 108, 160, 162
Vigh, Henrik, 101
Village Act (1887), 77
violence, 10, 24, 31; armed, 101–2; gender-based, 82; political, ix
Viveiros de Castro, Eduardo, 45
Voluntary Guidelines on the Responsible Governance of Tenure of Land, Fisheries, and Forests, 149

Wade, Jonathan, 17
war zones, 3, 4, 156; agriculture and, 100
Way Pgha (forest), 65, 131, 137, 138, 139, 172; described, 129; hunting/fishing in, 130, 133; protecting, 130, 132
Wee Hta Baw Mu (oracle), 180, 181
West, Paige, 116, 159, 160
white zones, 15, 108, 208
Winichakul, Thongchai, 73, 107, 108
witchcraft law, 72
Woods, Kevin, 11, 104, 109, 113
World Bank, 101

World War II, 14, 17, 31

Yadana pipeline, 112
Yu Wah Duh, 41, 98, 180
Yunzalin River, 38, 52, 81
Y'wa (demiurge), 19, 36–38, 89, 135, 184n8, 187n3; origin of, 17–18; winnowing by, 181
Y'wa Ma Htu Lay (Y'wa's Deadfall Trap Rocks), 36–38, 59, 62, 65, 86

zoning, 114

CULTURE, PLACE, AND NATURE
Studies in Anthropology and Environment

Possessed Landscapes: Experiments in Conservation and Sovereignty in Southeast Myanmar, by Tomas Cole

Amphibious Anthropologies: Living in Wet Environments, edited by Alejandro Camargo, Luisa Cortesi, and Franz Krause

Viable Ecologies: Conservation and Coexistence on the Galápagos Islands, by Paolo Bocci

Crafting a Tibetan Terroir: Winemaking in Shangri-La, by Brendan A. Galipeau

China's Camel Country: Livestock and Nation-Building at a Pastoral Frontier, by Thomas White

Sustaining Natures: An Environmental Anthropology Reader, edited by Sarah R. Osterhoudt and K. Sivaramakrishnan

Fukushima Futures: Survival Stories in a Repeatedly Ruined Seascape, by Satsuki Takahashi

The Camphor Tree and the Elephant: Religion and Ecological Change in Maritime Southeast Asia, by Faizah Zakaria

Turning Land into Capital: Development and Dispossession in the Mekong Region, edited by Philip Hirsch, Kevin Woods, Natalia Scurrah, and Michael B. Dwyer

Spawning Modern Fish: Transnational Comparison in the Making of Japanese Salmon, by Heather Anne Swanson

Upland Geopolitics: Postwar Laos and the Global Land Rush, by Michael B. Dwyer

Misreading the Bengal Delta: Climate Change, Development, and Livelihoods in Coastal Bangladesh, by Camelia Dewan

Ordering the Myriad Things: From Traditional Knowledge to Scientific Botany in China, by Nicholas K. Menzies

Timber and Forestry in Qing China: Sustaining the Market, by Meng Zhang

Consuming Ivory: Mercantile Legacies of East Africa and New England, by Alexandra Celia Kelly

Mapping Water in Dominica: Enslavement and Environment under Colonialism, by Mark W. Hauser

Mountains of Blame: Climate and Culpability in the Philippine Uplands, by Will Smith

Sacred Cows and Chicken Manchurian: The Everyday Politics of Eating Meat in India, by James Staples

Gardens of Gold: Place-Making in Papua New Guinea, by Jamon Alex Halvaksz

Shifting Livelihoods: Gold Mining and Subsistence in the Chocó, Colombia, by Daniel Tubb

Disturbed Forests, Fragmented Memories: Jarai and Other Lives in the Cambodian Highlands, by Jonathan Padwe

The Snow Leopard and the Goat: Politics of Conservation in the Western Himalayas, by Shafqat Hussain

Roses from Kenya: Labor, Environment, and the Global Trade in Cut Flowers, by Megan A. Styles

Working with the Ancestors: Mana and Place in the Marquesas Islands, by Emily C. Donaldson

Living with Oil and Coal: Resource Politics and Militarization in Northeast India, by Dolly Kikon

Caring for Glaciers: Land, Animals, and Humanity in the Himalayas, by Karine Gagné

Organic Sovereignties: Struggles over Farming in an Age of Free Trade, by Guntra A. Aistara

The Nature of Whiteness: Race, Animals, and Nation in Zimbabwe, by Yuka Suzuki

Forests Are Gold: Trees, People, and Environmental Rule in Vietnam, by Pamela D. McElwee

Conjuring Property: Speculation and Environmental Futures in the Brazilian Amazon, by Jeremy M. Campbell

Andean Waterways: Resource Politics in Highland Peru, by Mattias Borg Rasmussen

Puer Tea: Ancient Caravans and Urban Chic, by Jinghong Zhang

Enclosed: Conservation, Cattle, and Commerce among the Q'eqchi' Maya Lowlanders, by Liza Grandia

Forests of Belonging: Identities, Ethnicities, and Stereotypes in the Congo River Basin, by Stephanie Rupp

Tahiti beyond the Postcard: Power, Place, and Everyday Life, by Miriam Kahn

Wild Sardinia: Indigeneity and the Global Dreamtimes of Environmentalism, by Tracey Heatherington

Nature Protests: The End of Ecology in Slovakia, by Edward Snajdr

Forest Guardians, Forest Destroyers: The Politics of Environmental Knowledge in Northern Thailand, by Tim Forsyth and Andrew Walker

Being and Place among the Tlingit, by Thomas F. Thornton

The Tropics and the Traveling Gaze: India, Landscape, and Science, 1800–1856, by David Arnold

Ecological Nationalisms: Nature, Livelihoods, and Identities in South Asia, edited by Gunnel Cederlöf and K. Sivaramakrishnan

From Enslavement to Environmentalism: Politics on a Southern African Frontier, by David McDermott Hughes

Border Landscapes: The Politics of Akha Land Use in China and Thailand, by Janet C. Sturgeon

Property and Politics in Sabah, Malaysia: Native Struggles over Land Rights, by Amity A. Doolittle

The Earth's Blanket: Traditional Teachings for Sustainable Living, by Nancy J. Turner

The Kuhls of Kangra: Community-Managed Irrigation in the Western Himalaya, by J. Mark Baker